Domestic Violence
Law and Practice

FIFTH EDITION

Domestic Violence
Law and Practice

FIFTH EDITION

Roger Bird

 Family Law

Published by
Jordan Publishing Limited
21 St Thomas Street
Bristol BS1 6JS

British Library Cataloguing-in-Publication Data

A catalogue record for this book is available from the British Library.

ISBN 0 85308 974 4

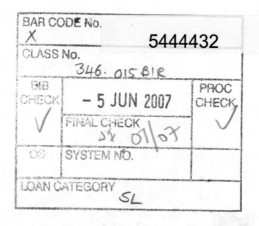
Typeset by Etica Press Ltd, Malvern

Printed and bound in Great Britain by Antony Rowe, Chippenham

PREFACE

It is now some three years since the last edition of this book, in which period the practice of the law has been changed by judicial decisions, and it is therefore appropriate to amend the work for the assistance of practitioners in this difficult field. However, the principal factor dictating publication of a new edition is the Domestic Violence, Crime and Victims Act 2004. Most of this statute is not, in fact, concerned with the law relating to domestic violence but the changes in this field which the Act does effect are important and wide-ranging.

However, the publishers have been faced by a dilemma. It is now well-known that important changes to the law are to be effected at some time in the future, and there have been a number of false alarms concerning the date of implementation. Publishers, and family lawyers, have to be alert to the new developments and to be ready to accommodate them when, as is likely, they are brought in at fairly short notice. The problem is that, whereas it was confidently thought that the delayed implementation date of April 2006 would be met, it now transpires that this will not be so and no one is able to predict the precise date; clearly government in this area is less joined-up than it might be.

The decision has therefore been taken to publish now with all the changes included in the text as if the changes effected by the 2004 Act were in force. Care is taken in the text to explain where it refers to prospective changes only, so that the reader will not be misled. The only other word of caution must be that references to the amended Rules are to draft rules which are awaiting signature at the time of writing. There is no reason to think that these rules are controversial nor that they will not be implemented, but readers must be aware of the position.

It has to be said that most practitioners involved in this area of law find the changes contained in the 2004 Act puzzling. There is no reason to think that the county courts have dealt with enforcement of the orders which they have made in anything other than a proper and effective way (it is difficult to be categoric about Family Proceedings Courts since they deal with such a small volume of work), yet the power to enforce their own orders by the remedy most valued by practitioners, namely the power of arrest, is to be removed and replaced with reliance on the prosecuting authorities. The obvious gaps and inconsistencies which will result are explained in the text and need not be considered here. Confidence in the ability of our legislators to grasp the issues involved was not increased by a reading of the parliamentary debates, from which the impression is derived that the same self-congratulatory unanimity of opinion had previously been achieved only in the debates on the Child Support Bill in 1989.

Roger Bird

16 January 2006

CONTENTS

TABLE OF CASES

References are to paragraph numbers.

TABLE OF STATUTES

References are to paragraph numbers and Appendices.

TABLE OF STATUTORY INSTRUMENTS

References are to paragraph numbers and Appendices.

TABLE OF FORMS

References are to paragraph numbers and Appendices.

TABLE OF ABBREVIATIONS

CA 1989	Children Act 1989
CCR	County Court Rules 1981
CPR 1998	Civil Procedure Rules 1998
DVCVA 2004	Domestic Violence, Crime and Victims Act 2004
DVMPA 1976	Domestic Violence and Matrimonial Proceedings Act 1976
FLA 1996	Family Law Act 1996
FPC (MP etc) R 1991	Family Proceedings Courts (Matrimonial Proceedings etc) Rules 1991
FPR 1991	Family Proceedings Rules 1991
MCA 1973	Matrimonial Causes Act 1973
MHA 1983	Matrimonial Homes Act 1983
MWPA 1882	Married Women's Property Act 1882
PD	Practice Direction (of the Civil Procedure Rules 1998)
PHA 1997	Protection from Harassment Act 1997
RSC	Rules of the Supreme Court 1965

CHAPTER 1

INTRODUCTION – HOW TO USE THIS BOOK

1.1 The purpose of this book is to provide a quick and reliable guide to practitioners and others relating to the various forms of personal protection available through the court process. The remedies which will be described are those which are designed to protect the individual from some wrong which has been committed against them or which is threatened. These wrongs include assault, molestation, harassment and interference with occupation of a home. The common element in all these remedies is normally that the victim and the perpetrator have, at some stage, been 'associated' in a family or quasi-family sense although, as will be seen, even this is not always the case where 'stalking' is alleged under the Protection from Harassment Act 1997 (PHA 1997).

1.2 The remedies available are provided partly by statute and partly by the general law. Part IV of the Family Law Act 1996 (FLA 1996) as amended by the Domestic Violence, Crime and Victims Act 2004 (DVCVA 2004) provides a comprehensive code for applications for personal protection from molestation by a member of the family or other associated person, and also for occupation of a family home. A person who is not associated cannot apply under FLA 1996. However, there remain cases of harassment and violence between persons who are not included in the class of associated persons eligible under FLA 1996. Here, the position may be remedied by injunctions, made in actions under the PHA 1997 or founded on common law torts.

1.3 The various sections of this book are designed to deal with each of the separate possibilities which may arise. In many cases, of course, there may be overlapping remedies but it is hoped that this approach will provide the quickest solution for the reader.

The reader should be aware of one very important feature of this book, to which reference will be made where appropriate. The current law and procedure are set out in the fourth edition of this work, which remains an accurate guide to the law as it is in March 2006. It had been thought that the DCVCA 2004, mentioned above, would come into force in November 2005. It was then thought that it would be in force in April 2006. In the event, neither date has been met, and the changes effected by the DCVCA 2004 are therefore still prospective. However, it was thought right to publish this book now, so that readers will be aware of what the law will be as and when the Act is brought into force, which will probably be some time in the coming 12 months. This edition is of course also required because of the changes in the existing law effected by case-law.

Step One: Is the victim 'associated'?

1.4 It has already been shown that victims and potential applicants for relief are divided into those who are associated and those who are not. This is the first question the adviser has to deal with. This division into associated and non-associated persons is one of the key concepts of FLA 1996. Section 62(3) of FLA 1996 provides that a person is associated with another person if:

(a)   they are or have been married to each other;
(b)   they are cohabitants or former cohabitants;
(c)   they live or have lived in the same household, otherwise than merely by reason of one of them being the other's employee, tenant, lodger or boarder;
(d)   they are relatives;
(e)   they have agreed to marry each other (whether or not that agreement has been terminated);
(ea) they have, or have had, an intimate personal relationship with each other which is or was of significant duration. [prospective change]
(f)   in relation to any child, they are both persons falling within subs (4). Subsection (4) provides that a person falls within its scope if:

> '(a)   he is a parent of the child; or
> (b)   he has or has had parental responsibility for the child';

(g)   they are parties to the same family proceedings (other than proceedings under Part IV of the FLA 1996).

This definition introduces further terms, some of which must themselves be defined.

Cohabitation

1.5 Section 62(3)(a) presents no problems. The first term requiring definition is 'cohabitant'. Section 62(1) defines 'cohabitants' thus:

> '(a)   Cohabitants are two persons who, although not married to each other, are living together as husband and wife or (if of the same sex) in an equivalent relationship; and
> (b)   "former cohabitants" is to be read accordingly, but does not include cohabitants who have subsequently married each other.'

It will be remembered that before the amendments made by the DVCVA 2004, s 62(1) of the FLA 1996 required cohabitants to be 'a man and a woman'. The amended section extends the definition to include same-sex couples. With that difference in mind, the position is clear; the parties must have lived together as if husband and wife or the same-sex equivalent. This would involve a shared life and living arrangements and, normally, a sexual element in the relationship. In most cases, the meaning of cohabitant will be clear enough, although it has to be said that, given the almost infinite variety of conditions of married life, there may be room for interesting arguments about what does and does not come within 'living together as husband and wife'.

The question of what constitutes cohabitation is not only relevant in the field of family law; there is a body of jurisprudence on the subject in social security law, which is frequently overlooked by family practitioners. The issue to be determined is normally whether an applicant for income support is disqualified because of cohabitation.

In *Crake v Supplementary Benefits Commission*,[1] Woolf J approved six factors as 'admirable signposts' for the existence of cohabitation. These are membership of the same household, stability, financial support, sexual relationship, children and public acknowledgment. However, in *Re J (Income Support: Cohabitation)*,[2] a Social Security Commissioner held that to consider only these factors placed a wholly inadequate emphasis on the parties' 'general relationship'. The parties' sexual and financial relationship was relevant only for the light it cast on this general relationship. Where there had never been a sexual relationship, there must be strong alternative grounds for holding that there existed a relationship akin to that of husband and wife.

In *G v G (Non-molestation Order: Jurisdiction)*,[3] justices found that the applicant and respondent were not associated because they had never lived in the same household, were not cohabitants and there was insufficient evidence of agreement to marry. Wall J allowed the appeal and directed a rehearing, saying that the court should adopt a purposive construction of the FLA 1996 and jurisdiction should not be declined unless the facts of the case were plainly incapable of being brought within the statute. In this case, three of the 'signposts' set out in *Crake* (see above) were present.

1.6 Section 62(3)(c) introduces a new class of applicants into the law. The previous law, taken as a whole, recognised present or former spouses and cohabitants as potential applicants; this provision broadens the range of applicants.

---

[1]   [1982] 1 All ER 498.
[2]   [1995] 1 FLR 660.
[3]   [2000] 2 FLR 533.

The 1995 Bill introduced by the Government did not accept the totality of the recommendations which had been made by the Law Commission. On the second reading, the Lord Chancellor explained:

> 'The other significant policy departure from the recommendations of the Law Commission concerns the categories of people entitled to apply for orders. The categories proposed by the Law Commission of – persons who had at any time agreed to marry each other; and persons who have or have had a sexual relationship with each other were rejected, because the persons within them may not have the same domestic link as those in the other categories. In some cases, the relationship might have been brief and the parties would never have lived together. There might also be problems for the courts of definition and proof, which would not apply to the other categories. If that happened, it would undermine the principle that domestic violence remedies should be able to be obtained swiftly in emergencies. Of course, that does not mean that there would not be other remedies available to such people; but it means that the simplified form of procedure available under the Bill would not be available to them for the reasons that I have given.'[1]

The essential characteristic of this class of person is, therefore, that they have lived in the same household as the other person.

Household

1.7 'Household' had been considered by the Law Commission, which, when defining the relationships to be protected in addition to spouses and cohabitants, began with:

> 'The phrase "living in the same household" may be expected to retain the usual meaning which it has acquired in matrimonial proceedings. Thus, it is possible for people to live in different households, although they are actually living in the same house. The crucial test is the degree of community life which goes on. If the parties shut themselves up in separate rooms and cease to have anything to do with each other, they live in separate households. But if they share domestic chores and shopping, eat meals together or share the same living room, they are living in the same household, however strained their relations may be.' (Law Com, para 3.21)

The term implies some shared living arrangements; people living under the same roof, for example by occupying flats or bedsits in the same building, would not be living in the same household. The class clearly could overlap with cohabitants, in the sense that someone could qualify under this classification and as a cohabitant; however, one could not qualify as a cohabitant without being of the opposite sex to the other party, and without the relationship being similar to that of husband and wife.

---

1   Official Report (HL), 23 February 1995.

In the same way, the class would overlap with that of relatives, so it must be taken that, in attempting to define those intended to qualify here, relatives should be excluded. Section 62(3)(c) specifically excludes people who live in the same household 'merely by reason' of their being employer and employee, landlord and tenant (although it is difficult to see how a landlord and tenant, properly so called, could live in the same household), and 'landlord' and lodger or boarder. It would be possible for someone to argue that, although he or she was an employee or boarder, that was not the only reason for living in the same household as someone else; for example, it might be argued that there was some sexual relationship which made it convenient for them to be close at hand.

It seems, therefore, that people who might be associated with each other would in any event include homosexual couples, and also people who share a home for reasons of friendship, convenience or some other reason.

'Relative'

1.8 'Relative' is defined in s 63(1). In relation to a person, 'relative' means:

'(a)   the father, mother, stepfather, stepmother, son, daughter, stepson, stepdaughter, grandmother, grandfather, grandson or granddaughter of that person or of that person's spouse or former spouse, or

(b)   the brother, sister, uncle, aunt, niece or nephew (whether of the full blood or of the half blood or by affinity) of that person or of that person's spouse or former spouse,

and includes, in relation to a person who is living or has lived with another person as husband and wife, any person who would fall within paragraph (a) or (b) above if the parties were married to each other.'

The significance of this last provision is, therefore, that the word 'cohabitant' or 'former cohabitant' can be substituted for 'spouse' in the definition. Apart from this, the definition needs little further elaboration, save for a consideration of the effect of s 62(4) and (5).

Section 62(4) begins 'A person falls within this subsection in relation to a child ...'. Pausing there, it will be remembered that the purpose of the section is to define 'associated persons', relatives are associated persons, and, of course, parents are relatives of their children. It is unsurprising, therefore, to find that subs (4) continues:

'if—

(a)   he is a parent of the child; or

(b)   he has or has had parental responsibility for the child.'

By s 63(1), 'parental responsibility' has the same meaning as in the Children Act 1989.

Section 62(5) deals with the position where a child has been adopted or freed for adoption by virtue of any of the enactments mentioned in s 16(1) of the Adoption Act 1976. In such circumstances, two persons may be associated for the purposes of this Act if:

'(a) one is a natural parent of the child or a parent of such a natural parent; and
(b) the other is the child or any person—

(i) who has become a parent of the child by virtue of an adoption order or has applied for an adoption order, or
(ii) with whom the child has at any time been placed for adoption.'

Engaged couples

1.9 Section 62(3)(e) introduces another class of associated persons, namely the former engaged couple.

Section 44, the marginal note to which is 'Evidence of agreement to marry', provides, in subs (1), that the court shall not make an order under s 33 (an occupation order in favour of an entitled person) or s 42 (a non-molestation order) by virtue of s 62(3)(e) unless there is produced to it evidence in writing of the existence of an agreement to marry. However, this is subject to subs (2), which provides as follows:

'Subsection (1) above does not apply if the court is satisfied that the agreement to marry was evidenced by—

(a) the gift of an engagement ring by one party to the agreement to the other in contemplation of their marriage, or
(b) a ceremony entered into by the parties in the presence of one or more other persons assembled for the purpose of witnessing the ceremony.'

The practical circumstances under which these provisions are likely to have to be considered are, therefore, either where an applicant entitled by some freehold, leasehold or contractual interest in a property is seeking an occupation order against a person to whom he was engaged, or where someone seeks a non-molestation order against someone to whom he was engaged; the latter is likely to be the more common. In either case, the court will have to be satisfied of the agreement to marry, and s 44 establishes that there are only three ways to do this.

First, the applicant may produce written evidence of the agreement; this does not mean a written agreement as such, but some written evidence of the fact that there was an agreement to marry. This could take the form of letters passing between the parties referring to their engagement, press announcements, wedding invitations or such other evidence as might satisfy the court; it would be for the court in each case to find as a fact that the written evidence put before it tended to prove the existence of the agreement, and this would have to be considered together with the oral evidence of the parties. The written evidence would be necessary but not, of itself, sufficient.

Secondly, where no such written evidence existed, the applicant could seek to prove that an engagement ring had changed hands, by way of gift. This would be a matter of evidence, no doubt oral in most cases. It would be helpful if the ring still existed. There might be room for argument as to whether a ring was an engagement ring, a mere gift, or a demonstration of affection and intent falling short of a commitment to marry.

Thirdly, the applicant could seek to prove that there had been a ceremony in the presence of others at which the agreement to marry had been made. This would be most likely to have happened where the parties belonged to one of the minority ethnic communities. The important element is that the agreement to marry itself is made at a formal ceremony; this would distinguish it from, say, an engagement party.

Where none of these three possibilities exists, the court may not entertain an application under s 33 or s 42. There could be an army of witnesses to prove an agreement to marry, but without proof in one of the three specified ways the court would be precluded from acting. What would happen if there was no such evidence but the respondent appeared before the court and admitted the engagement is unclear. At the very least, his verbal admission would be of no effect if he did not commit it to writing. If he did so, could it be argued that the court should not have allowed the matter to proceed so far in the absence of the pleading of one of the three specified grounds, and that the application should have been refused ad limine? This has not been adjudicated upon since the coming into force of the FLA 1996 and may be a matter for future debate.

Non-cohabiting couples [prospective change]

1.10 The class of associated persons is now extended by s 4 of the DVCVA 2004 so that s 62(3) of the FLA 1996 reads as follows:

'For the purposes of this Part, a person is associated with another person if—

(ea) they have or have had an intimate personal relationship with each other which is or was of significant duration'.

1.11   When explaining the possible meaning of this clause in debates on the Bill leading to the 2004 Act in Standing Committee,[1] the Parliamentary UnderSecretary of State Mr Goggins said that it was the government's intention to close a significant loophole in the protection afforded by the FLA 1996 by including within it non-cohabiting couples. The Bill defined the meaning of this in the broadest terms and it would be for the court in individual circumstances to determine whether it applied. It was not the government's intention to include platonic friendships or brief sexual encounters such as one-night stands. Intimacy and duration were the key elements. For short or non-intimate relationships the Protection from Harassment Act 1997 was available.

1.12   It seems, therefore, that the intention of the legislation is to include the boyfriend and girlfriend who had not actually lived together. It is easy to see the problems of definition which might be encountered, and it has to be said that the court may be faced with significant difficulties in certain cases. While it may not have been the government's intention to include platonic relationships, the word 'intimate' has a variety of meanings and cannot be taken always to import a sexual connotation. Again, what is 'significant duration'? Would one month, or one week, suffice?

Mr Goggins' view was clearly that the judges would recognise a suitable candidate for this description when they saw one, and this may well be true in the majority of cases, but there is certainly room for argument in peripheral cases.

Family proceedings

1.13   'Family proceedings' are defined by s 63(2) as any proceedings under the inherent jurisdiction of the High Court in relation to children, and any under the following enactments:

(a)   Part II of the 1996 Act;
(b)   Part IV of the 1996 Act;
(c)   the Matrimonial Causes Act 1973 (MCA 1973);
(d)   the Adoption Act 1976;
(e)   the Domestic Proceedings and Magistrates' Courts Act 1978;
(f)   Part III of the Matrimonial and Family Proceedings Act 1984;
(g)   Parts I, II, and IV of the Children Act 1989;
(h)   s 30 of the Human Fertilisation and Embryology Act 1990.

'Family proceedings' also includes proceedings in which the court has made an emergency protection order under s 44 of the Children Act 1989 which

---

[1]   Official Report (HC) Standing Committee 22 June 2004 cols 54 and 55.

includes an exclusion requirement as defined in s 44A(3) of that Act (see Chapter 6).

By s 62(2), 'relevant child' means:

'(a)   any child who is living with or might reasonably be expected to live with either party to the proceedings;

(b)   any child in relation to whom an order under the Adoption Act 1976 or the Children Act 1989 is in question in the proceedings; and

(c)   any other child whose interests the court considers relevant.'

The Law Commission had concluded that it was unnecessary for the court to have to have regard to the interests of every child of every party; it was clearly desirable for the court to have a discretion to make orders in relation to as wide a range of children as possible, without necessarily being required to consider the position of children whose interests might be completely unaffected by the matters before the court; hence the somewhat broad definition.[1]

Checklist

1.14   It may be helpful to set out in summary form the classes of persons with whom an applicant may be related. Such application may be made if the respondent is in one of the following categories:

(a)   in relation to the applicant:
spouse
former spouse
cohabitant
former cohabitant;

(b)   in relation to the applicant or to any class of person in (a):
father
mother
stepfather
stepmother
son
daughter
stepson
stepdaughter
grandmother
grandfather
grandson
granddaughter
brother
sister

---

[1]   Law Com, para 3.27.

half- or step-brother or sister
uncle
aunt
niece
nephew;

(c)   in relation to any of the persons in (b):
spouse
former spouse
cohabitant
former cohabitant;

(d)   someone who lives, or has lived, in the same household (for detail see **1.7**);

(e)   someone whom the applicant has agreed to marry (for detail see **1.9**); where agreement terminated, only within 3 years of termination;

(f)   a person with whom the applicant has had an intimate personal relationship of significant duration;

(g)   where the applicant is the parent of a child or has parental responsibility for a child, any other parent or person having parental responsibility;

(h)   where a child has been adopted or freed for adoption:

   (i)   a natural parent, or the parent of such a natural parent,
     is associated with
   (ii) the child, or
     a parent of the child by virtue of an adoption order, or
     a person who has applied for an adoption order, or
     any person with whom the child has at any time been placed for adoption.

Anyone in class (i) may apply for an order against anyone in class (ii);

(i)   the other party to any family proceedings.

Step Two: Is the victim 'entitled'?

1.15   The other preliminary classification, which relates to occupation orders made under FLA 1996 only, is whether or not the applicant is, in the terms of FLA 1996, 'entitled'. A person who is entitled makes her application for an occupation order under a different section of FLA 1996 from one who is not entitled; entitled applicants are then subdivided further according to whether or not they are or have been married. The reason for this complication is that Parliament was anxious not to confer on someone who had been in a casual relationship the same rights as a person who was or had been married, and it was thought necessary to take account of the various gradations of permanence of relationship.

1.16 The simple distinction between entitled and non-entitled applicants is that an entitled applicant is someone who has a legal right to occupy the property in question by reason of being the freehold owner, the tenant or a contractual licensee, or by reason of some statutory provision (this is rare). Section 33(1) of FLA 1996 therefore defines a 'person entitled' as one who:

(a) is entitled to occupy a dwelling house by virtue of a beneficial estate or interest or contract or by virtue of any enactment giving him the right to remain in occupation; or

(b) has matrimonial home rights in relation to a dwelling house.

A non-entitled person has no such legal right and is therefore in the position of asking the court to give her such a right. However, a person who would not otherwise be regarded as entitled may be so regarded because she has 'matrimonial home rights'. Such rights arise by virtue of a marriage and are lost on the grant of decree absolute unless an order is made before decree absolute to the effect that they survive.[1]

By FLA 1996, s 30(1), matrimonial home rights are conferred where:

'(a) one spouse is entitled to occupy a dwelling-house by virtue of—

   (i) a beneficial estate or interest or contract; or

   (ii) any enactment giving that spouse the right to remain in occupation; and

(b) the other spouse is not so entitled.'

These rights are conferred on the spouse 'not so entitled', and consist of the following:

'(a) if in occupation, a right not to be evicted or excluded from the dwelling-house or any part of it by the other spouse except with the leave of the court given by an order under section 33;

(b) if not in occupation, a right with the leave of the court so given to enter into and occupy the dwelling-house.'

Certain other consequential provisions are contained in the section, and these will be considered at more appropriate places in this book. For the moment, it is necessary only to mention s 30(7), which provides that the section does not apply to:

'a dwelling-house which has at no time been, and which was at no time intended by the spouses to be, a matrimonial home of the spouses in question.'

The words 'and which was at no time intended by the spouses to be' represent a change in the law effected by the FLA 1996. Under the Matrimonial Homes

---

1   FLA 1996, ss 31(8) and 33(5).

Act 1983 (MHA 1983), there was no power to regulate the occupation of a property which the parties intended to be their home, but in which they had never actually lived together. The Law Commission gave the example of a couple who had sold their existing house and were living in temporary rented accommodation while renovating a new house bought in the sole name of the husband. In such a case, the wife would have had no occupation rights over the new property if the relationship broke down in the meantime, since they had never lived in it together.[1] Section 30(7) of FLA 1996 corrects this gap in the law, so that matrimonial home rights may be acquired in respect of such a property.

The effect of matrimonial home rights is, therefore, that a spouse who occupies a dwelling-house which is, has been, or was intended to be the matrimonial home, and which is vested in the sole name of the other spouse, whether as beneficial owner or tenant, has a right of occupation and a right not to be evicted by the other spouse; where she is not in occupation, for example if the other spouse had evicted her, she is entitled to apply to the court for an order under s 33 of FLA 1996.

In summary therefore, if the victim is associated but not entitled she may apply under the FLA 1996 for a non-molestation order and for an occupation order; the exact kind of occupation order will depend on the section under which she is able to apply.

If the victim is not associated she can make no application under the FLA 1996. She may be able to apply for personal protection though not for any kind of occupation order. In practical terms, such protection is likely to be limited to that available under the PHA 1997.

---

[1]   Law Com, para 4.4.

Quick checklist

1.17 The following might be an instant checklist for use in conjunction with the information given above:

Non-molestation order

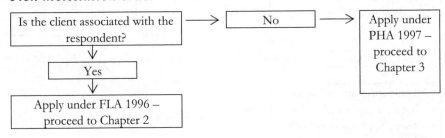

Occupation orders

Question 1: Preliminaries

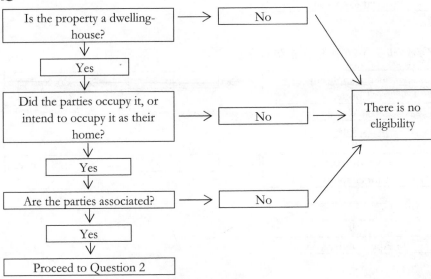

Question 2: Section 33 orders

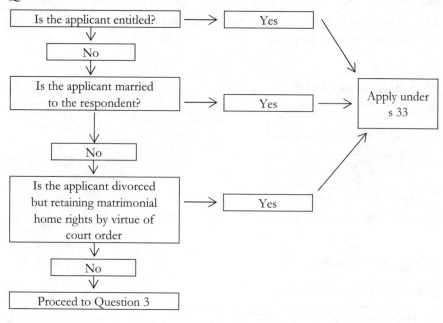

Question 3: Section 35 and 36 orders

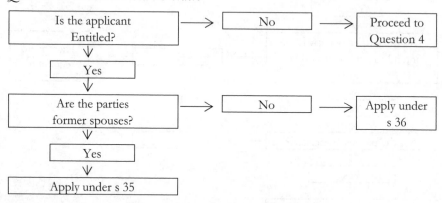

Question 4: Section 37 and 38 orders

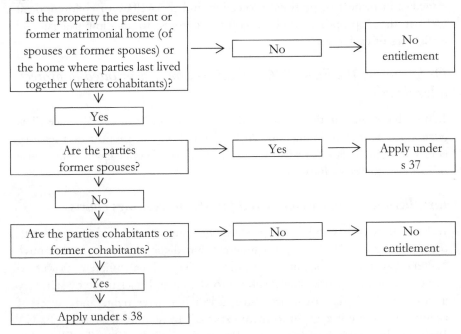

General note as to procedure and jurisdiction

Applications under Part IV of FLA 1996 may be 'free-standing' or made within family proceedings

1.18 Most applications for personal protection or regulation of occupation of the family home under the FLA 1996 will be 'free-standing', but protection under the Act is also available on applications made within other family proceedings.[1] In particular, sometimes an order under the powers in the FLA 1996 for protection of children is appropriate within proceedings under the Children Act 1989 (CA 1989). The court may make a non-molestation order in other family proceedings whether or not a formal application has been made and, in appropriate cases, of its own motion.[2]

Concurrent jurisdiction

1.19 FLA 1996, Part IV, follows the approach of CA 1989 in creating, with small exceptions, a structure of unified remedies and procedures available in the High Court, county courts and family proceedings courts. Parliament has chosen to achieve concurrent jurisdiction in different tiers of our historical

---

[1] Family Law Act 1996 (Part IV) (Allocation of Proceedings) Order 1997, art 4(3); Family Proceedings Rules 1991, SI 1991/1247 (FPR 1991), r 3.8(3).

[2] FLA 1996, s 42(2).

court structure as the best way to create a flexible system of family law remedies in respect of personal protection and the welfare of children, dealt. with at the appropriate level of court according to the importance and difficulties of each case.

Orders under the FLA 1996 and injunctions are granted to protect a legal right

1.20 This is not at the whim of the court or on 'palm-tree' justice. The general law is that an injunction can be granted only in support of a legal or equitable right. This was reaffirmed in the context of family law by the House of Lords in *Richards v Richards*.[1]

Jurisdiction of county courts and family proceedings courts

1.21 County courts and family proceedings courts have jurisdiction given to them by statute. They have no inherent jurisdiction over any substantive matters beyond their statutory jurisdiction. They have inherent power to regulate their own proceedings,[2] subject to statute and rules made by statutory instrument. Both tiers of courts have jurisdiction over rights and causes of action only where it is given to them expressly by statute, such as by the CA 1989 and the Children (Allocation of Proceedings) Order 1991, the FLA 1996 and the Family Law Act 1996 (Part IV) (Allocation of Proceedings) Order 1997, art 4(1) and, in county courts in relation to torts, by the County Courts Act 1984, s 15(1).

As far as family proceedings courts are concerned, there is no inherent jurisdiction or provision within rules to enable magistrates to exercise any general form of supervisory control over their own final orders or over the parties' arrangements. They are left with orders for taking charge and delivering a child under FLA 1986, s 34 and enforcement penalties under the Magistrates' Courts Act 1980, s 63(3). Unlike a judge in the High Court or a county court, magistrates in a family proceedings court may not make a final order with 'liberty to restore' nor adjourn proceedings which have been concluded for review at a later date. Proceedings are pending only for such time as it takes for the court to make a final order. Upon the making of a final order, the original proceedings cease and the magistrates become functus officio. Any subsequent orders sought in the context of those proceedings, including an application for committal or for taking charge and delivery of a child, must be sought by a fresh application being lodged and new proceedings issued.

---

[1]   [1984] AC 174, [1984] FLR 11 at 16H–17C, 17F, 23B, 29H, 32A and 35H.
[2]   *Langley v North West Water Authority* [1991] 3 All ER 610.

1.22 Magistrates' courts remain unable to decide contested matters of title to property[1] and the Lord Chancellor has power to restrict the level of court to which an application may be made.[2] However, in general, whether an application is made in a family proceedings court, a county court or the High Court, the remedies and procedures are essentially the same. Thus, magistrates now have the same power to accept an undertaking in proceedings under Part IV of FLA 1996 as the High Court and county courts,[3] and magistrates are provided with penal enforcement procedures similar to the High Court and county courts, for example penal or warning notices,[4] Notice to Show Good Reason,[5] order or committal[6] and purging contempt.[7]

Similarly, statutory provisions, designed to ensure that enforcement powers are the same for each tier of courts, include new powers for the High Court and county courts (and re-enactment of existing family proceedings courts' powers) to issue a warrant of arrest, where no power of arrest had been attached to the provision of the order alleged to have been breached,[8] also to remand an alleged contemnor until a full hearing can be conducted[9] and to remand a contemnor who appears to be mentally unbalanced for the purpose of obtaining a medical report .[10]

The 'parens patriae' inherent jurisdiction for the protection of minors and mentally incompetent adults is vested in the High Court alone.

Injunction powers of the High Court under the Supreme Court Act 1981 and of county courts under the County Courts Act 1984

1.23 The High Court has general powers, under s 37(1) of the Supreme Court Act 1981, to grant an injunction where it is 'just and convenient to do so'. These general powers are also available in a county court, under the County Courts Act 1984, s 38(1), provided that the county court has jurisdiction over the rights and obligations in support of which an injunction may be just and convenient. Where such rights and obligations are not within the jurisdiction conferred on county courts, a county court cannot assume or draw down the inherent jurisdiction of the High Court.

---

1   FLA 1996, s 59(1).
2   Ibid, s 57(3).
3   Ibid, s 46(1).
4   Form FL404.
5   Form FL418.
6   Form FL419.
7   Form FL421.
8   FLA 1996, s 47(8).
9   Ibid, s 47(7), (10), Sch 5, bail notice (Form FL412).
10   Ibid, s 48.

Injunctions for protection under the PHA 1997 and under the general law of torts

1.24 There remain some situations where a person seeks a remedy against harassment by someone who is not within the scope of the FLA 1996, for example a former lover who has not lived with the applicant and they have not produced any children. Such victims of harassment may be able to obtain a remedy under the PHA 1997 or under the general law of torts.

Because county courts have jurisdiction in cases founded in torts, they can grant an injunction to prevent a threatened tort or repetition of a tortious harm.

CHAPTER 2

NON-MOLESTATION ORDERS UNDER THE FAMILY LAW ACT 1996

The law

What is 'molestation'?

2.1 The FLA 1996 does not define 'molestation'. In *C v C (Non-molestation Order: Jurisdiction)*,[1] Sir Stephen Brown P held that molestation:

> 'implies some quite deliberate conduct which is aimed at a high degree of harassment of the other party, so as to justify the intervention of the court. ... It does not include enforcing an invasion of privacy per se; there has to be some conduct which clearly harasses and affects the applicant to such a degree that the intervention of the court is called for.'

This is consistent with the case-law in force before the FLA 1996, which established that 'molestation' means deliberate conduct which interferes with the victim, whether by violence, intimidation, harassment, pestering or interference that is sufficiently serious to warrant the intervention of the court.[2]

The Family Proceedings Rules Committee decided to adopt as part of Prescribed Form FL404 language similar to precedents in common use which avoided using the word 'molestation'. However, under s 47(2) of FLA 1996, there is a presumption in favour of a power of arrest where there has been actual or threatened violence, which is why threats of violence have been included in orders 38 and 40, rather than in orders 39 and 41, in Form FL404.

The words of the non-molestation menu of orders 38–41 in Prescribed Form FL404 give the convenient definition of 'molestation'.

> '38. The respondent [name] is forbidden to use or threaten violence against the applicant [name] [and must not instruct, encourage or in any way suggest that any other person should do so]. AND/OR

---

[1] [1998] 1 FLR 554.
[2] See *Davis v Johnson* [1979] AC 264 at 334A, *Vaughan v Vaughan* [1973] 3 All ER 449 at 452E, *Horner v Horner* (1983) FLR 50 at 51G.

39. The respondent [name] is forbidden to intimidate, harass or pester [or [*specify*]] the applicant [name] [and must not instruct, encourage or in any way suggest that any other person should do so]. AND/OR

40. The respondent [name] is forbidden to use or threaten violence against the relevant child(ren) [*name(s) and date(s) of birth*] [and must not instruct, encourage or in any way suggest that any other person should do so]. AND/OR

41. The respondent [name] is forbidden to intimidate, harass or pester [or [*specify*]] [the relevant child(ren) [*name(s) and date(s) of birth*]] [and must not instruct, encourage or in any way suggest that any other person should do so].'

Note that psychological harm can amount to actual bodily harm,[1] and silent phone calls can amount to an assault under s 47 of the Offences Against the Person Act 1861.[2]

Who may apply for non-molestation orders?

2.2   The FLA 1996 extends substantially the class of persons eligible to apply for non-molestation orders. The Act was designed as a family law statute and to protect persons with a family connection. Any person, including a child if he obtains leave of the High Court[3] can apply for a non-molestation order.[4] 'Associated persons' are defined in s 62(3) and the concept of family connection is not restricted to a nuclear family or to relatives.

Is the applicant eligible (being associated with the proposed respondent) for a non-molestation order?

2.3   See **1.4**.

The class of associated persons is considerably wider than the class eligible under the previous law, which was for practical purposes restricted to married persons and cohabitants of different sex. Under the previous law, after decree absolute of divorce, the family law remedies in relation to occupation of the family home ceased unless an order had been made extending a right to occupy the matrimonial home, and all the family law remedies between cohabitants ceased when cohabitation ended or after a limited period of about 3 months thereafter.

In *G v G (Non-molestation Order: Jurisdiction)*,[5] Wall J urged courts to adopt a purposive construction of Part IV of FLA 1996. In that case, justices had found that the applicant and respondent were not associated because they had never lived in the same household, they were not cohabitants and there was

---

1   *Kendrick v Kendrick* [1990] 2 FLR 107.
2   *R v Ireland; R v Burstow* [1998] 1 FLR 105, HL.
3   FLA 1996, s 43; Family Law Act 1996 (Part IV) (Allocation of Proceedings) Order 1997, art 4(2); FPR 1991, r 3.8(2).
4   FLA 1996, s 42(1).
5   [2000] 2 FLR 533.

insufficient evidence of agreement to marry. Wall J said that jurisdiction should not be declined unless the facts of the case were clearly not capable of being brought within the statute. In the instant case, three of the six 'signposts' set out by Woolf J in *Crake v Supplementary Benefits Commission*[1] (membership of the same household, stability, financial support, sexual relationship, children and public acknowledgement) were present.

Exclusion orders in respect of a defined area around a home or place of work

2.4   An occupation order (or, arguably, a non-molestation order) can include provision to 'exclude the respondent from a defined area in which the dwelling-house (the subject of the occupation order) is included'.[2]

In *Burris v Azadani*,[3] it was held that where a personal protection injunction is granted against torts, in order to make it effective the order can be supplemented by an order that the defendant shall not be within a defined area around the home of the plaintiff. This power should also enable the High Court or a county court to add to a non-molestation injunction an order excluding the respondent from a defined area around the home or place of work of the applicant, even if an occupation order is not available. There seems to be no reason in principle why a non-molestation order granted under Part IV of FLA 1996 should not include an order to exclude the respondent from a defined area around the applicant's place of work if such order is necessary to prevent molestation.

Care should be taken when drafting orders excluding a respondent from a defined area around a home. The distance should never be such as might lead to unintentional breach by the respondent. In any event, the distance must not exceed that which is necessary for the protection of the applicant. When the respondent has contact with a child residing in the house, consideration must be given to how this would be affected by a restriction as to radius.

Own motion non-molestation orders

2.5   Section 42(2)(b) of FLA 1996 enables the court when dealing with other family proceedings to make a non-molestation order in favour of one party, or a relevant child, against another party even though no application for such an order has been made.

---

[1]   [1982] 1 All ER 498.
[2]   FLA 1996, ss 33(3)(g), 35(5)(d), 36(5)(d), 37(3)(d), 38(3)(d).
[3]   [1996] 1 FLR 266.

Duration of non-molestation orders

2.6   Section 42(7) of FLA 1996 provides:

> 'A non-molestation order may be made for a specified period or until further order.'

The courts are likely to make initial orders of up to 6 months, following the practice before the FLA 1996.[1] A longer order may be appropriate where the respondent persists in molesting the applicant after the initial injunctive order. In *M v W (Non-Molestation Order: Duration)*,[2] Cazalet J held that justices had erred in making an open-ended non-molestation order. Unless there are exceptional circumstances, such an order should be for a fixed period; in the instant case, 18 months was reasonable. However, this decision was expressly disapproved by the Court of Appeal in *Re B-J (Power of Arrest)*,[3] where it was held that it was not helpful to seek to limit the making of indefinite non-molestation orders to circumstances which were exceptional or unusual; there were a great variety of cases where non-molestation orders might be required, and the statute clearly provided for indefinite orders if appropriate in the circumstances.

An (interim) without notice order need not last only until the return day. Indeed, to avoid problems of service, it would be wise for the order to last at least until 2 weeks after the return day. There is no reason in principle why the without notice order should not last for the whole (normal) period (eg 6 months), provided the return day is fixed as soon as possible.

Power of arrest

2.7   Section 47(2) of FLA 1996 provided that a power of arrest must be attached to one or more provisions of a non-molestation order if it appeared to the court that the respondent had used or threatened violence against the applicant or a relevant child, unless the court was satisfied that in all the circumstances of the case the applicant or child would be adequately protected without such a power of arrest. This provision enabled a constable to arrest without warrant a person whom he reasonably suspected had disobeyed the non-molestation order, and was regarded as a most important weapon for the protection of victims of domestic violence.

The effect of DVCVA 2004, Sch 10, para 38 is to amend FLA 1996, s 47 so that as from the date of implementation of the Act the power to attach a

---

[1]   See *Practice Note* [1978] 2 All ER 1056, [1978] 1 WLR 1123; *Practice Direction* [1981] 1 All ER 224, [1981] 1 WLR 27.
[2]   [2000] 1 FLR 107.
[3]   [2000] 2 FLR 443.

power of arrest to a non-molestation order will be removed, while allowing it to remain for occupation orders.

2.8 This provision might seem puzzling at first sight. However, the reason for it is that breach of a non-molestation order is to become a criminal arrestable offence (see **7.2** below) and it was thought that it would be unduly confusing for police officers to have to decide whether a person arrested by them should be dealt with under the previous procedure of bringing before the family court within 24 hours, or as a criminal defendant to be dealt with in the magistrates' court.

The result is that the court will no longer be able to attach a power of arrest to a non-molestation order. Methods of enforcement will be considered below, and the position relating to occupation orders is considered at **5.23**.

Procedure

2.9 Having established that the client is eligible under FLA 1996 and determined the kind of order to be sought, how does the practitioner go about obtaining such an order? The following Quick Procedural Guide will explain, though it should be noted that there is a detailed chapter on procedure at Chapter 5.

Which court?	Any county court or FPC (see **1.20**).
Documents to be filed at court.	Form FL401
	Written statement (FPC) or affidavit (county court).
	Draft order
Fees.	None in FPC. £ in county court.
Without notice hearing (where appropriate).	Applicant attends court with solicitor. NB statement must state why the application is being made without notice.
	Court will either make order, abridge time for service or decline to make order.
	The without notice order must provide for an on notice hearing.
Service.	The documents listed above, plus any without notice order, must be served personally on respondent allowing 2 clear days' notice (unless time for service has been abridged).
	A statement of service in Form FL415 must be filed at court.

	Where a power of arrest has been attached to a without notice order the applicant must file notice in Form FL406 at the applicant's local police station forthwith after service.
On notice hearing.	Applicant, witnesses and solicitor or counsel attend court.
	Court either makes order, accepts undertaking, or dismisses application. (See **5.25** as to undertakings.)
	Where undertaking accepted, respondent should be served with a sealed copy of the undertaking before leaving court.
Service.	As before, except where undertaking accepted and served at court.

CHAPTER 3

OCCUPATION ORDERS

Introduction

If the client is an associated person with proposed respondent, is the client eligible for an occupation order (or for a non-molestation order under s 42)?

3.1   As was seen at **1.14**, the structure of classification of rights of occupation in the FLA 1996, vested or contingent on grant of an order of the court, is governed first by property rights and, secondly, by the personal relationship between the parties. The appropriate category for the client can be found as follows.

The applicant can apply for an occupation order in respect of the family home if he or she is:

- the person in occupation who has a legal right of occupation, against any associated person (s 33, see **3.8**);
- the spouse who is in occupation but has no legal right of occupation against the spouse who has a right of occupation (ss 30(2)(a), 33(3), (4), see **3.8–3.11**);
- the spouse who is not in occupation and has no legal right of occupation against the spouse in occupation who has a right of occupation (ss 30(2)(b), 33(3), (4), see **3.8–3.11**);
- the spouse in occupation against the other spouse also in occupation where neither spouse has a right of occupation (s 37, see **3.23**);
- the previous spouse, whether or not in occupation against the previous spouse in occupation who has a right of occupation (s 35; see **3.13–3.17**);
- a cohabitant or former cohabitant where either party has a right of occupation (s 36, see **3.18–3.21**);
- a cohabitant or former cohabitant where both parties in occupation but neither party has a right of occupation (s 38, see **3.25**).

Expiration of s 30 matrimonial home rights on death or divorce

3.2   Where a spouse, who has no legal title, has matrimonial home rights under FLA 1996, s 30(1) and (2)(a), or is granted such rights under s 30(2)(b), under s 33(8) the rights expire on divorce or death of the other party unless:

(a)　an order is made to charge the rights on an estate or interest in the home under s 31; or

(b)　an order is made before the divorce or death, under s 33(5), extending the rights beyond the divorce or death.

Therefore, if divorce or death of the respondent who has the legal title is anticipated, it may be wise to seek an order under s 31 or s 33(5).

What criteria apply for the grant of an occupation order?

3.3　The criteria vary between s 33 and ss 35–38. They vary according to who has legal title (if either party does) and according to a 'balance of harm' test.

It will be necessary in each case to be clear which criteria are required by the applicable section to be taken into account by the court.

The criteria common to all applications are:

'(a)　the housing needs and housing resources of each of the parties and of any relevant child;

(b)　the financial resources of each of the parties;

(c)　the likely effect of any order, or any decision by the court not to exercise its powers [to make an occupation order], on the health, safety or well-being of the parties and of any relevant child; and

(d)　the conduct of the parties in relation to each other and otherwise.'

The 'balance of harm' test

3.4

'In considering whether to make an occupation order, the court will have to apply a "balance of harm" test. Under this test, in the case of spouses [where at least one has a legal right of occupation (ss 33(7), 35(8)), or neither has such right (s 37(4))], and others who have a right to occupy the home [s 33(7)], the court has a duty to make an occupation order where the applicant or a relevant child is likely to suffer significant harm attributable to conduct of the respondent if the order is not made, greater than the respondent or a relevant child is likely to suffer if the order is made. This power is discretionary in the case of cohabitants who do not have existing property rights [ss 36(7), (8), 38(5)] so that the court has additional flexibility in dealing with these situations.'[1]

In its report, the Law Commission explained the reasoning behind its recommendation, and how this would work in practice:

---

[1]　Consultation Paper on Part IV, Draft Rules and Forms, LCD, March 1997, at p 43, para 133.

'In cases where the question of significant harm does not arise, the court would have power to make an order taking into account the three factors set out above; but, in cases where there is a likelihood of significant harm, this power becomes a duty and the court must make an order after balancing the degree of harm likely to be suffered by both parties and any children concerned. This approach would still work in the case of cross applications, where the court would firstly consider who would suffer the greatest risk of harm if the order were not made. In the event of the balance of harm being equal, the court would retain power to make an order, but would have no duty to do so, and so would still be able to reach the right result. Harm has a narrower meaning than hardship. It is defined as "ill-treatment or impairment of physical or mental health". In relation to children, the term will attract the definition used in section 31 of the Children Act 1989. It is likely that a respondent threatened with ouster on account of his violence would be able to establish a degree of hardship (perhaps in terms of difficulty in finding or unsuitability of alternative accommodation or problems in getting to work). But he is unlikely to suffer significant harm, whereas his wife and children who are being subjected to his violence or abuse may very easily suffer harm if he remains in the house. In this way the court will be treating violence or other forms of abuse as deserving immediate relief, and will be directed to make an order where a risk of significant harm exists. However, by placing an emphasis on the need for a remedy rather than on the conduct which gave rise to that need, the criteria will not actually put a premium on allegations of violence and thus may avoid the problems which would be generated by a scheme which focuses upon it. The proposed test also has the advantage that it will avoid giving rise to a situation in which the court is put in the undesirable position of having to choose between the interests of a child and those of an adult, as, in cases where there is a risk of significant harm to a child, the duty to make an order will come into operation and the child's welfare will effectively become the paramount consideration.'[1]

It will be seen, therefore, that the first decision which the court has to make is whether or not to make any order at all; having decided to make an order, it must then decide which of the menu of orders contained in s 33(3) it should make. If the decision-making process anticipated by the Law Commission were adopted, the chain of reasoning would be as follows.

(1) The first consideration will be the direction contained in subs (7), namely to decide whether the applicant has established that she, or a relevant child, is likely to suffer significant harm attributable to conduct of the respondent if an order is not made (the meaning of 'significant harm' is considered below). The harm which may be taken into account is limited to harm which is attributable to the conduct of the respondent; other harm is not to be taken into consideration.

(2) Next, the court would have to consider whether the respondent had established that he or any relevant child would suffer significant harm if the order were made. Here, there is no requirement that the harm to be considered be attributable to the conduct of the applicant; the court may

---

[1] Law Com, para 4.34.

consider harm in the widest sense, for example, the harm which might be suffered as a result of being evicted.

(3) Finally, the court would have to decide which party would suffer the greater harm; the applicant or a child if the order were not made, or the respondent or child if the order were made.

The process therefore has a cumulative effect; if the applicant fails to clear the first hurdle, subs (7) does not apply at all, and subs (6) alone would govern the decision. If the applicant passed that stage, but the respondent failed to satisfy the court as to the second test, the court would have to find in favour of the applicant. It would only be if both hurdles were crossed that the court would be faced with the 'balance of harm' test.

3.5 With those principles in mind, the cases decided since the implementation of the act can be considered.

In *B v B (Occupation Order)*,[1] the wife and daughter of the marriage had left the home because of the husband's severe violence; he remained in occupation with his son from a previous marriage. It was held that the harm which he and his son would suffer if an order were made outweighed that which the wife and daughter would suffer if an order were not made, because they, being unintentionally homeless, would be rehoused by the local authority, whereas he would not be rehoused.

In *Chalmers v Johns*,[2] Mr Johns had been ordered to leave the home after a series of relatively minor incidents which were the culmination of a long and stormy relationship. His appeal was allowed. The Court of Appeal stated that this was not 'in any ordinary forensic language a domestic violence case' and that a less drastic order would have dealt with the problem.

Thorpe LJ observed that the wider provisions of Part IV did not obliterate the previous authorities to the effect that to require someone to vacate a family home was a Draconian order which should be restricted to exceptional cases. 'It remains an order which overrides proprietary rights and it seems to me that it is an order that is only justified in exceptional circumstances'.[3] For other examples of the exercise of the court's discretion.[4]

3.6 The various authorities have been considered, and helpful guidance as to approach of the court given, in *G v G (Occupation Order: Conduct)*.[5] The significant aspects may be summarised as follows:

---

[1] [1999] 1 FLR 715, CA.
[2] [1999] 1 FLR 392, CA.
[3] Ibid, at 397.
[4] See *Banks v Banks* [1999] 1 FLR 726; *S v F (Occupation Order)* [2000] 1 FLR 255.
[5] [2000] 2 FLR 31, CA.

(1) An exclusion order is Draconian and should be made only in exceptional circumstances.
(2) When considering an application under s 33, the court must first consider s 33(7). Then, if the precondition of significant harm is found not to be satisfied, the court may move to s 33(6).[1]
(3) Under s 33(7), significant harm must be attributed to the respondent's conduct. However, it does not have to be intentional conduct.
(4) The 'balance of harm' test involves comparison of the harm which would be suffered by the applicant and the relevant child if the order were not made with that which would be suffered by the respondent and any relevant child if the order were made. In the instant case, the judge had erroneously compared both situations from the applicant's perception.
(5) The discretionary exercise under s 33(6) is a precise one, which is strictly governed by the specific factors in the checklist. The court must make express reference to those factors; a generalised consideration of all the circumstances will not suffice.

Types of occupation orders in detail

3.7 The ingredients of an occupation order in respect of the family home, the criteria for an order, and the duration of an order all depend on the relationship between the parties and whether and what legal rights either of them have to occupy the home. See **3.3–3.4** for the general criteria which apply upon an application for an occupation order.

Section 33 orders

3.8 Occupation orders under s 33 are available to:

(1) a party in occupation who has a legal right of occupation, against any associated person (s 33); this includes cases where both parties are in occupation and both have a legal right of occupation;
(2) a spouse who is in occupation but has no legal right of occupation against the spouse who has a right of occupation (s 33(3), (4)); such an applicant has vested 'matrimonial home rights' under s 30(2)(a);
(3) a spouse who is not in occupation and has no legal right of occupation against the spouse in occupation who has a right of occupation (s 33(3), (4)); such an applicant has a right to apply for leave to enter and occupy, ie contingent 'matrimonial home rights' under s 30(2)(b).

3.9 The menu of possible orders under s 33(3) is set out in Form FL404, as follows:

'1. The court declares that the applicant [name] is entitled to occupy [address of home or intended home] as [his/her] home. OR

---

[1] See also *Chalmers v Johns* [1999] 1 FLR 392, CA.

2. The court declares that the applicant [name] has matrimonial home rights in [address of home or intended home]. AND/OR

3. The court declares that the applicant [name]'s matrimonial home rights shall not end when the respondent [name] dies or their marriage is dissolved and shall continue until ... or further order.

It is ordered that:

4. The respondent [name] shall allow the applicant [name] to occupy [address of home or intended home] OR

5. The respondent [name] shall allow the applicant [name] to occupy part of [address of home or intended home] namely: [specify part]

6. The respondent [name] shall not obstruct, harass or interfere with the applicant [name]'s peaceful occupation of [address of home or intended home]

7. The respondent [name] shall not occupy [address of home or intended home] OR

8. The respondent [name] shall not occupy [address of home or intended home] from [specify date] until [specify date] OR

9. The respondent [name] shall not occupy [specify part of address of home or intended home] AND/OR

10. The respondent [name] shall not occupy [address or part of address] between [specify dates or times]

11. The respondent [name] shall leave [address or part of address] [forthwith] [within _____ [hours/days] of service on [him/her] of this order] AND/OR

12. Having left [address or part of address], the respondent [name] shall not return to, enter or attempt to enter [or go within [specify distance] of] it.'

3.10 The detailed effect of these provisions will be considered in turn.

(a) Enforce the applicant's entitlement to remain in occupation

An order in these terms would be required where the respondent had interfered, or threatened to interfere with the applicant's right to occupy the dwelling-house. The order would, where necessary, declare the applicant's right of occupation, and take the form of an injunction restraining the respondent from interfering with that right. It would be for the court to decide whether any of the other classes of order contained in subs (3) should also be made.

(b) Require respondent to permit applicant to enter and remain in dwelling-house or part

This would apply where the applicant had been excluded from the home, or where the respondent threatened to exclude her. It would take the form of a mandatory order requiring the respondent to allow the applicant back into possession, and/or a restraining order requiring him not to exclude her.

Such an order could direct that the applicant be permitted to occupy part only of the house; this might be appropriate where, for example, the house was large enough for the respective quarters of the parties to be defined, and it was in their best interests to be kept apart.

(c) Regulate the occupation of dwelling-house by either party

This overlaps, to some extent, with the final comments in para (b) above. In theory, to 'regulate' the occupation of a house could involve excluding one party from it. However, the fact that there is specific provision in this section for exclusion suggests that this provision is designed to enable the court to dictate which parts of a house may be used by one or other party, and to prescribe areas which one party may not enter.

(d) If respondent entitled, prohibit, suspend or restrict the exercise of his right to occupy

This applies where the respondent is 'entitled' under s 33(1)(a)(i); that is to say, he is entitled to occupy because he is a freehold or beneficial owner, or tenant, or contractual licensee. He does not need the protection of the FLA 1996 in order to occupy; he occupies as of right.

This provision, therefore, enables the court to override his legal property rights, and to deny him the right to occupy the house. This can be a complete denial ('prohibit'), a temporary denial ('suspend'), or a partial denial ('restrict').

(e) If respondent has matrimonial home rights, restrict or terminate those rights

To some extent, this is a mirror image of the previous provision. Whether or not a person has matrimonial home rights is a matter of law, not discretion. Where the parties are spouses, and one of them is 'entitled' because of general legal rights, the other automatically acquires matrimonial home rights by virtue of s 30(2). If these rights could not be interfered with, there would be the absurd position that such a person would be in a stronger position than the spouse who was 'entitled'.

Accordingly, this provision permits the court to order that a person with matrimonial home rights may be excluded from the home either partially, temporarily or permanently.

(f) Require respondent to leave the dwelling-house or part thereof

This is self-explanatory, and clearly fits in with the general array of powers conferred on the court. This provision would be the specific authority for making an ouster order.

(g) Exclude respondent from a defined area in which the dwelling-house is included

This is a power which derives from the DVMPA 1976, there being no corresponding provision in the MHA 1983; it is clearly sensible that it is to be included in the unified powers of the court. The tendency has been for courts to approach such orders with caution. On the one hand, it may obviously be wise to prevent a potential molester from lurking in the vicinity of the home and intimidating by his very presence. However, it is necessary to have regard to and protect the liberty of the subject, and also to avoid the possibility of unintentional breaches of orders. Accordingly, it is submitted that any order of this kind should be made only where a clear need for it, in order to protect the applicant and family, has been demonstrated, and then only in the most limited terms consistent with the safety of the applicant. Having said that, it must also be said that the specimen orders attached to Form FL404 include, at nos 12, 19 and 23, an appropriate order for use in such cases.

3.11 By s 33(7), the 'balance of harm' test applies . For the effect of this, and the matters contained in s 33(6), see **3.3** and **3.4**.

(h) Duration of s 33 orders

3.12 An order under s 33(3) may be indefinite or for a defined period.[1] However, where a spouse, who has no legal title, has matrimonial home rights under s 30(1) and (2)(a), or is granted such rights under s 30(2)(b), under s 33(8) the rights expire on divorce or death of a party unless:

(a) an order is made to charge the rights on an estate or interest in the home under s 31; or

(b) an order is made before the divorce or death, under s 33(5), extending the rights beyond the divorce or death.

Therefore, if divorce or death of the respondent who has the legal title is anticipated, it will be wise to seek an order under s 31 or s 33(5).

Section 35 orders

3.13 Section 35 orders are available to a former spouse, whether or not in occupation, who has no right of occupation against the former spouse who has a right of occupation of a dwelling-house in which they lived or intended to live (s 35(1), (2)).

Section 35 deals with cases where the applicant is non-entitled, the respondent is entitled and the applicant is a former spouse. Subsection (1) applies where:

---

[1] FLA 1996, s 33(10).

'(a) one former spouse is entitled to occupy a dwelling-house by virtue of a beneficial estate or interest or contract, or by virtue of any enactment giving him the right to remain in occupation; and

(b) the other former spouse is not so entitled; and

(c) the dwelling-house was at any time their matrimonial home or was at any time intended by them to be their matrimonial home.'

Subsection (2) then provides that, in such cases, the former spouse, not so entitled, may apply for an order under this section against the entitled former spouse.

The section will never apply to spouses, since they have matrimonial home rights. Applicants under this section will therefore always be former spouses; the respondent will always be 'entitled'.

3.14 The menu of possible orders under s 35(3), (4) and (5) is set out in Form FL404.

If the court grants an order, it must (s 35(3), (4)), include menu orders 13 and 14:

13. 'The applicant [name] has the right to occupy [address of home or intended home] and the respondent [name] shall allow the applicant [name] to do so'.

14. 'The respondent [name] shall not evict or exclude the applicant [name] from [address of home or intended home] or any part of it namely [specify part]'.

These orders are mandatory. If the court makes any order at all under s 35, it must include these orders. In addition, the possible supplementary orders under s 35(5) are set out in menu orders 15–19:

'15. The respondent [name] shall not occupy [*address of home or intended home*]. OR

16. The respondent [name] shall not occupy [*address of home or intended home*] from [*specify date*] until [*specify date*] OR

17. The respondent [name] shall not occupy [*specify part of address of home or intended home*] OR

18. The respondent [name] shall leave [*address or part of address*] [forthwith] [within _____ [*hours/days*] of service on [*him/her*] of this order.] AND/OR

19. Having left [*address or part of address*], the respondent [name] shall not return to, enter or attempt to enter [or go within [*specify distance*] of] it.'

3.15 It will be seen that the provisions of subss (3) and (4) are similar to, but not identical with, matrimonial home rights. The similarities are obvious, and may be demonstrated by comparing this subsection with s 30(2).

The differences are as follows. First, there is no mention of 'leave of the court'. The reason for this is that matrimonial home rights are an entitlement conferred by statute, whereas the protection under a s 35 order is always contained in an order of the court.

Secondly, whereas matrimonial home rights are a general protection, with no time-limit (save that they disappear on decree absolute), the rights under a s 35 order will subsist only for 'the period specified in the order'. Courts will, therefore, have to ensure that every order under s 35 specifies a period for the duration of the rights conferred.

3.16   The criteria applicable in deciding whether to make a s 35 order are set out in s 35(6) and are:

'all the circumstances including—

(a)   the housing needs and housing resources of each of the parties and of any relevant child;

(b)   the financial resources of each of the parties;

(c)   the likely effect of any order, or of any decision by the court not to exercise its powers under subsection (3) or (4), on the health, safety or well-being of the parties and of any relevant child;

(d)   the conduct of the parties in relation to each other and otherwise;

(e)   the length of time that has elapsed since the parties ceased to live together;

(f)   the length of time that has elapsed since the marriage was dissolved or annulled; and

(g)   the existence of any pending proceedings between the parties—

(i)   for an order under section 23A or 24 of MCA 1973 (property adjustment orders in connection with divorce proceedings etc.);

(ii)   for an order under paragraph 1(2)(d) or (e) of Schedule 1 to the Children Act 1989 (orders for financial relief against parents); or

(iii)   relating to the legal or beneficial ownership of the dwelling-house.'

If the court decides to grant a s 35 order, then the 'balance of harm' test is applied by s 35(8) in relation to whether the court includes in the order a supplementary order under s 35(5):

'(8) If the court decides to make an order under this section and it appears to it that, if the order does not include a subsection (5) provision, the applicant or any relevant child is likely to suffer significant harm attributable to conduct of the respondent, the court shall include the subsection (5) provision in the order unless it appears to the court that—

(a)   the respondent or any relevant child is likely to suffer significant harm if the provision is included in the order; and

(b)   the harm likely to be suffered by the respondent or child in that event is as great as or greater than the harm attributable to conduct of the respondent which is likely to be suffered by the applicant or child if the provision is not included.'

Further criteria apply for deciding whether, if the 'balance of harm' test does not apply, to make a supplementary order under s 35(5). The further criteria are items (a) to (e) in the list from s 35(6) set out above.

Duration of s 35 orders

3.17 By s 35(10), a s 35 order 'must be limited so as to have effect for a specified period not exceeding 6 months, but may be extended on one or more occasions for a further specified period not exceeding 6 months'. Further, an order under s 35:

> '(a) may not be made after the death of either of the former spouses; and
> (b) ceases to have effect on the death of either of them.'

Where an occupation order is granted without notice, and is renewed at a hearing on notice, the period it may remain effective is calculated from the date on which the initial without notice order is granted.[1]

Section 36 orders

3.18 Section 36 orders are available, at the discretion of the court, to a person who is a cohabitant or former cohabitant where one of them only has a right of occupation in the home where they live or intended to live together as man and wife.[2] If both cohabitants have a right of occupation, the application should be made under s 33.

It may be remembered that FLA 1996, s 41 provided that where the parties were cohabitants or former cohabitants, in considering the nature of the parties' relationship the court 'is to have regard to the fact that they have not given each other the commitment involved in marriage'. This always was a meaningless provision, and it will come as no surprise to learn that this was not part of the government's original draft Bill but was accepted as a backbencher's amendment when the progress of the Bill was in difficulty.

Section 2(1) of DVCVA 2004 has repealed FLA 1996, s 41 so this will no longer be an issue to trouble the court.

The menu of possible orders under s 36(3), (4) and (5) is set out in Form FL404, orders 13–19.

If the court grants an order, it must (s 36(3), (4)) include menu orders 13 and 14. Orders 13 and 14, made under s 36(3) or (4) give the applicant the right to live in and not to be excluded from the home:

---

1   FLA 1996, s 45(4).
2   Ibid, s 36(1).

'13. The applicant [name] has the right to occupy [*address of home or intended home*] and the respondent [name] shall allow the applicant [name] to do so. OR

14. The respondent [name] shall not evict or exclude the applicant [name] from [*address of home or intended home*] or any part of it namely [specify part].'

The court can add orders 15–19 under s 36(5), to regulate the occupation of the home by the respondent. Orders 15–19 are:

'15. The respondent [name] shall not occupy [*address of home or intended home*] OR

16. The respondent [name] shall not occupy [*address of home or intended home*] from [*specify date*] until [*specify date*] OR

17. The respondent [name] shall not occupy [*specify part of address of home or intended home*] OR

18. The respondent [name] shall leave [*address or part of address*] [forthwith] [within _____ [*hours/days*] of service on [*him/her*] of this order] AND/OR

19. Having left [*address or part of address*], the respondent [name] shall not return to, enter or attempt to enter [or go within [*specify distance*] of] it.'

3.19 Orders under s 36 are discretionary. The criteria applicable in deciding whether to make a s 36(3) or (4) order in orders 13 and 14 are set out in s 35(6). The matters to be considered under s 36(6) are:

'all the circumstances including—

(a) the housing needs and housing resources of each of the parties and of any relevant child;

(b) the financial resources of each of the parties;

(c) the likely effect of any order, or of any decision by the court not to exercise its powers under subsection (3) or (4), on the health, safety or well-being of the parties and of any relevant child;

(d) the conduct of the parties in relation to each other and otherwise;

(e) the nature of the parties' relationship and in particular the level of commitment attached to it;

(f) the length of time during which they have lived together as husband and wife;

(g) whether there are or have been any children who are children of both parties or for whom both parties have or have had parental responsibility;

(h) the length of time that has elapsed since the parties ceased to live together; and

(i) the existence of any pending proceedings between the parties—

    (i) for an order under paragraph 1(2)(d) or (e) of Schedule 1 to the Children Act 1989 (orders for financial relief against parents); or

    (ii) relating to the legal or beneficial ownership of the dwelling-house.'

If the court decides to grant orders 13 or 14 under s 36(4), then further criteria apply as to whether the court should add orders 15–19 under s 36(5). The further criteria are set out in s 36(6) and (8).

The considerations in s 36(6) are:

'(a) the housing needs and housing resources of each of the parties and of any relevant child;

(b) the financial resources of each of the parties;

(c) the likely effect of any order, or of any decision by the court not to exercise its powers under subsection (3) or (4), on the health, safety or well-being of the parties and of any relevant child;

(d) the conduct of the parties in relation to each other and otherwise.'

3.20 If the court decides to grant a s 36 order then the 'balance of harm' test is applied by s 36(7) and (8) in relation to whether the court includes in the order a supplementary order under s 36(5) to regulate the occupation of the home by the respondent. The court must consider:

'(a) whether the applicant or any relevant child is likely to suffer significant harm attributable to conduct of the respondent if the subsection (5) provision is not included in the order; and

(b) whether the harm likely to be suffered by the respondent or child if the provision is included is as great as or greater than the harm attributable to conduct of the respondent which is likely to be suffered by the applicant or child if the provision is not included.'

3.21 Comparison with s 35(6) shows that s 36(6)(h) has its counterpart in subs 6(e) of that section. The real differences are therefore contained in (e), (f) and (g). Given that the parties have never married, the court has, in effect, to make a value judgement on the nature of the relationship; cohabitants may vary from those who have entered into a fleeting relationship to those who have lived together in a stable relationship for many years and have brought up children together. In deciding who is to occupy the home, and for how long, the court will have to take these matters into account.

A potentially more significant difference from the s 35 provisions is contained in s 36(7), which deals with whether or not to include any of the subs (5) provisions in an order which the court has decided to make which contains the matters mentioned in subs (3) or (4); this is, essentially, the significant harm test. By subs (7), the court is directed to have regard to:

'… all the circumstances including—

(a) the matters mentioned in subsection (6)(a) to (d); and

(b) the questions mentioned in subsection (8).'

By subs (8), the questions are:

'(a) whether the applicant or any relevant child is likely to suffer significant harm attributable to conduct of the respondent if the subsection (5) provision is not included in the order; and

(b)   whether the harm likely to be suffered by the respondent or child if the provision is included is as great as or greater than the harm attributable to conduct of the respondent which is likely to be suffered by the applicant or child if the provision is not included.'

This is similar in some respects to the 'greater harm' test contained in s 35. However, there is one obvious difference. Under s 35(8), which applies the 'greater harm' test to former spouses, the court must include a subs (5) provision where the first limb of the 'greater harm' test is satisfied, unless satisfied as to the second limb; once significant harm is established, the onus passes to the respondent to show why a subs (5) provision should not be included.

Under s 36(8), applicable to cohabitants or former cohabitants, there is no such requirement on the court. The issue of the balance of significant harm is a 'question' for the consideration of the court; the court must consider it, but there is no obligation on the court to exercise its discretion in any particular direction once it has made a finding.

It might be argued that the court would be acting unreasonably, or unjudicially, if it did not include a subs (5) provision after making a finding in favour of one party as to one of the subs (8) questions. However, the difference in wording between the two provisions is deliberate and it might be thought, therefore, that the intention of Parliament was that the protection to be afforded to a cohabitant is less than that which the court is obliged to afford to a former spouse.

Duration of s 36 orders

3.22 Section 36(9) contains provisions identical with those in s 35(9). Subsection (10) provides that an order under s 36 must be limited so as to have effect for a specified period not exceeding 6 months, but may be extended on one further occasion for a further specified period not exceeding 6 months. This is the second principal difference between these provisions and the s 35 provisions. A cohabitant or former cohabitant is limited to an occupation order for one year; then she must leave.

The intention is clearly that, if the applicant is unable to justify occupation on other grounds in other proceedings (eg under the Children Act 1989, or by proving a beneficial or equitable interest), an occupation order should not in the long term displace the interest in the property of the entitled party.

Finally, s 36(13) provides that, so long as the order remains in force, subss (3)–(6) of s 30 apply in relation to the applicant as if he were a spouse entitled to occupy the dwelling-house by virtue of that section and the respondent were the other spouse. These provisions relate to payment of rent, mortgage, etc.

Section 37 orders

3.23 Section 37 orders are available to a spouse in occupation against other spouse also in occupation where neither have a right of occupation.[1]

The menu of possible orders under s 37(3) is set out in Form FL404 orders 20–23:

> '20. The respondent [name] shall allow the applicant [name] to occupy [*address of home or intended home*] or part of it namely: [*specify*]. AND/OR
> 21. [One or both of the provisions in paragraphs 6 and 10 above may be inserted] AND/OR
> 22. The respondent [name] shall leave [*address or part of address*] [forthwith] [within _____ [*hours/days*] of service on [*him/her*] of this order] AND/OR
> 23. Having left [*address or part of address*], the respondent [name] may not return to, enter or attempt to enter [or go within [*specify distance*] of] it.'

The criteria applicable in deciding whether to make a s 37 order are the same as in s 33(6).

> '(a) the housing needs and housing resources of each of the parties and of any relevant child;
> (b) the financial resources of each of the parties;
> (c) the likely effect of any order, or of any decision by the court not to exercise its powers under subsection (3) or (4), on the health, safety or well-being of the parties and of any relevant child;
> (d) the conduct of the parties in relation to each other and otherwise.'

By s 37(4) and s 33(7), the 'balance of harm' test applies to create a presumption that a s 37(3) order should be made 'if it appears to the court that the applicant or any relevant child is likely to suffer significant harm attributable to conduct of the respondent if an order containing one or more of the provisions mentioned in subsection (3) is not made'. If this appears to the court, the court must make an order:

> 'unless it appears to the court that—
> (a) the respondent or any relevant child is likely to suffer significant harm if the order is made; and
> (b) the harm likely to be suffered by the respondent or child in that event is as great as, or greater than, the harm attributable to conduct of the respondent which is likely to be suffered by the applicant or child if the order is not made.'

---

[1] FLA 1996, s 37(1), (2).

Duration of s 37 orders

3.24   By s 37(5), a s 37 order 'must be limited so as to have effect for a specified period not exceeding six months, but may be extended on one or more occasions for a further specified period not exceeding six months'.

Where an occupation order is granted without notice and is renewed at a hearing on notice, the period it may remain effective is calculated from the date on which the initial without notice order is granted (s 45(4)).

Section 38 orders

3.25   Section 38 orders are available where the client is cohabitant or former cohabitant and where both parties in occupation but neither has a right of occupation.[1]

The menu of possible orders under s 38(3) is set out in Form FL404 orders 20–23.

The criteria applicable in deciding whether to make a s 38 order are set out in s 38(4) and (5).

By s 38(4), the court must 'have regard to all the circumstances including:

'(a)   the housing needs and housing resources of each of the parties and of any relevant child;
(b)   the financial resources of each of the parties;
(c)   the likely effect of any order, or of any decision by the court not to exercise its powers under subsection (3), on the health, safety or well-being of the parties and of any relevant child;
(d)   the conduct of the parties in relation to each other and otherwise; and
(e)   the questions mentioned in subsection (5).'

By s 38(5), the 'balance of harm' test applies when the court is considering whether to grant a s 38 order. The court must 'have regard to':

'(a)   whether the applicant or any relevant child is likely to suffer significant harm attributable to conduct of the respondent if the subsection (3) provision is not included in the order; and
(b)   whether the harm likely to be suffered by the respondent or child if the provision is included is as great as or greater than the harm attributable to conduct of the respondent which is likely to be suffered by the applicant or child if the provision is not included.'

---

[1]   FLA 1996, s 38.

Section 38(4) provides that in the exercise of its discretion the court must have regard to all the circumstances including the matters which it goes on to set out. These are, in fact, identical to those contained in s 36(7) and (8) (see **3.21**), with five exceptions.

There is no reference to:

(1) children;
(2) the nature of the relationship;
(3) the length of the relationship;
(4) the length of time since they ceased to live together;
(5) other proceedings.

This, in effect, leaves needs, resources, effect of order and conduct as the relevant factors. Significant harm is dealt with as a 'question' the court must consider but, as in s 36, there is no requirement on the court to make any particular order as a result of that inquiry.

Duration of s 38 orders

3.26 By s 38(6):

'An order under this section shall be limited so as to have effect for a specified period not exceeding six months, but may be extended on one occasion for a further specified period not exceeding six months.'

Where an occupation order is granted without notice, and is renewed at a hearing on notice, the period it may remain effective is calculated from the date on which the initial without notice order is granted.[1]

Penal notice incorporated in an occupation order

3.27 Where no non-molestation order is included in an occupation order, the court has a discretion as to whether to attach a penal notice, but where a non-molestation order is included a penal notice is to be incorporated.[2]

Power of arrest attached to occupation order

3.28 As was seen in Chapter 2, breach of a non-molestation order is now a criminal offence and the power to attach a power of arrest to such an order has been removed. To that end, s 46 of FLA 1996 has been amended.

It should be made clear, however, that the court retains the power to attach a power of arrest to an occupation order, so that the procedure for arrest and

---

[1] FLA 1996, s 45(4).
[2] FPR 1991, r 3.9(6)(b), FPC(CA)R, r 12A(1)(b), Form FL404, Notices A and B.

bringing a contemnor before the county court remains the same. One of the several difficulties this might bring is where the court chose to make both a non-molestation order and an occupation order. In the event of a breach, a person could be arrested under the power of arrest for breach of the occupation order but not the non-molestation order. It will be interesting to see how the police deal with this difficulty. A further difficulty might be where the court had made an occupation order with a radius clause, eg not to attempt to enter the former home nor to come within 100 metres of it. Breach of such an order might well involve violence but, in the absence of a non-molestation order, would be dealt with under the power of arrest, which is normally attached to such a provision.

What was previously an interesting issue of whether such a radius clause should be classed as an occupation order or a non-molestation order will now become much more relevant, not to say vital, and will have important practical effects. The following guidance is offered somewhat tentatively. If the order is, for example, to leave the property and then not to return within 100 metres of it, it will certainly be an occupation order. However, what about an order where the parties do not live together and there is no ouster involved? Here, the radius clause would be imposed as an adjunct to the non-molestation order and would therefore be a non-molestation order itself. The way in which such orders are drafted will therefore be of great practical significance.

Forms of order

3.29   As a result of the changes effected by DVCVA 2004, the forms of order (formerly Form FL404) have had to be changed. For a full explanation see **5.23** below.

Supplementary orders providing for maintenance, repair, mortgage or rent payments and care and use of furniture, available for orders under s 33, s 35 or s 36

3.30   FLA 1996, s 40 provides for certain supplementary orders to be available when an occupation order is made under s 33, s 34 or s 35. These are to be found in the menu of orders in Form FL404, orders 24 to 31.

'24. The [*applicant [name]*] [*respondent [name]*] shall maintain and repair [*address of home or intended home*] AND/OR
25. The [*applicant [name]*] [*respondent [name]*] shall pay the rent for [*address of home or intended home*]. OR
26. The [*applicant [name]*] [*respondent [name]*] shall pay the mortgage payments on [*address of home or intended home*]. OR
27. The [*applicant [name]*] [*respondent [name]*] shall pay the following for [*address of*

home or intended home]: [*specify outgoings as bullet points*].

28. The [*party in occupation*] shall pay to the [*other party*] £   each [*week, month, etc*] for [*address of home etc*].

29. The [*party in occupation*] shall keep and use the [*furniture*] [*contents*] [*specify if necessary*] of [*address of home or intended home*] and the [*applicant [name]*] [*respondent [name]*] shall return to the [*party in occupation*] the [*furniture*] [*contents*] [*specify if necessary*] [*no later than [date/time]*].

30. The [*party in occupation*] shall take reasonable care of the [*furniture*] [*contents*] [*specify if necessary*] of [*address of home or intended home*].

31. The [party in occupation] shall take all reasonable steps to keep secure [*address of home or intended home*] and the furniture or other contents [*specify if necessary*].'

In *Nwogbe v Nwogbe*,[1] it was held that an order made under FLA 1996, s 40 cannot be enforced by committal and that, indeed, it seems that there is no obvious way to enforce such an order.

It will be noted that these provisions do not apply to s 37 or s 38 orders; the reason is that in those cases neither party has any legal right of occupation, and therefore the question of liability for outgoings does not arise.

3.31   Section 40(2) contains guidelines to govern the exercise of the court's discretion. It is provided that in deciding whether and, if so, how to exercise its powers, the court shall have regard to all the circumstances of the case, including:

'(a)   the financial needs and financial resources of the parties; and
(b)   the financial obligations which they have, or are likely to have in the foreseeable future, including financial obligations to each other and to any relevant child.'

No particular comment is needed on these provisions.

By subs (3), any order under this section ceases to have effect when the occupation order to which it relates ceases to have effect.

Suggested draft order/checklist in Part IV of the Family Law Act 1996

3.32   As has been seen, in applications for injunctions, it is the duty of the applicant to supply the court with a draft order. Part IV of the Family Law Act 1996 provides a somewhat bewildering menu of possible orders, and in many county courts the practice has arisen of handing up a checklist with the appropriate orders ticked. This is entirely acceptable to most county courts

---

1   [2000] 2 FLR 744, CA.

because the orders themselves are available on a computer programme used by the court service. The form is also useful for the judge and for court staff to ensure that all necessary matters have been considered.

The tick box form which is set out below was originally the work of District Justice Gordon Ashton of the Preston County Court and was first published in the *Bulletin of the Association of District Judges*.

			Case No			
Applicant			and			Respondent
Date	....		CJ/DJ	....		[name]
Ex parte	Yes/No					
Applicant	counsel	solicitor	in person	no attendance	Present	Yes/No
Respondent	counsel	solicitor	in person	no attendance	Present	Yes/No
Statements						[name/date]
Evidence						[name/date]

NOTICE   Type A – *non-molestation order (includes penal notice)*   OR

Type B – *no non-molestation order*   Delete penal notice   Yes/No

DURATION *of non-molestation orders*   the order shall continue until

NON-MOLESTATION ORDERS

It is ordered that:

1.   The *Respondent* is forbidden to use or threaten violence against the *Applicant* [and must not instruct, encourage or in any way suggest that any other person should do so] AND/OR

2.   The *Respondent* is forbidden to intimidate, harass or pester [*or specify*] the *Applicant* [and must not instruct, encourage or in any way suggest that any other person should do so] AND/OR

3.   The *Respondent* is forbidden to use or threaten violence against the children [*specify name(s) and date(s) of birth of relevant children*] [and must not instruct, encourage or in any way suggest that any other person should do so] AND/OR

4.   The *Respondent* is forbidden to intimidate, harass or pester [*or specify*] the children [*specify name(s) and date(s) of birth of relevant children*] [and must not instruct, encourage or in any way suggest that any other person should do so]

5.   The *respondent* is forbidden to approach within   metres of

COSTS

Respondent/Applicant to pay assessed costs of £

Respondent/Applicant to pay costs to be determined by detailed assessment

Public funding detailed assessment *Applicant/Respondent/both parties*   Certificate for counsel

Costs reserved   No Order as to costs

HEARING – *for ex parte orders*

Next available date after .... days   Time estimate .... *hours/minutes*

Service abridged to   *days/hours*

OCCUPATION ORDERS

ARREST   The power of arrest applies to paragraphs   below and remains
in force until [date]

Home: [address]

Section 33 – *Applicant has estate or interest or matrimonial home rights*

6.   The court declares that the *Applicant* is entitled to occupy [*home*] as *his/her* home OR

7.   The court declares that the *Applicant* has matrimonial home rights in [*home*] AND/OR

8.   The court declares that the *Applicant's* matrimonial home rights shall not end when the *Respondent*
dies or their marriage is dissolved and shall continue until .... [*date*] or further order

It is ordered that:

9.   The *Respondent* shall allow the *Applicant* to occupy [*home*] OR

10.   The *Respondent* shall allow the *Applicant* to occupy part of [*home*] namely:

.... [specify part]

11.   The *Respondent* shall not obstruct, harass or interfere with the *Applicant's* peaceful occupation of
[*home*]

13.   The *Respondent* shall not occupy [*home*] from .... [*date*] until .... [*date*] OR

14.   The *Respondent* shall not occupy .... [specify part] AND/OR

15.   The *Respondent* shall not occupy [*home*] between .... [*date*] and .... [*date*]

16.   The *Respondent* shall leave [*home*] [forthwith] [within .... [hours/days]] of service on
him/her of this order AND/OR

17.   Having left [*home*] the *Respondent* shall not return to, enter or attempt to enter [or go within ....
        [specify distance] of] it

Sections 35 – former spouse – 36 (former) cohabitant – No existing right to occupy

It is ordered that:

18.   The *Applicant* has the right to occupy [*home*] and the *Respondent* shall allow the *Applicant* to do so
        OR

19.   The *Respondent* shall not evict or exclude the *Applicant* from [*home*] or any part of it namely:
        .... [specify part] AND/OR

20.   The *Respondent* shall not occupy [*home*] OR

21.   The *Respondent* shall not occupy [*home*] from .... [date] until .... [date] OR

22.   The *Respondent* shall not occupy .... [specify part] OR

23.   The *Respondent* shall leave [*home*] [forthwith] [within .... [hours/days]] of service on
        him/her of this order AND/OR

24.   Having left [*home*] the *Respondent* shall not return to, enter or attempt to enter [or go within ....
        [specify distance] of] it

Sections 37 & 38 – No rights to occupy – refer to Family Law Act 1996 when required

ADDITIONAL PROVISIONS *– for sections 33, 35 & 36 Orders only*

It is ordered that:

25.   The *Applicant/Respondent* shall maintain and repair [*home*] AND/OR

26.   The *Applicant/Respondent* shall pay the rent for [*home*] OR

27.   The *Applicant/Respondent* shall pay the mortgage payments on [*home*] OR

28.   The *Applicant/Respondent* shall pay the following for [*home*]:

        .... [specify outgoings]

29.   The *Applicant/Respondent in occupation* shall pay to the *other party* £ .... each [*week/month*] for [*home*]

30.   The *Applicant/Respondent in occupation* shall keep and use the [*furniture/contents*] of [*home*] and the
        Applicant/Respondent shall return to the *Applicant/Respondent in occupation* the
        [furniture/contents/specify] no later than [date/time]

31.   The Applicant/Respondent in occupation shall take reasonable care of the [*furniture/contents/specify*]
        of [*home*]

32.   The *Applicant/Respondent in occupation* shall take all reasonable steps to keep secure [*home*] and the
        furniture or other contents [*specify if necessary*]

DURATION – *of occupation Orders*

Under section 33

33.   This Order shall last until .... [date or event] OR

34.   This Order shall last until a further Order is made

Under sections 35 & 37

35.   This Order shall last until .... [date up to 6 months hence]

36.   The occupation Order made on .... [date] is extended until .... [extension of up to 6 months]

Under sections 36 & 38

37.   This Order shall last until .... [date up to 6 months hence]

38.   The occupation Order made on [date] is extended until .... [extension of up to 6 months] and must end on that date

Procedure

3.33   The basic procedural steps for obtaining an occupation order under any of the sections set out above are identical with those for applying for a non-molestation order (see **2.9**). However, there are certain additional provisions which must be observed, arising out of the fact that, as a property is always involved in an occupation order, the rights of third parties may have to be observed. These provisions are contained in FPR 1991, r 3.8(11) which provides that a copy of an application for an occupation order under s 33, s 35 or s 36 must be served by the applicant by first class post on the mortgagee or, as the case may be, the landlord of the dwellinghouse in question with a notice in Form FL416 informing him of his right to make representations in writing or at any hearing. For a more detailed account of procedure, see Chapter 5.

CHAPTER 4

PROTECTION FROM HARASSMENT ACT 1997

Introduction

4.1   The protection available under Part IV of FLA 1996 is not the only remedy for the victim of domestic violence. Soon after the FLA 1996 was enacted, the PHA 1997 was also enacted.

It is open to doubt whether the PHA 1997 was drafted with domestic violence in mind, but this seems to be its result.

The PHA 1997 was introduced after widespread public concern over the apparent inability of the law to control the practice known as 'stalking'. The essential characteristics of this phenomenon are the obsessive harassment of a victim, usually female, by someone who pursues her by following her movements, telephoning and so on. Any relationship between the parties has ended, if, indeed, it ever existed outside the imagination of the perpetrator. Several well-publicised cases led to a pledge by the government of the day to legislate to provide protection from this form of harassment. Unfortunately, whether or not the Act succeeded in achieving the aims of its proponents, it provides a system of law and procedure which is overlapping and parallel with Part IV of the Family Law Act 1996, which may result in some confusion. Whether Parliament ignored the scope for confusion, or was unaware of the fact that it had recently debated at some length a measure providing very similar remedies is a matter for speculation.

The operation of the PHA 1997 is further complicated by the fact that it creates an offence of harassment which is the subject of the criminal law, and also provides civil remedies for the restraining of and damages for such offences, so that an unusual hybrid has come into being.

The offences

4.2   The foundation of the PHA 1997 is laid in s 1, which provides that:

'A person must not pursue a course of conduct—

(a)   which amounts to harassment of another, and

(b)   which he knows or ought to know amounts to harassment of the other.'[1]

Section 1(2) then provides that, for the purposes of the section:

'the person whose course of conduct is in question ought to know that it amounts to harassment of another if a reasonable person in possession of the same information would think the course of conduct amounted to harassment of the other.'

In other words, the test of the 'reasonable person' applies and an offender would not be able to pray in aid any particular obsession from which he suffered.

Section 2(1) then provides that a person who pursues a course of conduct in breach of s 1 commits an offence. 'A course of conduct' must involve conduct on at least two occasions,[2] and 'conduct' includes speech.[3]

Criminal penalties

4.3   A person guilty of an offence under s 1 is liable on summary conviction to imprisonment for not more than 6 months or to a fine not exceeding level 5 on the standard scale or to both.[4] An offence under s 2 is an arrestable offence.[5]

A person guilty of an offence under s 4 is liable on conviction on indictment to imprisonment for up to 5 years or a fine or both, and on summary conviction to imprisonment for up to 6 months or a fine not exceeding the statutory maximum or both.[6]

Civil remedies

4.4   The civil remedies available under the PHA 1997 all relate to ss 1 and 2, and not to s 4. Accordingly, it is no longer necessary to consider s 4, save to note that a court dealing with a person convicted under s 2 or s 4 may make a restraining order against such a person; a restraining order will prohibit the convicted person from further conduct which causes harassment or will cause

---

[1]   PHA 1997, s 1(1).
[2]   Ibid, s 7(3).
[3]   Ibid, s 7(4).
[4]   Ibid, s 2(2).
[5]   Police and Criminal Evidence Act 1984, s 24(2)(n), as amended by PHA 1997, s 2(3).
[6]   PHA 1997, s 4(4).

a fear of violence.[1] Breach of such a restraining order is an offence under s 5(6).

An order under s 5 would be made at the request of the prosecution, no doubt with the encouragement or acquiescence of the victim.

Civil remedies properly so-called arise under s 3, which provides as follows.

(1) An actual or apprehended breach of s 1 may be the subject of a claim in civil proceedings by the person who is or may be the victim of the course of conduct in question.

(2) On such a claim, damages may be awarded for (among other things) any anxiety caused by the harassment and any financial loss resulting from the harassment.

The PHA 1997 therefore provides a cause of action in damages. The right to apply for an injunction, which will probably be the most common civil remedy to be sought, is not specifically mentioned in the PHA 1997, but the general law as to interlocutory and final injunction orders applies.

4.5 Harassment therefore became a statutory tort on 16 June 1997, when most of the civil remedy provisions of the PHA 1997 were implemented. The scope of protection afforded by the law of torts has substantially been expanded by the PHA 1997. The remedy available under the Act may be supplemented by the general law of torts, in particular the torts of harassment amounting to nuisance, harassment at work amounting to interference with a contract of employment, personal injury by molestation, assault, battery and trespass. Before considering the detailed provisions of PHA 1997, some essential principles of the law of tort must be considered.

Personal injury by molestation, which became fully established in *Khorasandjian v Bush*,[2] is wider than, but includes conduct amounting to assault and battery.

No general remedy for invasion of privacy

4.6 There is 'no general remedy for invasion of privacy'.[3] 'It is well known that in English law there is no right to privacy, and accordingly there is no right of action for breach of a person's privacy'.[4] The practical effects of this are substantially mitigated by the new statutory tort of harassment, which provides a remedy against a 'course of conduct'[5] which amounts to

---

[1] Ibid, s 5.

[2] [1993] QB 727, [1993] 2 FLR 66.

[3] Lord Denning MR in *Re X (A Minor) (Wardship: Restriction on Publication)* [1975] 1 All ER 697 at 704E.

[4] Glidewell LJ in *Kaye v Robertson & Sport Newspapers Ltd* [1991] FSR 62.

[5] PHA 1997, s 1(1).

harassment. However, the new tort does not cover a single act of invasion of privacy.[1] The courts might be ready to infer an intended course of conduct where a person, having once perpetrated a serious invasion of the privacy of another, threatens to repeat the invasion, in which case injunctive relief might be granted after only one actual invasion. However, the case-law which establishes that there is no tort of invasion of privacy in general is still good law.

Factual basis of an actual or threatened tort needed for grant of an injunction

4.7   An application based in tort must be supported by evidence that a tort has been committed or threatened.[2] Further, in general, no court can either grant an injunction against a person who is not a party to the proceedings[3] or join as a party someone against whom the plaintiff has no justiciable claim or lis.[4]

As to the standard of proof to be applied, see *Hipgrave and Hipgrave v Jones* [2004] EWHC 290, where it was held that in an action under s 3 of the Protection from Harassment Act 1997, the civil standard of proof applied. For a recent decision as to 'course of conduct' see *R v Patel* [2004] EWCA Crim 3284.

Orders to exclude the defendant from an area surrounding the plaintiff's home and place of work

4.8   An injunction can be granted to forbid the defendant from entering a defined area within which the home of the plaintiff is situated. Such an injunction can be based on the plaintiff's right not to suffer harassment or, if she has a legal title to the home, any other relevant tortious acts which interfere with her peaceful enjoyment of her home.

In *Burris v Azadani*,[5] the Court of Appeal held that an order prohibiting the defendant from being in a defined area in which the plaintiff's home was situated was possible, in support of an injunction forbidding tortious harassment. The court determined that the deletion of such an order in *Patel v Patel*[6] was not conclusive in principle, and that a person's right to exercise a public right of way can be over-ridden by an injunction prohibiting him from being within a specified area around the home of the applicant if his presence there is likely to lead to him committing some tortious harassment of the

---

1   Ibid, s 7(3).
2   *South Carolina Insurance Co v Assurantie Maatschappij 'De Zeven Provincien' NV* [1987] AC 24, [1986] 3 All ER 487; *Khorasandjian v Bush* [1993] QB 727, [1993] 2 FLR 66.
3   *Marengo v Daily Sketch and Sunday Graphic Ltd* [1948] 1 All ER 406.
4   See *Kalsi v Kalsi* [1992] 1 FLR 511 at 502A.
5   [1996] 1 FLR 266, [1995] 4 All ER 802.
6   [1988] 2 FLR 179.

applicant. The court held that the general powers of the High Court in s 37(1) of the Supreme Court Act 1981 enable the court, where it appears necessary to ensure that an injunction forbidding tortious conduct shall be effective, to forbid coming within an exclusion zone around the home of the plaintiff. Sir Thomas Bingham MR said that such an order should not be made at all readily or without good reason, however, if the plaintiff has a legal right not to be harmed by the defendant, the court can grant such injunction as may be needed to protect the plaintiff from that harm.

Although in *Hunter v Canary Wharf Ltd*,[1] it was held that a licensee cannot sue in nuisance, a licensee such as the daughter of the tenants in *Khorasandjian v Bush* (above),[2] who can persuade the court that harassment is being perpetrated outside the home where she lives, may be able to obtain an injunction which forbids such harassment.

The powers of the court to prohibit harassment can extend to prohibition of the exercise of a general public right in specified circumstances and may extend to forbidding any behaviour which may be likely to result in the person enjoined harassing or tortiously harming the applicant. Thus an exclusion zone could be imposed around the plaintiff's place of work as well as her home, provided that the court is satisfied that this is needed to protect the plaintiff from tortious harm.

Harassment under PHA 1997

The ingredients of and civil remedies against the statutory tort of harassment

4.9 The statutory tort of harassment, introduced by the PHA 1997, is a 'course of conduct' pursued by a person[3] 'which amounts to harassment of another'[4] and 'which he knows or ought to know amounts to harassment of the other [person]'.[5] Thus it must be a deliberate course of behaviour, which the perpetrator knew or should have known would amount to harassment, and which in fact harasses the other person.

The test for whether the perpetrator of conduct, which in fact amounts to harassment of the victim, knows or ought to know that the conduct amounts to harassment is objective. '... the person whose course of conduct is in question ought to know that it amounts to harassment of another if a

---

[1]   [1997] 2 All ER 426.
[2]   [1993] QB 727, [1993] 2 FLR 66.
[3]   PHA 1997, s 1(1).
[4]   Ibid, s 1(1)(a).
[5]   Ibid, s 1(1)(b).

reasonable person in possession of the same information would think the course of conduct amounted to harassment of the other'.[1]

PHA 1997 provides a civil remedy for the victim of harassment,[2] in which damages may be awarded[3] for 'any anxiety caused by the harassment and any financial loss resulting from the harassment'. An injunction may be granted.[4] The Act also enables a restraining order to be granted by a criminal court sentencing or dealing with a person convicted of a criminal offence of harassment under s 2, or convicted under s 4 of putting another in fear of violence on at least two occasions.

Definition of 'harassment'

4.10   Harassment includes, but is not restricted to 'alarming the person' or 'causing the person distress'.[5] 'Harassment ... includes within it an element of intent, intent to cause distress or harm', per Lord Donaldson MR in *Johnson v Walton*.[6]

Harassment is a 'course of conduct'.[7]

'"Conduct" includes speech'.[8]

In *Huntingdon Life Sciences Ltd v Curtin and Others*,[9] Eady J said that the courts would resist any wide interpretation of the PHA 1997, and held that it could not be used to restrain public discussion and demonstration about matters of public interest.

The tort of harassment is not complete unless the conduct amounting to harassment happened 'on at least two occasions'.[10] However, an 'apprehended' harassment 'may be the subject of a claim in civil proceedings by the person who is or may be the victim of the course of conduct in question'.[11] Therefore, where the evidence enables the court to conclude that the perpetrator is likely to conduct a course of harassing conduct, the court may restrain such anticipated conduct. However, the evidence would have to justify such a conclusion.

---

[1]   Ibid, s 1(2).
[2]   Ibid, s 3(1).
[3]   Ibid, s 3(2).
[4]   Ibid, s 3(3).
[5]   Ibid, s 7(2).
[6]   [1990] 1 FLR 350 at 352H.
[7]   PHA 1997, s 1(1).
[8]   Ibid, s 7(4).
[9]   [1997] TLR 646, (1997) *The Times*, December 11.
[10]   PHA 1997, s 7(3).
[11]   Ibid, s 3(1).

Two recent cases on the criminal aspects of harassment cast some further light on the meaning of the term. In *R v Hills*,[1] the indictment was based on two assaults some 6 months apart, between which times the couple had frequently come back together and sexual intercourse had taken place. It was held that the necessary cogent link between the assaults had not been made out and there was not the requisite 'course of conduct'.

In *R v Colohan*,[2] it was held that (to justify a criminal conviction) it was necessary for the jury to answer the question of whether the defendant ought to have known that what he was doing amounted to harassment by the objective test of what a reasonable person would think. Section 1(3) of PHA 1997 posed an even more objective test, namely whether the conduct was reasonable.

Threatened repetition of a single harassing act

4.11 Although the tort is incomplete until the conduct complained of has happened 'on at least two occasions',[3] the courts have power to restrain a threatened tort. This is consistent with the availability of the civil remedy, provided under s 3(1), for an apprehended harassment.

By s 6 of PHA 1997, the standard limitation period of 3 years for bringing an action for personal injuries is disapplied. Therefore, where an act of harassment happened more than 3 years, and not more than 6 years, before civil proceedings are begun for harassment, that earlier act may be relied on as part of the conduct amounting to a course of conduct.

Justifiable harassment

4.12 By s 1(3) of PHA 1997, a person who pursues a course of conduct which might otherwise amount to harassment, is excused from liability, civil and criminal, if the person who pursued it shows:

'(a) that it was pursued for the purpose of preventing or detecting crime,

(b) that it was pursued under any enactment or rule of law or to comply with any condition or requirement imposed by any person under any enactment, or

(c) that in the particular circumstances the pursuit of the course of conduct was reasonable.'

---

[1] [2001] 1 FLR 580, CA.
[2] [2001] 2 FLR 757, CA.
[3] PHA 1997, s 7(3).

Harassment amounting to nuisance

4.13   Nuisance is based on infringement of a right to peaceful occupation of real property or exercise of an easement. Therefore, nuisance cannot provide the legal basis for personal protection against conduct which does not interfere with a legal right of occupation of property or exercise of an easement. In *Hunter v Canary Wharf Ltd*,[1] overruling *Khorasandjian v Bush*[2] on this point, it was confirmed that a licensee (a daughter of the parents with legal title in *Khorasandjian v Bush*) has insufficient legal interest in occupation of a house to found the tort.

Loitering near a person's home, where the plaintiff has legal title to the home, also can be forbidden if the court considers that the loitering seriously interferes with the plaintiff's enjoyment of her home.[3]

Noise can amount to nuisance. In *Soltau v De Held*,[4] it was held that excessive bell-ringing could amount to nuisance.

Persistent or abusive telephone calls can amount to nuisance.[5] Professor Flemming in the leading Australian book *The Law of Torts* (7th edn) says (at p 575):

> 'Clearly, no liability is warranted unless the intrusion is substantial and of a kind that a reasonable person of normal sensitivity would regard as offensive and intolerable. Merely knocking at another's door or telephoning on one or two occasions is not actionable, even when designed to cause annoyance; but if the calls are repeated with persistence, and in the midst of night, so as to interfere unreasonably with comfort or sleep, liability will ensue.'

Persistent 'silent telephone calls' causing psychiatric injury can amount to an assault.[6]

Persistent or abusive, harassing telephone calls which amount to interference with the peaceful occupation of the plaintiff's home could be held to be a nuisance, whether made by night or by day.[7]

---

1   [1997] 2 All ER 426, HL.
2   [1993] QB 727, [1993] 2 FLR 66.
3   See *J Lyons & Sons Ltd v Wilkins* [1989] 1 Ch 255; *Ward Lock & Co Ltd v Operative Printer's Assistants' Society* (1906) 22 TLR 327; *Hubbard v Pitt* [1976] QB 142, [1975] 3 All ER 1; *Pidduck v Molloy* [1992] 2 FLR 202 at 205H–206A.
4   (1851) 1 Sim (NS) 133.
5   *Khorasandjian v Bush* [1993] QB 727, [1993] 2 FLR 66; *Stoakes v Brydges* [1958] QWN 5, (1958) 32 Austral LJ 205; *Motherwell v Motherwell* (1977) 73 DLR (3d) 62 at 74.
6   *R v Ireland; R v Burstow* [1998] 1 FLR 105, [1997] 4 All ER 225, HL.
7   *Khorasandjian v Bush* [1993] QB 727, [1993] 2 FLR 66.

Harassment at the plaintiff's place of work: interference with a contract of employment

4.14 Sometimes, pestering a victim at or near his or her place of work can amount to harassment. Sometimes, the pestering is done to re-establish communication with the victim, sometimes to denigrate the victim in the eyes of his or her employer. Such conduct is susceptible of relief against the tort of harassment.

Following *Burris v Azadani*,[1] it would appear that where the court concludes that an injunction should be granted to forbid harassment, the injunction could include forbidding the defendant from harassing the plaintiff near his or her place of work, and from entering a specified area around the plaintiff's place of work.

Interference with a contract of employment by unlawful conduct intended to induce an employer to dismiss an employee is an actionable tort.[2] 'Molestation' and 'obstruction' can amount to unlawful interference with a contract of employment.[3] However, aggressive trade competition by a rival business, not amounting to unlawful interference with a contract, is neither actionable nor restrainable.[4]

No reported cases are known in which the court has given a remedy on the basis that a tortious interference with a contract has been committed by acts primarily motivated by a malignant personal relationship between the defendant and the plaintiff.[5] However, it may be that where the defendant harasses or molests the plaintiff by oppressive and injurious visits, letters or telephone calls to the premises of the plaintiff's employer, and the defendant's acts are of a character that enables the court to infer that the defendant must have known and intended that the employer will be driven to dismiss the plaintiff, such molestation could amount to a restrainable tort. In such a case, an appropriate formulation of an injunction might be:

> 'The defendant is forbidden to communicate with the employers of the plaintiff whether by visits, letters or telephone calls to their premises in any way calculated to cause the said employers to dismiss the plaintiff.'

---

1   [1996] 1 FLR 266, [1995] 4 All ER 802; see also **4.8**.
2   *Read v The Friendly Society of Operative Stonemasons of England, Ireland and Wales and Others* [1902] 1 KB 732; *Conway v Wade* [1909] AC 506.
3   *Mogul Steamship Co Ltd v McGregor, Gow & Co* (1889) 23 QBD 598 at 607, 614, 622 and 626, and *National Phonographic Co Ltd v Edison-Bell Consolidated Phonograph Co Ltd* [1908] 1 Ch 355 at 355, 361 and 369
4   See *Mogul Steamship Co Ltd v McGregor, Gow & Co* (above) at 614 and 620.
5   See *Glamorgan Coal Co Ltd and Others v South Wales Miners' Federation and Others* [1903] 2 KB 545 at 577 and *Crofter Hand Woven Harris Tweed Co Ltd and Another v Veitch and Another* [1942] AC 435 at 442–443.

Personal injury by molestation

4.15   In *Burnett v George*,[1] and *Khorasandjian v Bush*,[2] the tort of personal injury by molestation was recognised. Actual or threatened probable injury to physical or mental health must be proved or reasonably foreseeable. Psychological harm can amount to actual bodily harm.[3] The perpetrator must have intended or realised that his conduct was likely to cause impairment to the health of the victim.

The new statutory tort of harassment diminishes the circumstances in which it might be useful to resort to the tort of personal injury by molestation. However, where the victim of threatened further harassment, following a single severe act of harassment which caused harm to the mental health of the victim, seeks injunctive relief, the separate tort may provide a peg on which to hang an injunction if the court is reluctant to discern a 'course of conduct' within s 7(3) of PHA 1997.

Intentional bad behaviour, calculated to cause distress or harm, must be proved in support of the allegation of personal injury by molestation.[4]

Trespass

Removal of an obstreperous adult from the family home

4.16   The most convenient remedy for removal of an obstreperous adult from the home is an occupation order under s 33 of the FLA 1996 (see **3.8**).

An adult child, relative or friend living in the family home with the plaintiff can be ordered to leave and not to return on the basis of the tort of trespass, provided that the person has no legal right to stay there other than a revocable licence and that licence has been terminated.[5]

Provided that a licensee shares accommodation with the family, and the premises are the principal home of the licensor or another member of his family, the licence will be an 'excluded licence' within the meaning of the Protection from Eviction Act 1977, s 3A, and the licensee will not be entitled to protection under that Act.

---

[1]   [1992] 1 FLR 525, CA.

[2]   [1993] 2 FLR 66, CA.

[3]   *R v Ireland; R v Burstow* [1998] 1 FLR 105, [1997] 4 All ER 225, HL; *Kendrick v Kendrick* [1990] 2 FLR 107.

[4]   See Lord Donaldson MR in *Johnson v Walton* [1990] 1 FLR 350 at 352H.

[5]   See *Egan v Egan* [1975] Ch 218, [1975] 2 All ER 167; *Waterhouse v Waterhouse* (1905) 94 LT 133; and *Stevens v Stevens* (1907) 24 TLR 20.

Warrant for arrest for breach of injunction forbidding harassment

Availability of warrant

4.17   Under PHA 1997, s 3(3), (4) and (5) where, following the grant of an injunction forbidding harassment, a judge, including a district judge, 'has reasonable grounds for believing that the defendant has done anything which he is prohibited from doing by the injunction', which must be substantiated on oath, a warrant for the arrest of the defendant may be issued by the judge. A warrant of arrest cannot be granted for breach of an undertaking in respect of tortious harassment, as s 3(3), (4) applies only in respect of breach of an injunction.

A person who disobeys an injunction granted under s 3 of the 1997 Act cannot be both convicted of an offence under s 3(6) and punished for contempt in respect of the same conduct.[1]

The remedy of power of arrest is not available at the time when the injunction is granted.

Specimen clauses for forbidding tortious personal molestation

4.18   In the discussion above, it is demonstrated that the variety of relief available in the law of torts is more extensive than the conventional injunctions against assault and trespass. As the variety of possible injunctive clauses which may be helpful for an injunction where personal molestation or harassment by a relative or former cohabitant is complained of is so extensive, a menu of specimen clauses is offered at **4.19**. Some of the language in the menu, which appeared in the first edition of *Emergency Remedies* (Jordan Publishing), was adopted in *Pidduck v Molloy*[2] and *Khorasandjian v Bush*,[3] and was not criticised in the Court of Appeal.

---

1   PHA 1997, s 3(7), (8).
2   [1992] 2 FLR 202.
3   [1993] QB 727, [1993] 2 FLR 66.

Menu of specimen clauses for molestation injunctions in torts

4.19

The Plaintiff applies to the court for an injunction order in the following terms:

That the Defendant (name) ... be forbidden whether by himself or by instructing any other person to do any unlawful act of the kind listed below.

(1) harassing or harming the claimant, whether by actual or threatened violence, or any other conduct likely to cause her alarm, distress, physical or mental harm, and whether she is at home, at work, in any public place or anywhere else;

(2) wrongful damage to or interference with the personal possessions of the claimant (including any motor vehicle which belongs to or is being used by the claimant);

(3) coming or being within [200] metres of the home of the claimant.

[Additional possible detailed clauses]

(4 and 5 are available only to a claimant who has a legal title to the property)

(4) disturbing the peaceful occupation by the claimant of her home and property at .... (whether by [loitering outside or] [being within 200 metres thereof or] [making (abusive) telephone calls (persistently or) (late at night)] or in any other way]);

(5) trespassing on the home of the claimant;

(6) interfering with the employment of the claimant whereby the employers of the plaintiff may be induced to dismiss the claimant: the defendant is forbidden to harass or pester ...., the employers of the claimant, and is forbidden to harass or pester the claimant at or entering or leaving ...., her place of work.

Duration of injunction against, or undertaking about, torts

4.20   An injunction granted to forbid tortious harassment should be tailored in length to suit the circumstances of the case. Three and 6 months are common upon a first application.

Undertakings may be given for as long as the giver accepts; 3 months is common.

Procedure

4.21   There are no new rules relating to applications under PHA 1997, s 3(1), and the general rules of procedure apply. Proceedings may be issued in the High Court, but this is likely to be unusual and the procedure to be considered here will be that of the county courts, to which the great majority of applications are likely to be made. The Principal Registry of the Family

Division does not have jurisdiction since its jurisdiction is limited to family business.

Proceedings may be issued as follows.

(a) Liquidated claim where no injunction sought.
    Default summons (Form N1).
(b) Unliquidated claim, or liquidated claim with an injunction application.
    Fixed date summons (Form N2 or N3).
(c) Free-standing injunction (not linked to damages claim).
    Form N16a (as amended).

The requirements for applications for injunctions will be the same as those for any other injunction.

4.22   Where the damages sought are limited to £3,000, and a defence is filed, the action will be dealt with as a small claim. Where damages are limited to £5,000 (or such sum as is the district judge's current trial jurisdiction), or no damages are sought, the district judge will have jurisdiction.

The following quick guide may assist as a procedural check.

Which court?	Any county court. Where damages are sought, district judge has jurisdiction up to £15,000 and a circuit judge above that figure.
Documents to issue.	Claim form N1 (including particulars of claim and statement of truth where possible).
	Particulars of claim (where not endorsed on N1).
	Any medical report to be relied on.
	Draft order.
	Form N16A (where interim order sought).
	Affidavit in support of any interim order.
Interim orders.	Application without notice is made to District Judge in chambers.
	If order made, this must be served with the documents listed above. A return day giving at least two days' notice will be fixed.
Service.	Where no interim order made, court office serves documents on defendant.
	Where interim order made and return date fixed, claimant must serve all documents above plus the interim order.
	NB personal service of interim order is required.

	Claimant must file affidavit of service.
Hearing.	Where interim order made, hearing on return day. Order either continued, dismissed or varied. Where case continues, directions given as to filing of defence and evidence.
	Where no interim order, full hearing fixed (probably about 6 weeks ahead). Before that date defendant intending to oppose should have filed defence and evidence.
	Where final order made, claimant must serve on defendant.

Enforcement

4.23   Enforcement is dealt with in s 3(3)–(6). There is no provision for the attachment of a power of arrest to the order itself, and the procedure is very similar to that prescribed for the issue of a warrant of arrest under s 47 of FLA 1996.

Where the court grants an injunction for the purpose of restraining a defendant from pursuing any course of conduct which amounts to harassment, and the plaintiff considers that the defendant has done anything which he is prohibited from doing by the injunction, the plaintiff may apply for a warrant for the arrest of the defendant.[1] Where the injunction is granted by a county court, application may be made to a judge or district judge of that or any other county court.[2]

The judge or district judge may only issue a warrant if the application is substantiated on oath, and he has reasonable grounds for believing that the defendant has done anything which he is prohibited from doing by the injunction.[3]

The procedure set out above is of course in addition to what was the usual method of dealing with contempt, namely a notice to shew cause as to why the offender should not be committed.

Criminal penalty for breach of injunction

4.24   As an alternative to the civil contempt procedure, the PHA 1997 provides that when the High Court or a county court has granted an injunction for the purpose of restraining a defendant from pursuing any course of conduct which amounts to harassment, and, without reasonable excuse, the defendant does anything which he is prohibited from doing by the

---

1   PHA 1997, s 3(3).
2   Ibid, s 3(4).
3   Ibid, s 3(5).

injunction, he is guilty of an offence.[1] Such an offence attracts a penalty of up to 5 years' imprisonment or a fine or both, on conviction on indictment, or, on summary conviction, up to 6 months' imprisonment or a fine not exceeding the statutory maximum or both.[2]

However, a person cannot be convicted of an offence under subs (6) in respect of any conduct which has been punished as a contempt of court.[3] Similarly, where a person is convicted of an offence under subs (6), that conduct is not punishable as a contempt of court.[4]

A person seeking to punish breach of an injunction will therefore have to elect as to whether to deal with the matter by civil committal or to seek to bring about a criminal prosecution.

Limitation

4.25 A claim for harassment is, in effect, a claim for personal injuries, and would normally be subject to a limitation period of 3 years. To avoid any problems which this might cause, s 6 of PHA 1997 amends s 11 of Limitation Act 1980 by inserting a new subs (1A) which provides that s 11 (which contains the respective periods of limitation) does not apply to any action brought for damages under s 3 of PHA 1997.

It will therefore be possible to rely on events forming a course of conduct going back in time without limit.

Comparison of the PHA 1997 and Part IV of the FLA 1996

4.26 As has been seen, the PHA 1997 overlaps with Part IV of FLA 1996, and a victim of domestic violence may have to decide under which statute proceedings should be brought. The following considerations may be among those to be considered.

Availability of remedy

4.27 An applicant for an occupation order would not choose to bring proceedings under the PHA 1997 because it provides no remedy comparable with those in Part IV of the FLA 1996. The comparison is therefore limited to non-molestation orders.

---

1 Ibid, s 3(6).
2 Ibid, s 3(9).
3 Ibid, s 3(8).
4 Ibid, s 3(7).

Both statutes provide protection against harassment, the legal definition of which must be identical in both cases. Although the PHA 1997 is intended to provide for conduct falling short of physical assault, there can be little doubt that physical assault amounts to harassment. There is nothing in the PHA 1997 which makes it more difficult to establish harassment, save that it requires proof of a course of conduct, defined as conduct on at least two occasions.

Entitlement to apply

4.28   As was seen at **1.4** *et seq*, in order to apply for a non-molestation order under Part IV of FLA 1996, the applicant must be 'associated' with the other party, and there is a complicated list of who may be associated. There is no such requirement in respect of the PHA 1997; s 1 merely refers to 'a person' and 'another'. In this respect, therefore, there may be some advantage in the PHA 1997. Anyone may apply for an order against anyone else.

Nature of remedy

4.29   The first and most obvious advantage of the PHA 1997 is that, if a victim could persuade the police to become involved, there might be a prosecution under either s 2 or s 4, which would relieve the victim of the responsibility of taking civil action. However, it may be open to doubt that the police would wish to be involved in most domestic disputes where a civil remedy would be available.

Apart from this, the civil orders which could be obtained under the two statutes would seem to be identical; in neither case is there any limitation on the time during which the order will remain in force.

Section 42(5) of FLA 1996 sets out guidelines which the court must observe when deciding whether or not to grant a non-molestation injunction. The PHA 1997 contains no such guidelines so that, in theory, the court would be unconstrained.

Undertakings

4.30   As can be seen at **5.25** *et seq*, Part IV of FLA 1996 contains provision for an application to be resolved by one party giving an undertaking, which is then as enforceable as an order of the court. This is, in fact, how the great majority of domestic violence applications have always been resolved. There is nothing in the PHA 1997 which permits the court to accept an undertaking, and certainly nothing regarding its enforceability. It may be argued that there was nothing in the DVMPA 1976 to permit undertakings to be given; the court has an inherent jurisdiction to accept an undertaking, and the practice of the court evolved over a period of time and now reflected in, for example prescribed forms in the county court, clearly gives the court a discretion.

On the other hand, it may be said that there is nothing in the Act to support this, and it might be argued that, Parliament having gone to some lengths to prescribe the availability and enforceability of undertakings in Part IV of FLA 1996, it would not intentionally have left the question in doubt in the PHA 1997 so soon afterwards.

If the latter argument were to be accepted (which is probably unlikely, but possible in theory), the court would have the choice of either granting or refusing an application, with no room for 'settlement' or compromise.

Enforcement

4.31 One advantage of a Part IV order was that a power of arrest could be attached. This will no longer be the case when the DCVCA 2004 is implemented. Of course the system of applying for a warrant of arrest is common to both statutes.

Breach of non-molestation orders under both statutes will be an offence when the DVCVA 2004 is implemented.

Choice of court

4.32 Applications under FLA 1996, Part IV may be brought in magistrates' courts or in a county court or the High Court, whereas protection under the PHA 1997 is only available in a county court or in the High Court.

Combined applications

4.33 There would seem to be no reason in principle why the provisions of both statutes should not be relied on in the same application, and why, except in matters proceeding in the PRFD, the court should not make an order, or orders, drawing on its jurisdiction under both statutes (provided, of course, that the orders did not duplicate each other).

CHAPTER 5

PROCEDURES FOR PERSONAL PROTECTION ORDERS

Applications for personal protection orders and injunctions

Family proceedings court or county court? Choice of venue when starting proceedings under FLA 1996, Part IV

5.1 Part IV of FLA 1996 follows the CA 1989 in conferring concurrent jurisdiction to hear most applications on the High Court, specified county courts and family proceedings courts.[1] The Lord Chancellor has power to make rules about where proceedings should start or be transferred, and the Family Law Act 1986 (Part IV) Allocation of Proceedings Order 1997 makes such rules.

In London, only Lambeth, Shoreditch and Woolwich County Courts have family jurisdiction including Part IV of FLA 1996.[2] The Principal Registry of the Family Division has county court family jurisdiction including Part IV,[3] but it does not have general county court jurisdiction.

The effect of the Family Law Act 1986 (Part IV) Allocation of Proceedings Order 1997 with regard to the commencement of proceedings is that:

(a) proceedings under Part IV may be commenced in the Principal Registry or any county court or family proceedings court;[4] there are no geographical restrictions upon choice of venue;

(b) applicants aged under 18 years are required to commence proceedings in the High Court and, in the case of children under 16 years, they must apply for leave under s 43;[5]

(c) application to extend, vary or discharge an existing order, or any application which may have the effect of varying or discharging an order,

---

[1] FLA 1996, s 57(8).
[2] Family Law Act 1986 (Part IV) Allocation of Proceedings Order 1997, art 17.
[3] Ibid, art 16.
[4] Ibid, art 4(1).
[5] Ibid, art 4(2).

must be made to the court which made the original order;[1]

(d)   where family proceedings are already pending in either a county court or family proceedings court, application under Part IV may be made in those proceedings.[2]

In general, there is no obvious advantage to be gained in favouring the commencement of proceedings, under Part IV of the 1996 Act, in one level of court rather than another. The Act creates a structure of concurrent remedies and procedures in all three tiers of courts and, as far as associated persons are concerned, magistrates' powers to grant injunctive relief have been assimilated with those available in judge courts.[3]

With regard to occupation orders, s 59 places a limitation on the family proceedings courts' powers to the extent that magistrates are not competent to hear any application or to make an order involving a disputed question as to any party's entitlement to occupy any property unless it is unnecessary to determine the question in order to deal with the application or make the order. In practice, this provision is not likely to apply very often as such issues rarely arise in personal protection applications. Furthermore, as an emergency measure, a family proceedings court can always decide that it is unnecessary to determine a dispute as to title to property prior to making an initial occupation order for the protection of the applicant or a relevant child, allowing the dispute as to title to be dealt with later in a county court or the High Court, following transfer of the proceedings.

Since it is intended to achieve a neutral fees and legal aid position, applicants are free to apply in the court of their choice.

Actions for injunctions under the law of torts should be conducted in county courts.

Transfer of proceedings between courts

5.2   There is specific statutory provision to allow a family proceedings court to decline jurisdiction when it considers the case can be more conveniently dealt with in another court.[4] In addition, the Family Law Act 1986 (Part IV) Allocation of Proceedings Order 1997 permits transfer of proceedings under Part IV, so that:

(a)   one family proceedings court should, of its own motion or on application, transfer to another family proceedings court where it is

---

[1]   Family Law Act 1986 (Part IV) Allocation of Proceedings Order 1997, art 5.

[2]   Ibid, art 4(3).

[3]   Although it has to be said that orders made by magistrates are outnumbered by a ratio of nearly 50:1 to those made in county courts – see *Judicial Statistics 2001*.

[4]   FLA 1996, s 59(2).

appropriate for those proceedings to be heard together with pending family proceedings in the other court and the receiving court consents;[1]

(b) a family proceedings court may, of its own motion or on application, transfer proceedings to a county court, for example in order to be heard together with pending proceedings in that court or where proceedings involve some issue of general public interest or exceptional complexity;[2]

(c) a family proceedings court must transfer proceedings under Part IV to the nearest county court in cases where a child under the age of 18 is either a respondent or wishes to become a party to proceedings or where a party to proceedings is incapable by reason of a mental disorder of managing his property or affairs;[3]

(d) a county court may, of its own motion or on application, transfer proceedings to a family proceedings court where it considers that it would be appropriate for those proceedings to be heard together with pending proceedings in the family proceedings court or the difficulty or importance of the proceedings does not make them more appropriate for the county court;[4]

(e) a county court may, of its own motion or on application, transfer proceedings to another county court in order to be heard together with pending proceedings in the other court or where the property which is the subject of the dispute is situated in the district of another county court or where it is necessary or expedient to do so;[5]

(f) a county court may, of its own motion or on application, transfer proceedings to the High Court where it considers that it would be appropriate for those proceedings to be heard together with pending proceedings in the High Court;[6]

(g) the High Court may transfer proceedings to a county court;[7] where the High Court considers that it would be appropriate for proceedings to be heard together with pending proceedings in a family proceedings court, it may transfer to the family proceedings court.[8]

Standard form of application for non-molestation or occupation order

5.3 The standard Prescribed Form of application, Form FL401, for an order under Part IV of FLA 1996, is designed to elicit from the applicant the details which make him or her eligible to apply for an order and the details of what orders are sought. A new Form FL401 is included in the amendment rules and will be found in Appendix 3. While this entails more careful preparation than

---

1 Family Law Act 1986 (Part IV) Allocation of Proceedings Order 1997, art 7.
2 Ibid, art 8(1).
3 Ibid, art 8(2).
4 Ibid, art 11.
5 Ibid, art 10.
6 Ibid, art 12.
7 Ibid, art 14.
8 Ibid, art 13.

was the case under the previous law, the form really requires no more attention than would be necessary in any event to find the right pigeonhole for applications, given the complexity of the law in the Act. The form operates as a checklist and, in practice, facilitates applications being made appropriately. The separate menus of possible orders, in Prescribed Form FL404 *et seq*, specify which detailed occupation orders are available according to which section of the Act is applicable. See **5.23** below for further details. These menus enable someone advising a client, and preparing an application, to be clear about what is available for the client. They also operate as useful checklists for courts to see readily what they can order in each particular case. See **3.7–3.25**.

Evidence in support required for application for FLA 1996, Part IV order or injunction against torts

5.4 FPR 1991, r 3.8(4) requires a sworn statement in support of an application to a county court, which is required by r 3.8(6) to be served with the application in Form FL401. A different form of procedure has been preserved in family proceedings courts to take account of the likelihood that unrepresented applicants will apply in those courts. FPC (MP etc) R 1991, r 3A(3) makes provision for either a written statement, which is signed and declared to be true, to be filed in support of the application or for oral evidence to be adduced, with permission of the court. The rules do not give any guidance upon the circumstances in which permission of the court may be granted but the admission of oral evidence should not be used to circumvent the respondent's right to know the substance of the allegations being made against him. It is, therefore, likely that permission will be confined, in the main, to cases of real urgency, where permission has been granted for the application to proceed without notice.

An affidavit in support is required for an application for an injunction forbidding torts.[1]

General requirements appropriate for evidence in support of application

5.5 The evidence of the applicant and any corroborative witness, submitted in support of an application, should set out succinctly the essential facts relied on.

Special requirement where application begun without notice

5.6 No additional form is required in addition to the standard Form FL401 or Form N16A to begin an application without notice. However, the grounds

---

[1]   CCR Ord 13, r 6(3).

why an order without notice is needed are required to be set out in the statement in support.[1]

Special requirement for permission for child under the age of 16 to apply for a non-molestation or occupation order

5.7   A child under the age of 16 can make an application for a non-molestation order or an occupation order, but requires permission[2] of the High Court.[3] The circumstances relied on for obtaining permission must be set out adequately in support of the application.

Special requirement where applicant relies on agreement to marry

5.8   An applicant who is eligible to apply for a non-molestation order[4] or occupation order[5] by reason of an agreement to marry the respondent made within three years preceding the application, will need to assert the evidence required by s 44.

Under s 44(1), an agreement in writing to marry suffices. Under s 44(2), an agreement to marry may be proved by the gift of an engagement ring or a ceremony of betrothal witnessed by other persons.

Applications without notice, informal notice, and abridged and substituted service

The power to grant an initial order without notice

5.9   Section 45(1) of FLA 1996, reflecting the general law, allows a court 'in any case where it considers it just and convenient to do so, [to] make an occupation order or a non-molestation order even though the respondent has not been given such notice of the proceedings...'. The power is subject to criteria in s 45(2) (see **5.10**).

In county court actions founded in torts, an application can be begun without notice.[6]

---

1   FPR 1991, r 3.8(5); FPC (MP etc) R 1991, r 3A(4)(b); CCR Ord 13, r 6(3A).
2   FLA 1996, s 43(1).
3   Family Law Act 1996 (Part IV) (Allocation of Proceedings) Order 1997, art 4(2); FPR 1991, r 3.8(2).
4   FLA 1996, s 42(4).
5   Ibid, s 33(2).
6   CCR Ord 13, r 6(3A), CPR 1998, r 25.3(3) and PD 25, Interim Injunctions, para 4.

Before proceeding without notice, the applicant and the court should consider whether it would be better to give 'informal notice' (ie short notice), or abridge the time for service or provide for substituted service.[1]

For the situation of a respondent who objects to an order without notice, see **7.19**.

The statement in support of an application for an order without notice must contain reasons as to why the application is being made without notice to the respondent.

Criteria for applications without notice

5.10 Orders without notice should be the exception, not the norm. The criteria applicable when an application is begun without notice under FLA 1996, Part IV are set out in s 45(2). Section 45(2) reflects the policy in previous case-law in civil as well as family proceedings.

FLA 1996, s 45(2) states:

'In determining whether to exercise its powers under subsection (1) [to grant an occupation or non-molestation order without notice] the court shall have regard to all the circumstances including—

(a) any risk of significant harm to the applicant or a relevant child, attributable to the conduct of the respondent, if the order is not made immediately;

(b) whether it is likely that the applicant will be deterred or prevented from pursuing the application if an order is not made immediately; and

(c) whether there is reason to believe that the respondent is aware of the proceedings but is deliberately evading service and that the applicant or a relevant child will be seriously prejudiced by the delay involved—

(i) where the court is a magistrates' court, in effecting service of proceedings; or

(ii) in any other case, in effecting substituted service.'

The policy that orders without notice should be the exception, not the norm, has not always been respected in some courts, even though it is not legalistic theory. An order granted without notice inherently carries a risk of inflaming the situation, whereas at a hearing on notice the respondent frequently accepts that the applicant needs protection and is willing to submit to an injunction or give a binding undertaking. Most respondents do not know that an order without notice is only provisional and subject to early review as if nothing had been proved. Upon receiving service of an order without notice, it is likely that it will appear to most respondents that the court has assumed that the

---

[1]   See *Wookey v Wookey; Re S (A Minor)* [1991] 2 FLR 319 at 323G, quoted at **5.11**.

allegations made against him were accepted as true by the court without question.

A hearing on notice is an opportunity to address outstanding issues. For example, allegations of molestation are often answered by a respondent claiming that the applicant has frustrated contact with a child: if the first hearing is held urgently and on notice, mutually acceptable arrangements for contact with a child may be achieved and the problem defused. Orders which interfere with civil liberties ought not to be made without notice unless they are clearly warranted; audi alterem partem is a fundamental legal principle of great importance.

CPR 1998, r 25.3(1) enables the court to grant an order without notice 'if it appears to the court that there are good reasons for not giving notice', and the reasons for not giving notice must be set out in the applicant's evidence in support.[1] CPR PD 25, Interim Injunctions, para 4.3 prescribes further requirements of the applicant, and para 4.5 provides for urgent, out-of-hours telephone applications.

Case-law on the policy

'An ex parte order should be made only when either there is no time to give the defendant notice to appear, or when there is reason to believe that the defendant, if given notice, would take action which would defeat the purpose of the order.'[2]

'Ex parte applications for injunctions should, in general, only be made where there are strong grounds to justify such an application, where there is real urgency and impossibility of giving notice. It will often be preferable to abridge time, and the respondent may attend on short notice. In cases such as application for a non-molestation order, the presence of both sides may well lead to agreed undertakings and the opportunity for the judge to try to reduce the tension in family disputes and to underline the importance of compliance with the undertaking accepted or the order granted.'[3]

5.11 These words of Butler-Sloss LJ remain appropriate as a statement of the policy in relation to applications without notice.

Loseby v Newman[4] followed a clear line of case-law. An application for an injunction should not be made, or granted, without notice unless there is real immediate danger of serious injury or irreparable damage.[5] The principle that both sides must be heard can be displaced only where it appears to the court

---

1   CPR 1998, r 25.3(3).
2   Per Hoffmann LJ in *Loseby v Newman* [1995] 2 FLR 754 at 758C.
3   Per Butler-Sloss LJ in *Wookey v Wookey; Re S (A Minor)* [1991] 2 FLR 319 at 323G.
4   [1995] 2 FLR 754.
5   *Beese (Managers of Kimpton Church of England Primary School) v Woodhouse* [1970] 1 All ER 769; *Practice Note (Matrimonial Cause: Injunction)* [1978] 2 All ER 919.

that giving the other party an opportunity to be heard 'appears likely to cause injustice to the applicant, by reason either of the delay involved or the action which it appears likely that the respondent or others would take before the order can be made'.[1]

An application for an injunction without notice, including one for personal protection should not be made, or granted, unless either it is not reasonably practicable to give notice, even informal notice (see below), or giving notice would give the defendant time to defeat the purpose of the application and it is likely that he would do so.[2]

The most recent statement of principle on these issues is contained in the judgments of Munby J in *Re W (Ex Parte Orders)*[3] and *Re S (Ex Parte Orders)*.[4] The following guidelines were set out.

(1) Those who obtained injunctive relief without notice were under a duty to make the fullest disclosure of all the relevant circumstances known to them.
(2) The applicant is also under a duty to bring to the attention of the respondent at the earliest practicable opportunity the evidential and other persuasive materials on the basis of which the injunction had been granted.
(3) Generally, the court would require the applicant to give an undertaking to serve proceedings on the respondent at the earliest opportunity, such proceedings to include copies of all evidence and orders including a return date; where the order had been made otherwise than on the basis of sworn evidence, a statement or affidavit must be sworn and served. Where no such undertaking was obtained, the applicant and her solicitor still had an obligation to act in these terms.
(4) Any order without notice should set out on its face, whether by way of recital or in a schedule, a list of all affidavits, statements and other evidential materials read by the judge.

The dangers of making an occupation order on a without notice basis are well illustrated by *Chalmers v Johns*.[5] In fact, the decision at first instance was made not without notice but on an interim basis after hearing both parties, but that only reinforces the point. The judge ordered the husband to leave the home within seven days pending a final hearing of a residence application which was

---

[1] *Re First Express Ltd* [1991] BCC 782 at 785.
[2] *Ansah v Ansah* [1977] Fam 138, CA, [1977] 2 All ER 638; *G v G (Ouster: Ex Parte Application)* [1990] 1 FLR 395, CA; *Wookey v Wookey; Re S (A Minor)* [1991] 2 FLR 319, CA; *Practice Note (Matrimonial Cause: Injunction)* [1978] 2 All ER 919; *Re First Express Ltd* [1991] BCC 782; *Bates v Lord Hailsham of St Marylebone* [1972] 3 All ER 1019.
[3] [2000] 2 FLR 927.
[4] [2001] 1 FLR 308.
[5] [1999] 1 FLR 392, CA.

listed some 7 weeks ahead. On appeal, Thorpe LJ, referring to ouster orders, commented that:

> 'a string of authorities in this court emphasise the draconian nature of such an order and that it should be restricted to exceptional cases. I do not myself think that the wider statutory provisions contained in the Family Law Act 1996 obliterate that authority. The order remains draconian, particularly in the perception of the respondent. It remains an order that overrides proprietary rights and it seems to me that it is an order that is only justified in exceptional circumstances.'

The judge had misdirected herself in not going through the process contained in FLA 1996, s 33(6) and (7), and had never focused on the alternative nature of these subsections. The husband's appeal was allowed.

When may an occupation order which ousts the respondent from his home be made without notice?

5.12 The case-law under the MHA 1983 and the DVMPA 1976 was that removal of a party from his home was 'Draconian' and should rarely be granted without notice.[1] It can confidently be predicted that the Court of Appeal will continue to regard removal of a person from his home without notice as something which is so serious as seldom justifiable.

Mode of application begun without notice

5.13 It is not necessary to file a separate form of application to achieve an initial hearing without notice. The standard form of application FL401, or N16A in a tort action, will suffice, provided that the reasons for starting without notice are set out in the statement or evidence in support, unless leave is given for oral evidence to be given.

Grounds for application without notice required to be set out in statement in support

5.14 The grounds for starting without notice are required by FPR 1991, r 3.8(5) or CPR 1998, r 25.3(3) to be stated in the sworn statement or evidence in support of the application. In a family proceedings court, by FPC (MP etc) R 1991, r 3A(4)(b), the statement in support must state the reasons, unless permission is given for oral evidence to be given.

Ensuring issue and service of correct forms after grant of order without notice

5.15 Where a non-molestation order or occupation order is granted without notice under the FLA 1996, the application in Form FL401 and statement in

---

[1]   *G v G (Ouster: Ex Parte Application)* [1990] 1 FLR 395; *Masich v Masich* (1977) Fam Law 245.

support must be served with the order without notice, in order to comply with FPR 1991, r 3.8(6), FPC (MP etc) R 1991, r 3A(5). Where a power of arrest is granted without notice, the court is required to announce the order in open court at the earliest opportunity.[1]

In a tort action in a county court, if an order is granted without notice in Form N16, it is important to ensure that the court issues for service the application Form N16A with the correct return date entered, as well as the order without notice, or else the defendant will not receive notice of any additional clauses required in the order on notice, the client may not get the additional order at the first hearing on notice and the solicitor may be ordered to pay wasted costs.

'Informal' notice

5.16   In *G v G (Ouster: Ex Parte Application)*,[2] it was said at 402B that informal notice, ie notice which is too late to comply with the requirements of the rules for notice, is better than no notice at all.

Where a respondent attends having received informal notice, and does not object, or the court is satisfied that the matter can fairly be dealt with as a hearing on notice, the court can abridge time for service retrospectively under FPR 1991, r 3.8(7), FPC (MP etc) R 1991, r 3A(6).

Return date for hearing on notice where order granted without notice

5.17   Section 45(3) of FLA 1996 provides that where the court does grant an order without notice, it 'must afford the respondent an opportunity to make representations relating to the order as soon as just and convenient at a full hearing'. This reflects the general case-law about without notice orders in civil and family proceedings. The more drastic or invasive the order without notice, the greater the urgency for providing a hearing on notice.

Abridged time for service

5.18   The period required for notice to be given to the respondent of a hearing may be abridged by order under FPR 1991, r 3.8(7), FPC (MP etc) R 1991, r 3A(6), RSC Ord 3, r 5, or, in a torts action in a county court, CPR, r 6.9 enables the court to dispense with service. (CPR 1998, r 6.7 deals with the dates upon which documents served by the various means permitted by the rules are deemed served.)

---

[1]   *President's Direction (Children Act 1989: Exclusion Requirement)* [1998] 1 FLR 495 and *President's Direction (Family Law Act 1996, Part IV)* [1998] 1 FLR 496.

[2]   [1990] 1 FLR 395.

Substituted service

5.19 The standard requirement for personal service of an application for a non-molestation or occupation order, in FPR 1991, r 3.8(6), FPC (MP etc) R 1991, r 3A(7), 4, can be modified by an order under FPR 1991, r 3.8(8), FPC (MP etc) R 1991, r 4(5).

In an action based in torts, personal service is not required by the Rules, but judges are reluctant to grant an order without being satisfied that the respondent has been effectively served, whether personally or in some substituted way approved by the court.

CPR 1998, r 6.8 enables the court to provide for service by an alternative method where the court considers that 'there is a good reason to authorise service by a method not permitted by these Rules'. An application must be supported by evidence, but may be made without notice. If granted, the order will state the method of service and the date on which service is to be deemed.

Evidence in support of without notice (ex parte) applications

5.20 An applicant for a without notice order must make full disclosure of all matters known to him which may be material for the judge to know, both for and against the application:

> 'It is perfectly well settled that a person who makes an ex parte application to the court ... is under an obligation to the court to make the fullest possible disclosure of all the material facts within his knowledge, and if he does not make the fullest possible disclosure, then he cannot obtain any advantage from the proceedings.'[1]

Thus, disclosure extends to, and includes, any weaknesses in the applicant's case and points which it might be thought that the defendant would raise were the application being heard on notice. This is because an injunction is an equitable remedy: there is a duty on the applicant to come to the court with clean hands, in this instance by giving full disclosure to the court of all relevant facts. Further, advocates have a duty not to mislead the court, ie they must provide to the court all relevant information known to them. An injunction which has been made without full disclosure is likely to be set aside with costs, perhaps on the indemnity basis.[2]

---

1   *R v Kensington Income Tax Commissioners ex p Princess Edmond de Polignac* [1917] 1 KB 486, CA; and see, eg, *Rochdale Borough Council v A* [1991] 2 FLR 192, Douglas Brown J.
2   See, eg, *Burgess v Burgess* [1996] 2 FLR 34, CA.

Conduct of hearing

Procedure: evidence

5.21 The High Court or a county court may act on the sworn statement or affidavit in support of the application, if it is unopposed or made without notice and sufficient facts are given. Likewise, a family proceedings court may require no more than verification on oath of the statement in support. However, the applicant and any supporting witness should be ready to give oral evidence.

Announcement of a power of arrest granted without notice

5.22 Where a power of arrest is granted without notice, the court is required to announce the order in open court at the earliest opportunity.[1]

Forms of orders

5.23 Before DVCVA 20005, the standard form for a non-molestation order or an occupation order was Prescribed Form, FL404, which was required to be used by FPR 1991, r 3.9(6)(b) and FPC (MP etc) R 1991, r 12A(1)(b).

The fact that powers of arrest will no longer be attached to non-molestation orders has meant that this form has had to be amended and in fact from the date of implementation of the DVCVA 2004 there will now be three relevant forms, viz—

FL404 – (Occupation order)
FL404a – (Non-molestation order)
FL406a – (Record of non-molestation order)

In addition, the form of application for a non-molestation order or occupation order has been changed (see **5.3**).

All these forms are set out in Appendix 3.

Form FL406 will still be the form which contains details of the power of arrest. Rule 3.9A(1) provides that where the court makes an occupation order and a power of arrest is attached to one or more of the provisions ('the relevant provisions') of the order, the relevant provisions shall be set out in Form FL406 and the form shall not contain any provisions of the order to which the power of arrest was not attached.

---

[1]   *President's Direction (Children Act 1989: Exclusion Requirement)* [1998] 1 FLR 495 and *President's Direction (Family Law Act 1996, Part IV)* [1998] 1 FLR 496.

A new r 3.9A(1A) provides that where the court makes a non-molestation order, all the provisions of the order must be set out in Form FL406a. Rule 3.9A(1B) provides that where an occupation order containing a power of arrest or a non-molestation order have been made, a copy of Form FL406 or FL406a must be delivered to the police station for the applicant's address or any other police station which the court may specify, together with a statement showing service on the respondent or stating that he has been informed of its terms (whether by being present when the order was made or by telephone or otherwise).

The menu of forms of non-molestation order (see **2.1**) may be supplemented by specific directive orders, for example forbidding particular acts of molestation as permitted by s 42(6) of FLA 1996, Part IV, but should not otherwise be varied. Any variations must not exceed the powers of the court.

County court Form N16 remains the appropriate prescribed form for issue of an injunction in proceedings founded in torts. See **4.19** for menu of specimen clauses for molestation injunctions in torts.

Service or notification of orders required to make orders enforceable

5.24 An order which is capable of enforcement by committal must, in general, and subject to the court's powers to provide otherwise, be served personally on the respondent to make it enforceable.[1] This is dealt with substantively at **5.28**.

Undertakings: availability

5.25 By s 46(1) of FLA 1996 the court has power to accept an undertaking from any party where it has power to make an occupation order or non-molestation order. The only restriction on this power was that the court had to attach a power of arrest where violence had been used and a power of arrest cannot be attached to an undertaking. In those circumstances an order was mandatory.

Because the ability to attach a power of arrest to a non-molestation order is to be removed, this position has had to be rethought and the restriction on the right of the court to accept an undertaking redefined. First, s 46(3) has been amended to read as follows—

> 'The court shall not accept an undertaking under subsection (1) instead of making an occupation order in any case where apart from this section a power of arrest would be attached to the order'.

---

[1]   CCR Ord 29, r 1(2), FPC (MP etc) R 1991, r 20(6).

This recognises that a power of arrest may still be attached to an occupation order.

5.26   Secondly, a new subs (3A) is inserted,[1] which reads as follows—

'(3A) The court shall not accept an undertaking under subsection (1) instead of making a non-molestation order in any case where it appears to the court that—
(a)   the respondent has used or threatened violence against the applicant or a relevant child; and
(b)   for the protection of the applicant or child it is necessary to make a non-molestation order so that any breach may be punishable under section 42A'.

It will be seen that the restrictions on the court's powers and the standard to be applied by the court have not changed insofar as the principal matter is whether the respondent has used or threatened violence. However, the proviso in the old law, contained in s 47(2)(b) and applicable to s 46(3), namely that the court may decline to attach a power of arrest (and therefore feel able to accept an undertaking) if satisfied that the applicant would be adequately protected without a power of arrest, will go. Now the test will be whether the court considers that it is necessary to make a non-molestation order, breach of which is an arrestable offence, for the protection of the applicant. It may be that the end result will be very much the same as before, but the wording is different.

Undertakings: practice and the Prescribed Forms

5.27   Form FL422 for undertakings in family proceedings courts has been adapted from county court Form N117. These forms conveniently incorporate the procedural requirements of CCR Ord 29, r 1A(2) and FPC (MP etc) R 1991, r 20(14).

It is important that the court ensures that the giver of an undertaking understands both the ingredients of his promises to the court and the possible consequences of breach. See **5.24**, where the implications of committal proceedings are discussed.

Delivery of a form of undertaking

5.28   The record of the undertaking in county court Form N117 or FL422 should usually be delivered to the giver by the court. This is dealt with substantively at **7.20**.

---

[1]   By DVCVA 2004, Sch 10, para 37(3).

Interlocutory injunctions, free-standing injunctions and declaratory orders, in county court actions

5.29 An interlocutory injunction can, by reason of the County Courts Act 1984, s 38, be granted in any proceedings pending in the court. This includes proceedings in the family jurisdiction and other civil proceedings. CCR Ord 13, r 6(1) provides that:

'... an application for the grant of an injunction may be made by any party to an action or matter before or after trial or hearing, whether or not a claim for the injunction was included in that party's particulars of claim, originating application, petition, counterclaim or third party notice, as the case may be.'

CPR 1998, r 25.1(1) provides that the court may grant interim remedies, including injunctions and declarations, and such injunctions can be granted:

(a) whether or not there is a claim in the proceedings in question for a final remedy of the kind covered by the injunction;[1]
(b) before the proceedings have been started,[2] but only where the matter is urgent or the interests of justice require it;[3]
(c) after judgment has been given in the case.[4]

A free-standing injunction (ie in proceedings in which no other relief such as damages is claimed) can be granted in a county court since a new s 38 of the County Courts Act 1984 was substituted by the Courts and Legal Services Act 1990.

Although such a situation is unlikely in the context of personal protection, upon a claim for declaratory relief, such as who is legally entitled to occupy a house, the court can grant an interlocutory injunction in support of the claim for declaratory relief.[5]

In order for any court to have power to grant a free-standing injunction, there must be a lis, a legal right or basis for starting proceedings, which is within the jurisdiction of the court and which can be protected by an injunction.[6] The person against whom the injunction is sought must be someone who can properly be made a party in proceedings based on the lis, except where there

---

1   CPR 1998, r 25.1(4).
2   Ibid, r 25.2(1)(a).
3   Ibid, r 25.2(2)(b).
4   Ibid, r 25.2(1)(b).
5   *Newport Association Football Club Ltd v Football Association of Wales* [1995] 2 All ER 87.
6   *Richards v Richards* [1984] AC 174, [1984] FLR 11 at pp 17F, 23C, 29G, 32A and 35H; *Khorasandjian v Bush* [1993] QB 727, [1993] 2 FLR 66; *Chief Constable of Kent v V* [1983] QB 34, [1982] 3 All ER 36 at 40G, 42J, 45G and 46C–H; *Chief Constable of Hampshire v A* [1985] QB 132, [1984] 2 All ER 385 at 387E–H, 388C and 390A

is a specific statutory jurisdiction to grant an injunctive direction against a non-party.

Power to grant and enforce an injunction against a person aged at least 18 and less than 21

5.30 Anti-molestation injunctions sometimes are sought against people who are aged under 21, usually by parents or neighbours. An injunction can be granted against a person aged under 21 to protect a parent as well as in favour of any other person.[1]

There is power, where a person aged at least 18 and less than 21 is guilty of contempt of court, to commit him to detention under s 9(1) of the Criminal Justice Act 1981 as amended by the Criminal Justice Act 1991, s 63(1), (5).

Power to grant and enforce an injunction against a person aged less than 18

5.31 There is jurisdiction to grant an injunction against a person under the age of 18, whether to restrain molestation in a family case[2] or to restrain tortious behaviour.[3] In *Re L*, an injunction had been granted against a 17-year-old molester of a ward, and in *Shea v Shea*, an injunction against the plaintiff's 17-year-old son.

A person aged less than 18 cannot be committed to any form of detention for contempt of court: s 1(1) of the Criminal Justice Act 1981.[4]

Power to enforce an injunction against a person who is mentally disordered

5.32 In *Wookey v Wookey; Re S (A Minor)*,[5] the Court of Appeal said that a person who was incapable of understanding an injunction could not be guilty of contempt by disobeying it.

Suitability of injunction as remedy against person aged less than 18 or mentally disordered

5.33 In *Wookey v Wookey; Re S (A Minor)*,[6] the Court of Appeal said that it is not appropriate to grant an injunction against a person who, because he is aged less than 18, cannot be detained, if he has no income or money.

---

1   *Egan v Egan* [1975] Ch 218, [1975] 2 All ER 167.
2   *Re L (A Minor) (Injunction and Committal: Guardian ad Litem)* [1997] Fam Law 91 (1993) CAT No 0952.
3   *Shea v Shea* (1982) CAT No 387.
4   See *R v Selby Justices ex parte Frame* [1991] 2 All ER 344; *Mason v Lawton* [1991] 2 FLR 50.
5   [1991] Fam 121, [1991] 2 FLR 319.
6   [1991] 2 FLR 319.

Butler-Sloss LJ said:[1]

> '... in the vast majority of cases where the minor is still of school age, or
> unemployed, recourse to the civil courts is not the appropriate procedure ...
>
> 　Barristers and solicitors consulted by relatives of violent or unmanageable
> teenagers ought to think very carefully before advising the institution of civil
> proceedings to regulate their unacceptable behaviour.'

A mentally disordered person, against whom an injunction could be granted
because his condition is not so serious as to render him 'incapable of
managing and administering his property and affairs',[2] may, nevertheless, be
unlikely to respond appropriately to an injunction, and so careful
consideration should be given before seeking one.

Procedure where the defendant is a minor or mental patient

5.34　Where the defendant is a minor or is 'by reason of mental disorder ...
incapable of managing and administering his property and affairs',[3] unless the
defendant already has a guardian ad litem, the plaintiff must, after the time for
delivering a defence or admission has expired and before taking any further
step in the proceedings, apply to the court for a guardian ad litem to be
appointed for the defendant.[4] RSC Ord 80, r 16 and CCR Ord 10, r 4 deal
with service of proceedings on a minor or patient. RSC Ord 80, r 16(4) and
CCR Ord 29, r 2 require that an injunction must be served personally on a
minor or a patient unless the court otherwise orders.

In *Wookey v Wookey; Re S (A Minor)*, Butler-Sloss LJ discussed[5] the
considerations which apply, and the procedure to be followed, when it
appears that a person who is molesting the plaintiff may be suffering from a
mental disorder. In particular, it was stated that the Official Solicitor should be
notified as soon as possible if an application is to be made to a court for an
injunction, and the possible need for a guardian ad litem must be addressed.

In *Shea v Shea*,[6] the Court of Appeal directed that the 17-year-old son of the
plaintiff should be served personally with the injunction and that the Official
Solicitor should be invited to consider whether he should represent the child.

1　Ibid, at 328D–E.
2　RSC Ord 81, r 1.
3　Ibid.
4　Ibid, Ord 80, r 6(1); CCR Ord 10, r 6(1).
5　[1991] 2 FLR 319 at 325–326.
6　(1982) CAT No 387.

In *Re L (A Minor) (Injunction and Committal: Guardian ad Litem)*,[1] the Court of Appeal allowed the appeal against committal of the 17-year-old for breach of an injunction on procedural grounds, of which the failure to appoint a guardian was treated as the most significant. Neill LJ, with whom Russell and Rose LJJ agreed, indicated that a child against whom an injunction has been granted should have the benefit of a guardian following the grant of the injunction, to ensure that the child understands the consequences of disobedience.

---

1   [1997] Fam Law 91.

CHAPTER 6

TRANSFER OF TENANCIES

Introduction

6.1   The bulk of the provisions in Part IV of the FLA 1996 are concerned with the regulation of the occupation of a dwelling-house which is, or has been a family home, and with the behaviour of the parties towards each other; longer-term issues, such as transfers of title to property are not dealt with, because they are normally the subject of proceedings under the MCA 1973.

The exception to this, namely the provisions dealing with transfer of tenancies, concerns the position of cohabitants or former cohabitants, and, in effect, adapts the existing law which had previously applied only to spouses. This reflects the fact that the previous law relating to the position of cohabitants was unsatisfactory and, in some cases, unfair.

As will be seen, the provisions as to transfer of tenancies repeat, and are designed to improve, the existing law relating to former spouses, and extend that law to cohabitants and former cohabitants. In each case, the rights previously enjoyed by spouses are extended to unmarried people. These will be considered in turn.

6.2   The power to transfer a tenancy from one party to another has existed for some time in the case of former spouses whose marriage has been dissolved or annulled, or spouses to whom a decree of judicial separation has been granted. It was arguable that this power existed by virtue of s 24(1) of the MCA 1973, although a potential difficulty was that the court could not compel an unwilling landlord to accept a transfer of tenant where there was a covenant against assignment. However, there was no doubt that by virtue of s 7 of and Sch 1 to MHA 1983 the court did have the power to transfer tenancies between spouses or former spouses.

This power did not exist in the case of cohabitants, and the Law Commission considered that this anomaly should be rectified. Although the Family Law Reform Act 1987 gave the court jurisdiction to order the transfer or settlement of property between unmarried parents for the benefit of their children, this was thought to be unduly restrictive and unsatisfactory for a number of reasons.[1]

Such considerations led the Law Commission to:

> '... the firm conclusion that the power to transfer tenancies at present contained in the Matrimonial Homes Act 1983 should be extended to cohabitants, whether they are joint tenants or whether one party is a sole tenant and the other is non-entitled. We therefore recommend accordingly. There would, of course, be no entitlement to such a transfer in any particular situation. The court would simply have power to make such an order if the merits of the case justified it. If they did not, it would not be done.'[2]

This change was, therefore, brought about by s 53 of FLA 1996, which provides that Sch 7 to the Act shall have effect.

It should be noted that, by virtue of para 15(1) of Sch 7, the court's powers under this Schedule are in addition to the court's powers to make occupation orders under whatever section is appropriate. These powers are therefore additional to those arising under the remainder of the Act. It is interesting to note that unmarried couples are, in this respect, placed in a more favourable position with respect to rented property than to property which one of them might have owned.

Applicants for transfer of tenancy

6.3   The MHA 1983 is abolished in its entirety by the FLA 1996. As a result, the FLA 1996 has to confer on spouses and former spouses the rights which they enjoyed under the earlier legislation, as well as extending those rights to others. This part of the legislation is, therefore, of considerable significance to divorced couples whose matrimonial home has been tenanted property, within the classes of tenancy covered by Sch 7.

Schedule 7 begins by defining some terms. 'Cohabitant', except in one limited case which will be considered later, includes a 'former cohabitant'. 'Landlord' includes any person deriving title under the original landlord. 'Relevant tenancy' means:

> '(a)   a protected tenancy or statutory tenancy within the meaning of the Rent Act 1977;
> (b)   a statutory tenancy within the meaning of the Rent (Agriculture) Act 1976;
> (c)   a secure tenancy within the meaning of section 79 of the Housing Act 1985; or

---

[1]   See Law Com, para 6.5.
[2]   Ibid, para 6.6.

(d)   an assured tenancy or assured agricultural occupancy within the meaning of Part I of the Housing Act 1988.'

'Tenancy' includes a sub-tenancy, and 'spouse', except in one case, includes a former spouse.[1]

It will be noted that this list does not include assured shorthold tenancies, or long leases.

The orders for transfer which the court may make are collectively referred to as 'Part II orders'.[2]

Paragraph 2 of Part I of Sch 7 goes on to define the cases in which the court may make an order. These are as follows.

Spouses

Paragraph 2(1) applies if:

> '... one spouse is entitled, either in his own right or jointly with the other spouse, to occupy a dwelling-house by virtue of a relevant tenancy.'

Paragraph 2(2) goes on to provide that, at any time where it has power to make a property adjustment order under s 23A (divorce or separation) or s 24 (nullity) of MCA 1973 with respect to the marriage, the court may make a Part II order.

It follows from this that a spouse may apply for a transfer of tenancy under Part II only when she is in a position to apply for a property adjustment order; when the whole of the FLA 1996 comes into force, this will be, in the case of divorce or separation, at any time after the filing of a statement of marital breakdown. Until then, and in any event in the case of nullity, the appropriate time is on or after the grant of a decree. The applicant does not have to apply for a property adjustment order; the requirement is merely that she should be entitled to do so.

Paragraph 4 provides that the court shall not make such an order unless the dwelling-house is or was, in the case of spouses, a matrimonial home or, in the case of cohabitants, a home in which they lived together as husband and wife. A tenancy must therefore be contrasted with the much wider class of property which may be transferred under s 24 of MCA 1973.

---

1   FLA 1996, Sch 7, Part I, para 1.
2   Ie orders made under FLA 1996, Sch 7, Part II.

The 1995 Bill provided that only the court which granted the decree may make the order under Part II; that is no longer the case, so that the application may be brought in any county court.

Finally, it should be noted that para 13 of Sch 7 provides that a spouse who remarries cannot thereafter apply for an order under Part II. This has exactly the same effect as s 28(3) of MCA 1973, which prevents a spouse who has remarried from applying for a capital order under s 24 of that Act; however, as will be seen, this restriction does not apply to cohabitants, who may marry with impunity and not lose the right to apply.

Cohabitants

6.4   Paragraph 3(1) of Part I of Sch 7 applies if:

'... one cohabitant is entitled, either in his own right or jointly with the other cohabitant, to occupy a dwelling-house by virtue of a relevant tenancy.'

Paragraph 3(2) provides that:

'If the cohabitants cease to live together as husband and wife, the court may make a Part II order.'

As was seen above, by para 4, the court may not make an order unless the dwelling-house is or was a home in which the cohabitants lived together as husband and wife.

6.5   The meaning of 'cohabitant' has already been considered in Chapter 2 and need not be considered further here. There is, in the FLA 1996, no restriction on the time within which such an application may be made by a former cohabitant.

Principles to be applied

6.6   The orders which the court may make are set out at **6.10**. Paragraph 5 of Part I of Sch 7 sets out the matters to which the court shall have regard; these are:

'... all the circumstances of the case including—

(a)   the circumstances in which the tenancy was granted to either or both of the spouses or cohabitants or, as the case requires, the circumstances in which either or both of them became tenant under the tenancy;

(b)   the matters mentioned in section 33(6)(a), (b) and (c) and, where the parties are cohabitants and only one of them is entitled to occupy the dwelling-house by virtue of the relevant tenancy, the further matters mentioned in section 36(6)(e), (f), (g) and (h); and

(c)   the suitability of the parties as tenants.'

6.7   'All the circumstances of the case' gives the court a wide discretion to admit any evidence which may be relevant.

FLA 1996, Sch 7, para 5(a) directs the court to have regard to how the tenancy came into being, and to whom it was granted. It will, therefore, be relevant to consider which party is the tenant and how it was that he or she became the tenant.

Section 33(6)(a), (b) and (c) of FLA 1996 contains the matters to which the court is directed to have regard when deciding whether, and, if so, how, to exercise its powers to make an occupation order in favour of a person who is entitled or has matrimonial home rights; this is considered in more detail, in the context of occupation orders, in Chapter 3. It will be remembered that s 36 contains subs (7), which sets out the 'greater harm' test, but it might be thought that, if Parliament had intended subs (7) to apply, it would have said so, and the wording of para 5(b) of this Schedule seems to incorporate only s 33(6)(a), (b) and (c). It might seem, therefore, that the 'greater harm' test is not applicable.

In all cases, therefore, the court will have to have regard to the respective housing needs of the parties and of any relevant child, and the respective financial resources of the parties. By s 33(6)(c), the court must also have regard to:

> '... the likely effect of any order, or of any decision by the court not to exercise its powers under subsection (3) above, on the health, safety or well-being of the parties and of any relevant child.'

Subsection (3) of s 33 sets out the different kinds of occupation orders which a court may make. If the wording is read literally, it would seem that the court is directed to have regard to the consequences of making, or not making, an occupation order, which might broaden the scope of the court's enquiry. It may be that this difficulty is more apparent than real, since the consequences of an order for transfer of tenancy would be that the 'unsuccessful' party would have to leave, which would have the same effect as an occupation order; this provision would then be interpreted as meaning that the court must consider the effect on both parties of an order that one of them leave.

It is worth noting that s 33(6)(d), which directs the court to have regard to the conduct of the parties, is not applicable to Sch 7. Conduct, therefore, is irrelevant.

6.8   Paragraph 5(b) of Part I of Sch 7 then sets out further matters to which the court must have regard when the parties are cohabitants and only one of them is the tenant (it would not, therefore, apply when both were tenants); 'cohabitant' includes 'former cohabitant'.

These matters are those contained in s 36(6)(e), (f), (g) and (h), which are the factors to be considered by the court when deciding whether, and, if so, in what manner, to make an occupation order where the applicant was non-entitled; they are set out and considered in detail in Chapter 3. They are, where the parties are cohabitants or former cohabitants: the nature of their relationship; the duration of the cohabitation; whether there are children for whom they are responsible; and the length of time since they ceased to live together. Once again, the conduct of the parties, which is relevant to an issue of an occupation order, is not included as a relevant factor here.

These provisions are clearly designed to give the court wide discretion to make orders in accordance with the justice of the case.

6.9   The final matter to which the court must have regard is the suitability of the parties as tenants. It will be seen below that landlords will be entitled to be heard on applications for transfer of tenancies, and this provision enables the court to take account of the landlord's interests as well as those of the parties. It would also have some relevance as between the parties, since there would be little point, for example, in transferring a tenancy to someone who was incapable of paying the rent or who had proved to be a nuisance or annoyance to his neighbours.

Orders which may be made

6.10   By para 1 of Part I of Sch 7, 'the court' does not include a magistrates' court. Applications will therefore have to be brought in a county court.

The orders which the court may make will depend on the nature of the tenancy; these orders are, therefore, set out by reference to the type of tenancy which is involved. Part II of Sch 7 begins with one clarification of terms; whenever this part of the Schedule refers to a cohabitant or spouse being entitled to occupy a dwelling-house by virtue of a relevant tenancy, this applies whether the tenancy is sole or joint.[1]

It is, perhaps, also worth noting here the restrictions which apply in respect of some former spouses. As has already been noted above, a spouse who has remarried is not entitled to apply for an order under Sch 7.[2] If this is interpreted in the same way as other claims under the pre-1996 law for ancillary relief, it will mean that a petitioner who has applied for a transfer of a

---

[1]   FLA 1996, Sch 7, Part II, para 6.
[2]   Ibid, para 13.

tenancy in the prayer to her petition will be taken to have applied, and her claim will not be defeated by her remarriage. However, a respondent who had not filed an answer claiming relief would be barred from applying after remarriage. It remains to be seen what rules of court will provide for the new divorce law.

By para 12 of Sch 7, it is provided that the date on which an order for transfer of tenancy is to take effect may not be earlier than decree absolute.

Neither of these restrictions applies, of course, to cohabitants. A spouse whose marriage has not been dissolved, or to whom a decree of judicial separation has not been granted, has no right to apply under Sch 7.

The orders which the court may make are classified by reference to the nature of the tenancy to be transferred. This is not a textbook on the law of landlord and tenant; accordingly, no explanation is provided of the meaning of the various terms used, for example 'assured agricultural occupancy'. The reader who requires further information as to the rights and obligations attaching to such terms should therefore consult a more specialised publication.

In all cases, the interest to be transferred is the tenancy to which the transferor is entitled. They are as follows.

Protected tenancy, secure tenancy, assured tenancy, assured agricultural occupancy

6.11   These terms are defined by reference to their meaning in the Rent Act 1977, the Housing Act 1985, and Part I of the Housing Act 1988 respectively. It will be noted that an assured shorthold tenancy is not one which may be transferred, but a 'council tenancy' is. (The most common form of tenancy in the private sector is therefore excluded.) What is to be transferred is the estate or interest which the entitled spouse had in the dwelling-house immediately before the order for transfer:

'... by virtue of the lease or agreement creating the tenancy and any assignment of that lease of agreement, with all rights, privileges and appurtenances attaching to that estate or interest but subject to all covenants, obligations, liabilities and incumbrances to which it is subject ...'[1]

The transfer is effected by the order, and no further assurance or document in writing is needed.[2]

---

[1]   FLA 1996, Sch 7, para 7(1)(a).
[2]   Ibid, para 7(1).

Paragraph 7(1)(b) provides that where the entitled party is an assignee, his liability under any covenant of indemnity, whether express or implied, may also be transferred.

6.12   Paragraph 7(2) provides, in effect, that when an order for transfer is made, any liability or obligation to which the party whose tenancy has been transferred was liable shall no longer be enforceable against that party; this is only in respect of liabilities or obligations falling due to be discharged after the date of the transfer.

By para 7(3), (3A) and (4), where the entitled party is a successor within the meaning of Part IV of the Housing Act 1985, s 17 of the Housing Act 1988, or s 132 of the Housing Act 1996, his former spouse or cohabitant is also deemed to be a successor.

Paragraph 7(5) deals with the position where the transfer is of an assured agricultural occupancy. For the purposes of Chapter III of Part I of the Housing Act 1988, the agricultural worker condition shall be fulfilled with respect to the dwelling-house while the spouse or cohabitant to whom the occupancy is transferred continues to be the occupier under that occupancy, and that condition shall be treated as so fulfilled by virtue of the same paragraph of Sch 3 to the Housing Act 1988 as was applicable before the transfer.

Statutory tenancy within the meaning of the Rent Act 1977

6.13   The court may order that, as from the date specified in the order, the entitled party shall cease to be entitled to occupy the dwelling-house, and that the other party shall be deemed to be the tenant, or, as the case may be, the sole tenant, under the statutory tenancy.[1]

Paragraph 8(3) deals with the question of whether the provisions of paras 1–3, or, as the case may be, paras 5–7 of Sch 1 to the Rent Act 1977, as to the succession by the surviving spouse of a deceased tenant, or by a member of the deceased tenant's family, to the right to retain possession, are capable of having effect in the event of the death of a person deemed by an order under these provisions to be the tenant or sole tenant under the statutory tenancy. It is provided that this question shall be determined according as those provisions have or have not already had effect in relation to the statutory tenancy.

---

[1]   FLA 1996, Sch 7, para 8(2).

Statutory tenancy within the meaning of the Rent (Agriculture) Act 1976

6.14 The court may order that, as from such date as may be specified in the order, the entitled party shall cease to be entitled to occupy the dwelling-house and that the other party shall be deemed to be the tenant, or, as the case may be, the sole tenant under the statutory tenancy.[1] A spouse or cohabitant who is deemed under this provision to be the tenant under a statutory tenancy shall be (within the meaning of the Rent (Agriculture) Act 1976) a statutory tenant in his own right, or a statutory tenant by succession, according as the other spouse or cohabitant was a statutory tenant in his own right or a statutory tenant by succession.

Supplementary provisions

6.15 Part III of Sch 7 to the FLA 1996 contains what are described as 'supplementary provisions'. These are orders which may be made supplementary to the order for transfer of tenancy in any case. They are, in fact, potentially more important than their description might indicate.

The first of these relates to payment in return for transfer. By para 10(1), the court may order a party to whom a tenancy is transferred to make a payment to the other party. In deciding whether to exercise this power, and, if so, in what manner, the court is directed by para 10(4) to have regard to all the circumstances including:

'(a) the financial loss that would otherwise be suffered by the transferor as a result of the order;
(b) the financial needs and financial resources of the parties; and
(c) the financial obligations which the parties have, or are likely to have in the foreseeable future, including financial obligations to each other and to any relevant child.'

A wide discretion is therefore conferred on the court.

6.16 By para 10(2), the court may, in effect, order that the payment need not be made immediately. Instead, it may direct that payment of the sum, or part thereof, be deferred, or be paid by instalments. Further, by para 10(3), the court may vary any order for payment, or exercise its powers under para 10(2) at any time before payment in full has been made.

In deciding how to exercise its powers as to the method of payment, the court must have regard to the factors set out in para 10(4) above. However, this is subject to the overriding provision, contained in para 10(5), that the court

---

[1] FLA 1996, Sch 7, para 9.

shall not give any direction under para 10(2) unless it appears to the court that immediate payment of the sum required by the order would cause the transferee financial hardship which is greater than any hardship that would be caused to the transferor if the direction were given.

6.17 The second type of supplementary order relates to liabilities and obligations in respect of the dwelling-house. By para 11, the court may direct that both parties shall be jointly and severally liable to discharge and perform any obligation or liability in respect of the dwelling-house (whether arising under the tenancy or otherwise) which, before the order for transfer, may have fallen to be discharged or performed by only one of them, and which were due as at the date of the transfer. Where such a direction is given, the court may also direct that either party shall be liable to indemnify the other in whole or in part against any payment made or expenses incurred by the other in discharging or performing any such liability or obligation.

Rights of landlords

6.18 FLA 1996, Sch 7, para 14(1) provides that rules of court shall be made requiring the court to give the landlord of any dwelling-house, to which any order for transfer of tenancy will relate, an opportunity to be heard. The principal provision in Sch 7 which protects a landlord is para 5(c), which directs the court to have regard to the suitability of the parties as tenants when deciding how to exercise its powers.

For procedure, see **6.20**.

Date when order takes effect

6.19 There is no special provision as to when an order between cohabitants or former cohabitants is to take effect. However, provision has had to be made for orders made between spouses because of the provisions of the MCA 1973 introduced by the FLA 1996 as to the date on which a property adjustment order may take effect. Paragraph 12 of Sch 7 provides that, in the cause of nullity, the order may not take effect before decree absolute, and, in the case of divorce or separation, the date on which it may take effect is to be determined as if the court were making a property adjustment order under s 23A of MCA 1973, regard being had to the restrictions imposed by s 23B of that Act.[1]

---

[1]   See, generally, Cretney and Bird, *Divorce: The New Law* (Family Law, 1996).

Procedure

6.20 The procedure for applications for transfer of tenancies is different from the other applications under FLA 1996, Part IV. By FPR 1991, r 3.8(14), r 3.6(7)–(9) (which governs applications under the Married Women's Property Act 1882 (MWPA 1882)) applies to applications for the transfer of tenancy. The effect of this is as follows.

Issue and application

6.21 Rule 3.6(7) does not deal with applications for MWPA 1882 orders as such; this is dealt with by r 3.6(1), which is not deemed to apply to applications for transfer of tenancy. However, there is nothing in r 3.8 to govern applications for transfer of tenancy, nor any prescribed forms; Form FL401 is limited to applications for occupation orders or non-molestation orders.

It would seem, therefore, that application should be made by originating application supported by affidavit.

Respondent contesting

6.22 A respondent who wishes to contest an application must, within the time limited for sending the acknowledgement of service, file and serve an affidavit in reply.[1]

Interlocutory orders

6.23 If no affidavit in reply is served, the applicant may apply for directions.[2] A district judge may grant an injunction if it is incidental to the relief sought.[3]

The court has jurisdiction to order, for example discovery, further particulars etc as if the application were for ancillary relief.[4]

Service on landlords

6.24 Rule 3.8(12) provides that an application for transfer of tenancy must be served on the other cohabitant or spouse and on the landlord. Any person so served is entitled to be heard on the application. This is, therefore, a different requirement from that relating to third parties in applications for occupation orders where a landlord or mortgagee must be served with notice of an application rather than the application itself.

---

[1]   FPR 1991, r 3.6(7).
[2]   Ibid, r 3.6(8).
[3]   Ibid, r 3.6(9).
[4]   Ibid, r 2.62(4)–(6) and 2.63, applied by r 3.8(13)

CHAPTER 7

ENFORCEMENT

Enforcement procedures

Checklists for preparing for and conducting committal proceedings are provided at **7.39**.

Changes introduced by DVCVA 2004

7.1   The changes effected by the DVCVA 2004 in respect of the method of enforcing non-molestation orders and punishing breaches thereof are some of the most significant matters contained in that Act, and it seems appropriate therefore to consider these in some detail before the general principles of enforcement are considered.

Part IV of FLA 1996 laid down a comprehensive code for the enforcement of orders, consisting essentially of a power of arrest and provision for bringing offenders quickly before the relevant judicial authority, normally the court which had made the order. For cases where there was no power of arrest, or where that power had not been invoked, the complainant could issue a notice to show cause why the offender should not be committed.

The government's view was clearly that that system had been found wanting, though the evidence which led to that conclusion is elusive. The result of this is that, as described above, from the date of implementation of the DVCVA 2004, non-molestation orders will no longer bear a power of arrest, and breach of such an order will become a criminal offence.

The reasoning for this was that making a breach an offence would extend the range of sanctions available to the court. Contempt penalties are limited to fine or imprisonment, whereas a criminal court may impose the usual range of community sentences, such as curfew, mental health, drug treatment, voluntary activities etc. This would give the court an opportunity to deal with the offending behaviour.[1]

---

[1]   Official Report (HL), 29 January 2004, cols 237 and 238.

7.2   Section 1 of DVCVA 2004 inserts a new s 42A into the FLA 1996. This provides as follows—

> '(1)   A person who without reasonable excuse does anything that he is prohibited from doing by a non-molestation order is guilty of an offence.
>
> (2)   In the case of a non-molestation order made by virtue of section 45(1), a person can be guilty of an offence under this section only in respect of conduct engaged in at a time when he was aware of the existence of the order.
>
> (3)   Where a person is convicted of an offence under this section in respect of any conduct, that conduct is not punishable as a contempt of court.
>
> (4)   A person cannot be convicted of an offence under this section in respect of any conduct which has been punished as a contempt of court.'

7.3   Subsection (1) therefore contains the ingredients of the offence. The act complained of must be forbidden by the non-molestation order, and there must be no reasonable excuse for the breach; put another way, reasonable excuse is a defence to the charge.

It is interesting to note that breach of anything forbidden by the order will constitute a criminal offence and so render the offender liable to arrest and prosecution. Under the existing law, care has always been taken to distinguish between those matters involving violence or the threat of violence, to which a power of arrest could be attached, and other matters not involving violence, to which a power of arrest is not attached. For example, an order not to use or threaten violence would carry a power of arrest; this would not routinely be the case with an order prohibiting harassment, intimidation or pestering. The courts have been anxious to ensure that a person could not be arrested for, say, telephoning the applicant when he was enjoined not to.

There is no such distinction in the new Act, and this is deliberate. Speaking in the Grand Committee debate, the government spokesperson Baroness Scotland said—

> 'The police may be unclear to which part of the order any power of arrest may be attached … Our aim is to ensure the immediate safety of the applicant and any children, and we want to underline the seriousness of any breach. That is why [section] 1 makes a breach of the order a criminal offence.'[1]

The position is therefore that breach of any provision of the order, however comparatively insignificant, will constitute an offence.

In *Chechi v Bashier*[2] the court declined to make a non-molestation order where violence had been proved on the ground that it was mandatory to attach a

---

[1]   Official Report (HL), 19 January 2004, col GC238.
[2]   [1999] 2 FLR 489, CA, per Dame Elizabeth Butler-Sloss P.

power of arrest and that, in the particular circumstances of the case, arrest was a weapon which the parties should not have available to them. It will be interesting to see whether such reasoning is used in future when the issue of whether to make an order or accept an undertaking is being decided.

7.4 Subsection (2) refers to orders made under s 45(1) of FLA 1996, namely without notice orders. The significance of this is, therefore, that the respondent must be aware of the order before an offence can be committed. He will normally have been made aware by means of personal service of the order. However, the subsection merely says that he must be aware of the existence of the order and it is arguable that if, for example, he had learnt of the order in some other way, such as a telephone conversation with someone, he would be liable.

7.5 Subsections (3) and (4) deal with the overlapping of criminal proceedings and contempt proceedings.

The position with relation to this was clearly set out by the government spokesman in the parliamentary debates as follows—

> 'I was asked what action could be taken in relation to the breach with regard to the person who is protected by the order. Broadly speaking, there are two options. First, the police could be called and, because of the maximum five year imprisonment on conviction, the police will have automatically have the power of arrest for any breach of the terms of a non-molestation order ... The decision on whether to prosecute for the breach will be for the police and the Crown Prosecution Service – always of course in consultation with the victim herself. If the decision is not to prosecute for a criminal offence, the victim can still pursue an action through the civil court and breach remains contempt with the same penalties available as now.
>
> The second option is to pursue the civil route. The victim may decide that they do not want to involve the police at all. in those circumstances the victim will still be able to apply to the civil court for a warrant of arrest if the molestation (sic) order is breached, and to have the perpetrator arrested and brought back to the civil court for the judge to decide what should happen.'[1]

Even though the power of arrest is to be removed, therefore, there is no reason why a complainant should not seek to punish breach of an order by means of the issue of a warrant of arrest under FLA 1996, s 47(10) or by the issue and service of a notice to show good reason why the respondent should not be committed to prison (Form N78 in the county court, Form FL418 in magistrates' courts). The Act imposes no restrictions or time limits on either a prosecutor or a complainant wishing to enforce by a contempt application. Mr Goggins referred above to the warrant of arrest procedure only but it has

---

1   Mr Paul Goggins, Official Report, HC Standing Committee E, 22 June 2004, col 45.

to be said that this procedure has been little used and it is most likely that the notice to show good reason procedure would be more widely used. It remains to be seen whether the 'civil route' will be that adopted by most victims and their solicitors. Anecdotal evidence suggests that there are frequent delays while waiting for the Crown Prosecution Service to take action, and if such delays became commonplace it is likely that the notice to show cause procedure would be often used.

7.6 Subsections (3) and (4) provide, in effect, that a person who has been punished for contempt in the family proceedings may not be convicted of an offence and vice versa. This is obviously fair and sensible as far as it goes but it still leaves an unfortunate lacuna. There is nothing to prevent a complainant beginning contempt proceedings where the respondent has been arrested, and there is nothing to prevent prosecution of an alleged offender where contempt proceedings are pending. It may be that further rules of court will deal with this (though there is no sign of this at present) but it has to be said that, at present, there is room for confusion.

However, the position is potentially even worse than that. There is nothing to prevent a complainant who is dissatisfied by the acquittal of a respondent, or the dismissal of contempt proceedings against him, making a second attempt to punish him in the other court, perhaps armed with better evidence. The Act only prohibits duplicate proceedings in the event of a favourable outcome for the applicant; it does not contemplate the result of unsuccessful proceedings.

It cannot be said that the position is anything other than unsatisfactory.

7.7 Subsection (5) deals with the penalties for the offence. On indictment, an offender is liable to up to 5 years' imprisonment or a fine or both. On summary conviction, an offender is liable to up to 12 months' imprisonment or a fine not exceeding the statutory maximum of both. This contrasts with the maximum of 2 years' imprisonment or a fine in civil contempt proceedings.

7.8 Section 10 of DVCVA 2004 amends the Police and Criminal Evidence Act 1984 by inserting a new s 14A. This inserts common assault into the list of arrestable offences. This removes any doubt about whether a constable who would previously have had a power of arrest may arrest an alleged offender for breach of a non-molestation order, even though such doubt should have been removed by the new s 42A.

General principle

Disobedience of an order as a contempt of court

7.9   Disobedience of a directive order capable of enforcement by committal, or an undertaking to like effect, is a civil contempt of court.

Disobedience of a magistrates' order capable of enforcement under s 63(3) is a civil contempt.[1]

Directive orders made under FLA 1996, Part IV, in particular non-molestation orders and those parts of occupation orders which provide personal protection and the right to enjoy occupation of the family home, are enforceable by committal. Committal is available for breach of an injunction forbidding a common law tort or harassment within the PHA 1997, but if the contemnor has already been convicted of an offence of harassment, he cannot be punished for contempt in respect of the same conduct.[2]

Contempt consists of 'actus reus' and 'mens rea'. This means a deliberate act or neglect to act by the respondent who knew what the order was. It is *not* necessary to prove that the respondent's purpose was to breach the order or undertaking.

Orders not capable of enforcement by committal

7.10   Some orders are not capable of enforcement by committal (eg orders to attend court as witness). In the High Court or a county court, family financial support orders are enforceable only by judgment summons or enforcement as civil debts. Orders for payment of money also cannot be enforced as civil contempts under s 63(3) of the Magistrates' Courts Act 1980 (see **7.14**). Some parts of occupation orders, such as responsibility for maintaining the home cannot be enforced by committal.

In *Nwogbe v Nwogbe*[3] it was held that there was no power to commit a respondent who had failed to obey an order to pay the monthly rent on a property pursuant to s 40 of FLA 1996. It was observed that this revealed a statutory lacuna of real significance.

---

[1]   See *B (BPM) v B (MM)* [1969] P 103, [1969] 1 All ER 891, at 899H and the heading of the Contempt of Court Act 1981, Sch 3.

[2]   PHA 1997, s 3(7).

[3]   [2000] 2 FLR 744, CA.

Alternatives to applications for committal

7.11 Before making an immediate committal order, the court has a duty to consider whether an alternative means of disposal would be more appropriate.[1]

Where the contempt is serious and flagrant, the Court of Appeal has made it clear that there is no principle that 'a first breach [of an injunction] cannot result in a sentence of imprisonment'.[2] Where the first disobedience is a breach of a non-molestation injunction, an immediate custodial sentence may be imposed.[3]

Where the contempt is disobedience of a contact order, 'all remedies should be exhausted before this weapon [of committal] is wielded'.[4]

While in *A v N (Committal: Refusal of Contact)*,[5] the Court of Appeal has reaffirmed that in an extreme case a mother who prevents contact which is in the interests of a child may be sent to prison, practitioners should consider carefully whether some other remedy should be sought before launching an application for committal. The goal should be to achieve the optimum outcome for the client but, particularly where there are children, the client's interests are not separate from the welfare of the family. Where the client may have to have further dealings with the respondent, for example over contact with a child, penal proceedings involve an inherent risk of making future co-operation more difficult. Even where the complainant wishes to sever altogether any links with the respondent, if the respondent is given no cause for rancour or grievance, it may be less likely that he will cause further trouble.

For a complete review of the proper approach to committal and the alternatives which may be adopted see *Hale v Tanner*[6] at **7.35**.

Application for committal of a person aged less than 18 or who is a mental patient

7.12 A person aged less than 18 cannot be committed to any form of detention. Consideration should be given to whether committal is an appropriate remedy in the case of a contemnor who is aged 18 or is a mental patient, and to whether the Official Solicitor should be invited to act.

1   *Danchevsky v Danchevsky* [1975] Fam 17, at 417E; *Thomason v Thomason* [1985] FLR 214, at 216G–217A.
2   *Thorpe v Thorpe* [1998] 2 FLR 127, CA.
3   *Jordan v Jordan* [1993] 1 FLR 169, CA; *Neil v Ryan* [1998] 2 FLR 1068, CA.
4   *Re M (Contact Order: Committal)* [1999] 1 FLR 810, CA.
5   [1997] 1 FLR 533.
6   [2000] 2 FLR 879, CA.

Enforcement powers common to all courts

7.13   Upon hearing an application, and finding breach of a term in a directive order or an undertaking which is capable of enforcement by committal to prison, the court has a variety of possible disposals. The most common of these are set out in the forms of committal, Form N79 in a county court and FL419 in a family proceedings court. They are committal where the contemnor is aged at least 18, which may be immediate committal, for a total imposed on any one occasion not exceeding 2 years (Contempt of Court Act 1981, s 14(1)), or suspended committal of imprisonment, or adjournment of consideration of penalty and/or fine. The court also can make a further injunctive order or, if there is evidence of actual or threatened violence, add a power of arrest. Where an order to give up a child has not been obeyed, the court can order transfer of a child under s 34 of FLA 1986.

Additional enforcement powers of the High Court and county courts

7.14   Under the general injunctive powers in the Supreme Court Act 1981, s 37(1) and the County Courts Act 1984, s 38(1), the High Court and county courts have additional enforcement powers. The courts can authorise execution of an act to be done at the expense of the contemnor; can award damages; can order sequestration of assets for assisting the implementation of the injunctive order; a county court can provide for an occupation order, which requires the respondent to vacate the family home, to be implemented by a bailiff; see **7.38**.

The High Court enjoys the power at common law to commit for contempt, to suspend the sentence and to release; this is independent of any statutory power.[1]

Magistrates' enforcement powers and practice

7.15   Where a magistrates' court order has been disobeyed, then subject to certain exceptions, the order can be enforced under MCA 1980, s 63(3), by an order of committal to custody or an order for the payment of a sum of money. Section 63(3) restricts the maximum term of committal by magistrates to 'not … more than 2 months in all'.

Enforcement under s 63(3) is not available in respect of:

---

[1]   *Harris v Harris* [2001] 2 FLR 955.

(a)   an order for the payment of money;[1] or

(b)   an order which may be enforced under a provision of any other enactment;[2] or

(c)   an order made under any statute passed before 1880.[3]

Magistrates' powers under s 63(3), as respects disobedience of orders made under FLA 1996, Part IV, are extended by amendments incorporated by s 50 of FLA 1996, which enable magistrates to suspend the execution of an order of committal on terms or conditions, and to the new procedural requirements for enforcement process in FPC (MP etc) R 1991, r 20.

FPC (MP etc) R 1991, r 20(18) and Form FL419 'committal or other order upon proof of disobedience of a court order or breach of an undertaking' make provision for disposal by adjournment on terms of consideration of the penalty for any contempt found proved. This option is not mentioned in the 1996 Act, and is part of magistrates' inherent powers.

Where a person has been arrested under the powers in FLA 1996, s 47, whether under a power of arrest or a warrant, and is brought before a family proceedings court for breach of an occupation order, the powers of the court to punish the disobedience are those provided by s 63(3) of MCA 1980 and s 50 of FLA 1996.

The Prescribed Forms for enforcement of the Family Law Act 1996, Part IV orders correspond to county court Forms: Form FL418, 'Notice to Show Good Reason' to county court Form N78; Form FL419 'Order of Committal or Other Disposal' to county court Form N79, and Form FL420 'Warrant of Committal' to county court Form N80.

Procedure

Introduction – The importance of abiding by correct procedure

7.16   The Court of Appeal has stressed in several cases that, because committal for contempt of court is concerned with offences of a quasi-criminal nature and the liberty of the subject is at stake, the relevant rules of court must be complied with and the prescribed forms must be used. However:

---

[1]   MCA 1980, s 63(3)
[2]   Ibid, s 63(5).
[3]   Ibid, s 63(3).

'Any procedural defect in the commencement or conduct by the applicant of a committal application may be waived by the court if satisfied that no injustice has been caused to the respondent by the defect.'[1]

In *Nicholls v Nicholls*,[2] Lord Woolf MR, giving the judgment of the Court of Appeal, stated (at 655D) that: 'While the ... requirements of Ord 29, r 1 [County Court Rules] are there to be observed, in the absence of authority to the contrary, even though the liberty of the subject is involved, we would not expect the requirements to be mandatory, in the sense that any non-compliance with the rule means that a committal for contempt is irredeemably invalid'. Lord Woolf gave the following guidance:[3]

'(1) As committal orders involve the liberty of the subject it is particularly important that the relevant rules are duly complied with. It remains the responsibility of the judge when signing the committal order to ensure that it is properly drawn and that it adequately particularises the breaches which have been proved and for which the sentence has been imposed.

(2) As long as the contemnor has had a fair trial and the order has been made on valid grounds the existence of a defect either in the application to commit or in the committal order served will not result in the order being set aside except insofar as the interests of justice require this to be done.

(3) Interests of justice will not require an order to be set aside where there is no prejudice caused as the result of errors in the application to commit or in the order to commit. When necessary the order can be amended.

(4) When considering whether to set aside the order, the court should have regard to the interests of any other party and the need to uphold the reputation of the justice system.

(5) If there has been a procedural irregularity or some other defect in the conduct of the proceedings which has occasioned injustice, the court will consider exercising its power to order a new trial unless there are circumstances which indicate that it would not be just to do so.'

The checklists set out at **7.39** are designed to cover the practical points which most often arise, and need to be considered, in preparation for, and in the course of, committal hearings. They are not comprehensive of every point which has reached the Court of Appeal.

Penal or warning notice on orders capable of enforcement by committal

7.17 Any order which is capable of enforcement by committal may be thus enforced, subject to due service, if it has on it a penal notice,[4] warning the respondent of the consequences of breach.

---

1   CPR 1998, PD Committal, para 10, supplemental to RSC Ord 52 and CCR Ord 29.
2   [1997] 1 FLR 649.
3   Ibid, at 661E.
4   CCR Ord 29, r 1(3), FPC (MP etc) R 1991, r 20(7).

Prescribed Form FL404, for non-molestation and directive occupation orders, and county court injunction Forms N78 (general) and N138 (harassment) have a penal notice incorporated in the text. Prescribed Forms for undertakings, Form N117 in a county court and Form FL422 in a family proceedings court, also incorporate a penal notice.

The person who has the benefit of a non-molestation order or an injunction order against torts is entitled to have the order issued with a penal notice incorporated.[1]

Where an occupation order is made, which does not have a non-molestation order included, the court has a discretion as to whether to authorise a penal notice.[2]

Forms, rules and Practice Direction

7.18 Whichever prescribed form of committal application is required, the form 'must set out in full the grounds on which the committal application is made and should identify, separately and numerically, each act of contempt'.[3] This requirement and the need to support the application with suitable evidence and give due notice to the respondent are the most important steps to ensure that an application for committal can achieve an effective hearing.

CPR 1998 and PD Committal, supplemental to RSC Ord 52 and CCR Ord 29, have incorporated some of the previous case-law and practice, but have made the selection of appropriate forms and rules more complicated. This affects family practitioners as orders and committals under the PHA 1997 are governed by the CPR 1998.

Committal procedure is governed in the High Court by RSC Ord 52 (preserved in Sch 1 to CPR 1998) and, in civil proceedings, by PD Committal and, in the Family Division, by FPR 1998, r 7.2. In county courts, it is governed by CCR Ord 29 (preserved in Sch 2 to CPR 1998) and, in non-family proceedings, the same Practice Direction applies. In family proceedings courts, FPC (MP etc) R 1991, r 20 applies.

The prescribed form for initiating a committal application in family proceedings in county courts is Form N78. In family proceedings in the High Court, the application is made by summons (FPR 1991, r 7.2(1)). In civil proceedings in the High Court and county courts, it is made under CPR 1998, r 8.6 and PD Committal. Under CPR 1998, Part 8, if 'a final judgment has not yet been given' in civil proceedings, PD Committal, para 2.6 applies and a

---

[1]   FPR 1991, r 3.9A(5); FPC (MP etc) R 1991, r 20(7); CCR Ord 29, r 1(3).
[2]   Form FL404, Notice B; cf FPR 1991, r 4.21A in relation to an order under s 8 of CA 1989.
[3]   CPR 1998, PD Committal, paras 2.5, 2.6, and *Harmsworth v Harmsworth* [1988] 1 FLR 349.

committal application is made in the 'existing proceedings' by application notice in those proceedings, in Form N244. Where a 'final judgment' has been given in civil proceedings, CPR 1998, r 8.1(6) and PD Committal, paras 2.1 and 2.5 require an application for committal to be made by a claim form under Part 8 of CPR 1998, Form N208: this apparently applies where a free-standing injunction has been granted under the PHA 1997.

County court Forms N78 and N79 were designed to ensure that the procedural requirements of the rules were met, and the requirements for common disposals would be complied with. The forms can be used as checklists as they incorporate the essential requirements in all committal applications and, in the case of Form N79, the menu of common disposal orders. In family proceedings courts, similar Forms FL418 and FL419 apply. Practitioners are strongly recommended to use these forms as simple checklists for ensuring that the essential procedural requirements are followed. Form N78 remains a convenient guide as to the contents required for a committal application by summons in the Family Division or committal application under CPR 1998, Part 8, which must be issued in application notice in Form N244 or claim form in Form N208. The checklists appearing after this introduction provide a sequential and extended framework for following good practice.

Form N79, the prescribed form for a committal order in county courts, and Form FL419, for family proceedings courts, contain most of the usual orders made on proof of disobedience of an injunctive order or breach of an undertaking. The court (judge or justices and clerk) can delete the orders not required, and enter the precise details of the orders made. Forms N79 and FL419 are supplied to courts with explanatory guidance notes attached and they can be used as a checklist at the time of making an order.

Service or notification of orders required to make orders enforceable

7.19 An order which is capable of enforcement by committal must, in general, be served personally on the respondent to make it enforceable.[1]

The court can dispense with service of an order[2] or provide for some other form of service when exercising its powers under CCR Ord 29, r 1(7) or FPC (MP etc) R 1991, r 20(12). Such order must be made before a breach to make the breach punishable: there is no power to dispense with service of order at the time of a committal hearing.[3] However, if the order is *only a restraining order prohibiting conduct*, 'pending such service' the court does have power to commit,

---

[1]   CCR Ord 29, r 1(2); FPC (MP etc) R 1991, r 20(6).
[2]   CCR Ord 29, r 1(7); FPC (MP etc) R 1991, r 20(12).
[3]   *Lewis v Lewis* [1991] 2 FLR 43, [1991] 3 All ER 251.

provided that the respondent knew about the order by being present when it was made or had been adequately notified of it.[1]

In the case of a mandatory injunctive order, which directs an act to be done, the order incorporating the penal warning must be served in reasonable time before the time fixed by the order for the act to be done[2] unless service has been dispensed with[3] by the court before the time the act is directed to be done. In an exceptional case where the court is satisfied that the order can be adequately communicated without personal service, the court might provide for some form of alternative notification or substituted service.

In *Couzens v Couzens*,[4] the court had failed to serve a suspended committal order on the respondent in accordance with Form N79. It was held that this was a fundamental failure to meet the requirements of an essential rule and was incapable of cure; the sentence imposed for alleged breach could not stand.

Delivery of a form of undertaking

7.20 An undertaking duly given to the court and recorded in county court Form N117 or FL422, in terms which are within the powers of the court, by the giver who has been told by the court what the consequences of breach may be, is enforceable as soon as it has been given.

Following *Hussain v Hussain*,[5] CCR Ord 29, r 1A was introduced, as well as Form N117, to provide for delivery of a copy of the form of undertaking to the giver, usually by the court. This was to redress the problem identified in *Hussain v Hussain* that if, upon answering to a Notice to Show Good Reason, the giver of an undertaking asserts that he did not adequately understand the promises given to the court or the consequences of breach, it is difficult for the court to be sure what happened when the undertaking was given. Form N117 was adapted from a form devised by Her Honour Judge Counsell in Bristol, who led many developments in good family law practice. The rules specify that the form be 'delivered', not served, because delivery is an administrative act, and it is the giving of the undertaking which makes it enforceable, not delivery of the copy.

Contempt proceedings where criminal prosecution under way

7.21 Where criminal proceedings are pending in respect of the conduct alleged to be contempt, the court has a discretion as to whether to proceed

---

1   CCR Ord 29, r 1(6); FPC (MP etc) R 1991, r 20(11).
2   CCR Ord 29, r 1(2)(b); FPC (MP etc) R 1991, r 20(6)(b).
3   CCR Ord 29, r 1(7); FPC (MP etc) R 1991, r 20(12).
4   [2001] EWCA Civ 992, [2001] 2 FLR 701, CA.
5   [1986] Fam 134, [1986] 2 FLR 271.

with an application for committal. The principles have most recently been set out in *M v M (Contempt: Committal)*[1] by Lord Bingham of Cornhill CJ, giving the judgment of the court.

> 'It would appear that (the) authorities establish three principles. The first is that there is no absolute rule that civil proceedings (including contempt proceedings) should not proceed when criminal proceedings are pending. The second is that there is a general rule that contempt proceedings should be dealt with "swiftly and decisively" … The third principle is that the test as to whether or not contempt proceedings should proceed in advance of criminal proceedings is whether there is a risk of serious prejudice leading to injustice if the contempt proceedings go ahead … If the answer is that there is no real risk of serious prejudice leading to injustice, then in the ordinary way the contempt proceedings should go ahead. If, on the other hand, there is judged to be a real risk of serious prejudice leading to injustice if the contempt proceedings go ahead, the court may properly stay the contempt proceedings and would ordinarily do so.'

If the court does proceed upon a contempt where criminal charges are pending in relation to the same conduct, any sentence for the contempt must be based on the disobedience of the court rather than punishment for the crime.[2] However, in *Wilson v Webster*,[3] a sentence of 2 weeks for a violent assault was increased to 3 months on appeal and the court did not seek to discourage pursuit of criminal proceedings.[4]

Contempt proceedings for harassment where criminal charges pending or contemnor convicted

7.22 A person who disobeys an injunction forbidding harassment cannot be both convicted of a criminal offence and punished for contempt for the same disobedience.[5] A plaintiff victim of harassment who applies for a warrant of arrest for breach of an injunction forbidding harassment must disclose whether he has informed the police of the defendant's conduct and whether, to his knowledge, criminal proceedings are being pursued,[6] and at the hearing of committal proceedings, the court must be told if the contemnor has been convicted of an offence in respect of the same matters.

Issue and service of the 'Notice to Show Good Reason' and evidence in support

7.23 In county court Form N78, 'Notice to Show Good Reason why an order for your Committal to Prison should not be made' is issued by the court

---

1 [1997] 1 FLR 762, CA, at 764B.
2 *Smith v Smith* [1991] 2 FLR 55.
3 [1998] 1 FLR 1097.
4 Ibid, at 1100G and 1101B.
5 PHA 1997, s 3(7), (8)
6 CCR Ord 49, r 15A(5)(c), (d).

on a request by the applicant. The request for issue must:[1]

> '(a) identify the provisions of the injunction or undertaking which it is alleged have been disobeyed or broken;
> (b) list the ways in which it is alleged that the injunction has been disobeyed or the undertaking has been broken;
> (c) be supported by an affidavit stating the grounds on which the application is made.'

There is no separate form for the request for issue and county court practice is that the applicant drafts and submits Form N78, which is treated as the request for it to be issued, and the court will only revise it if it appears to be defective.

In magistrates' courts, the Notice to Show Good Reason in Form FL418 is issued pursuant to FPC (MP etc) R 1991, r 20(8), (9) at the request of the applicant. The requirements of r 20(9) follow CCR Ord 29, r 4A except that a statement signed and declared to be true is required instead of an affidavit. As in county courts, there is no separate form for requesting issue of the notice, and the applicant or the court may draw Form FL418. Under FPC (MP etc) R 1991, r 20(9), the request for issue is treated as a complaint for the purposes of MCA 1980, s 63(3).

The Notice instructs the respondent to attend the hearing of the application for an order of committal.

The Notice to Show Good Reason in Form N78 or Form FL418 and the affidavit or statement in support must be served personally on the respondent,[2] unless service is dispensed with under CCR Ord 29, r 1(7) or FPC (MP etc) R 1991, r 20(12).

---

[1] CCR Ord 29, r 4A.
[2] CCR Ord 29, r 1(4), FPC (MP etc) R 1991, r 20(8), (9).

Dispensation with service of 'Notice to Show Good Reason': committal without notice or waiving formality of service

7.24 Dispensation with service of the Notice to Show Good Reason[1] is exceptional, but may be allowed by the court where the respondent is shown to be evading service. If this course is taken and an order of committal is made, the court is required to announce the committal in open court at the earliest opportunity.[2] Also the court should provide for the respondent to be brought before it at the earliest opportunity after he has been arrested.[3]

Dispensation with service may also be ordered where the respondent is already before the court and he can reasonably be expected to conduct his case in answer to the alleged contempt.[4] However, in such a case, best practice is for the court to require a Notice to Show Good Reason to be issued and to authorise immediate service.

Drafting the 'Notice to Show Good Reason' and affidavit or statement in support

7.25 The Notice should be drafted and submitted as the request for it to be issued, by the solicitor for the applicant, as the solicitor must select the items to be alleged to amount to the breaches, and the rules require a list of the allegations. Where a litigant in person requests issue of a Notice to Show Good Reason in a family proceedings court, the clerk will have to be careful to identify the applicant's allegations.

Particular care must be taken in drafting the allegations of contempt. Clear particulars must be given.[5] The essential point is that the respondent must be given details adequate for him to know the case he has to answer.

The alleged breaches must be specified in the Notice in Form N78 or Form FL419.[6] The affidavit or statement in support is to narrate the events, not to specify the allegations. If the particulars of the alleged breaches have not been included in the Notice but are adequately particularised in the evidence in support, the court should be asked for leave to amend the Notice before the hearing begins. The court must not act on allegations of which notice has not

---

1   CCR Ord 29, r 1 (7).
2   *President's Direction (Children Act 1989: Exclusion Requirement)* [1998] 1 FLR 495 and *President's Direction (Family Law Act 1996, Part IV)* [1998] 1 FLR 496.
3   *Lamb v Lamb* [1984] FLR 278.
4   CCR Ord 29, r 1 (7).
5   *Williams v Fawcett* [1986] QB 604, 610E, [1985] FLR 935; *Chiltern District Council v Keane* [1985] 1 WLR 619, 622A; *Harmsworth v Harmsworth* [1988] 1 FLR 349, [1987] 3 All ER 816.
6   CCR Ord 29, r 1(4A)(b); FPC (MP etc) R 1991, r 20(9)(b).

been given unless exceptional circumstances justify an application being made ex parte.[1]

An affidavit in support is required in a county court by CCR Ord 29, r 1(4A)(c), and a statement signed and declared to be true is required in a family proceedings court by FPC (MP etc) R 1991, r 20(9).

Arrest under power of arrest attached to an occupation order under FLA 1996, s 47

7.26 Availability of power of arrest is dealt with at **3.28**. There is no power to attach a power of arrest to an injunction granted under the PHA 1997.

It is the occupation order which is required to be served on the respondent, and the order should include the provision of attachment of the power of arrest.

The power of arrest in Form FL406 is for delivery to the police, although it is sensible for the applicant to have a copy in case the police ask to see it when called to her assistance. The Form FL406 should recite the particular clauses of the order to which the power was attached and no others.[2]

Arrest under warrant of arrest for breach of an occupation order or an undertaking to like effect

7.27 There is doubt as to whether, where the court has accepted an undertaking to like effect as a non-molestation or occupation order, a warrant of arrest can be granted under s 47(8), (9) where the respondent has failed to comply with the undertaking: because although under s 46(4) an undertaking 'is enforceable as if it were an order', the court has not 'made a relevant order'.[3]

An application for a warrant of arrest is made in Form FL407 and must be substantiated on oath,[4] usually by affidavit in a county court, but oral evidence can be sufficient. The warrant is issued in Form FL408.[5]

A warrant of arrest is exercised by the Tipstaff in the High Court, usually assisted by the police, a bailiff of the court or the police upon a county court warrant, and the police where the warrant was granted by a family proceedings court.

---

[1]   *Tabone v Seguna* [1986] 1 FLR 591; *Wright v Jess* [1987] 2 FLR 373, [1987] 2 All ER 1067.
[2]   FPR 1991, r 3.9A(1)(a); FPC (MP etc) R 1991, r 20(1)(a).
[3]   FLA 1996, s 47(8).
[4]   Ibid, s 47(9).
[5]   FPR 1991, r 3.9A(3); FPC (MP etc) R 1991, r 20(3).

Following the grant of a warrant of arrest by a family proceedings court, responsibility for delivery to the police rests with the justices' chief executive who must cause the warrant to be delivered to the officer for the time being in charge of any police station for the respondent's address or such other police station as the court may specify.[1] Section 47(10) of the FLA 1996, which provides the power for issue of a warrant of arrest, unlike s 47(7), does not require a person arrested under a warrant to be brought before the court at any particular time. Form FL408, for warrants, authorises the person(s) who arrest the respondent 'to bring him before this court immediately'. The FPR do not further regulate this, so the wording of Form FL408 is the operative requirement. In practice, as attendance of the applicant will almost always be needed to enable the court to deal with the alleged breach, arrangements for her presence will have to be made urgently or, if she is not available within a reasonable time, the court should adjourn the matter and remand the respondent under s 47(10).

Power of the court

Procedural powers of court when arrested person brought before court under FLA 1996, s 47

7.28 When the respondent is brought before the court upon arrest under s 47 of FLA 1996, whether under a power of arrest or a warrant, the court may hear and deal with the alleged breach, or adjourn the hearing. The court may adjourn without having determined whether a breach has been proved, or after finding a breach proved. If the hearing is adjourned, the arrested person may be remanded under s 47(7)(b) or s 47(10), (11), or granted bail under s 47(12), or remanded for the purpose of enabling a medical examination to be made under s 48(1) or for a report on his mental condition under s 48(4).

FPR 1991, r 3.9A(4) and FPC (MP etc) R 1991, r 20(4) provide that when an arrested person is brought before the court, the court may:

'(a) determine whether the facts, and the circumstances which led to the arrest, amounted to disobedience of the order, or

(b) adjourn the proceedings and, where such an order is made, the arrested person may be released and—

(i) be dealt with within 14 days of the day on which he was arrested; and

(ii) be given not less than 2 days' notice of the adjourned hearing.

Nothing in this paragraph shall prevent the issue of a Notice (to Show Good Reason) if the arrested person is not dealt with within ... 14 days.'

---

[1] FPC (MP etc) R 1991, r 20(3).

The purpose of these provisions in FPR 1991, r 3.9A(4) and FPC (MP etc) R 1991, r 20(4) is to make it clear that:

(1) the court can deal with an arrested person forthwith without issue of, or dispensation with, a Notice to Show Good Reason;
(2) the court can adjourn and deal with the matter within 14 days without a Notice to Show Good Reason;
(3) if the court does deal with the matter forthwith or at an adjourned hearing within 14 days, it is restricted to the matter on which the person was arrested, and cannot deal with other alleged breaches; and
(4) if the court does not deal with the matter by virtue of the respondent being brought before it by arrest or adjournment following arrest, the victim can apply later upon a Notice to Show Good Reason.

The rules do not cut down the wider powers of remand in the statute.

Bail under the FLA 1996

7.29 FPR 1991, r 3.10 and FPC (MP etc) R 1991, r 21 provide for an application for bail by an arrested person, which may be with or without a surety. The prescribed forms for a recognisance of the person making an application (Form FL411), recognisance of a surety (Form FL411), and bail notice (Form FL412) should be referred to for the requirements for bail.

The penalty for non-attendance of the respondent in answer to bail is forfeiture of his recognisance and that of any surety. If the respondent fails to attend, it is submitted that the court may revert to the exercise of a power of arrest where one had been attached to a term of the order alleged to have been breached, otherwise it may grant a warrant of arrest if there are provisions of the original order to which no power of arrest was attached.

Warrant of arrest for breach of an injunction under the PHA 1997

7.30 The claimant victim of a breach of an injunction against harassment, granted under the PHA 1997, may apply for a warrant of arrest.[1] The application is made to the High Court if the injunction was granted there, or any county court if the injunction was granted in a county court.[2] A warrant is not available for breach of an undertaking as s 3(3), (4) refers only to injunctions.

A warrant under the PHA 1997 is appropriate:

(1) if the court considers that the breach needs to be dealt with promptly, for example where the court believes that the plaintiff is at risk of a further

---

[1] PHA 1997, s 3(3).
[2] Ibid, s 3(4).

breach;

(2) where the defendant has avoided service of a Notice to Show Good Reason; or

(3) where the defendant fails to appear for an adjourned hearing.

No special form is prescribed for the application,[1] so the general from of notice, Form N244, should be used in a county court. The application must set out the grounds for making the application, and state whether the plaintiff has informed the police of the conduct complained of and whether, to the plaintiff's knowledge, criminal proceedings are being pursued.[2] The evidence should normally be by affidavit, but in an emergency the court can act on oral evidence. The affidavit should state the believed address of the defendant, which is required to be entered in the warrant.

The warrant is issued in county court Form N140. It directs 'all police constables, [and] the district judge and bailiffs ... to arrest the defendant ... and bring him before this court immediately'. The defendant must be brought before the court the same day, if it can be reached while still sitting, or the next sitting day. Where no judge is sitting at the same courthouse, one nearby should be arranged. There is power to deal with the breach immediately, without issue and service of an application in Form N78,[3] or to adjourn for up to 14 days.[4] There is no power to remand under the PHA 1997.

As the PHA 1997 makes no provision for remand of a defendant, and the presence of the victim is usually needed to enable the court to deal with the breach then and there, the court before which the defendant is brought must either deal with him for the alleged breach or adjourn and release the defendant.

Further arrest where the respondent fails to appear at an adjourned hearing after being released following arrest under a power of arrest

7.31 Where a person has been arrested under a power of arrest under the FLA 1996 and the case has been adjourned and the respondent remanded or released, but the respondent fails to appear for the adjourned hearing, the court cannot grant a warrant of arrest under s 47(8) of the FLA 1996, unless the power of arrest was attached only to some of the terms of the non-molestation order. However, it is arguable that the respondent can be re-arrested under the original power of arrest, provided that he is again brought

---

[1]   CCR Ord 49, r 15A(5)(a).
[2]   Ibid, r 15A(5); the application must be supported by affidavit or evidence on oath (s 3(5)(a) of the 1997 Act and CCR Ord 49, r 15(5)(b).
[3]   Ibid, r 15A(7)(a).
[4]   Ibid, r 15A(7)(b).

before a judge within 24 hours of the second arrest. In *Wheeldon v Wheeldon*,[1] the Court of Appeal held that where a person had been arrested for a criminal offence of assault and released on bail, he was validly re-arrested under a power of arrest for domestic violence and brought before a judge within 24 hours of the second arrest, although the 'spirit (of the statutory power of arrest) requires that he be brought before the judge within 24 hours of the initial arrest where the circumstances clearly indicate two reasons for the arrest prevail' (per Ward LJ); thus a power of arrest is a procedural device which can be used for detaining the respondent and bringing him before the court even though the breach of the injunction is not continuing.

Warrant of arrest where the respondent fails to appear at an adjourned hearing, having appeared at the first hearing of a Notice to Show Good Reason, under FLA 1996, Part IV

7.32   Where a person appeared in answer to a Notice to Show Good Reason, and the case was adjourned and/or the respondent bailed, and he fails to appear at the adjourned hearing, and no power of arrest had been attached to the non-molestation order, a warrant for arrest under FLA 1996 can be granted in respect of the order.[2] If a power of arrest was attached to all of the terms of the order, and a warrant of arrest cannot be granted because there are no terms of the injunction to which it was not attached, it is arguable that the respondent can be arrested under the original power of arrest (see the reasoning at **7.30**).

Application by contemnor or respondent who objects to an injunctive order

7.33   An injunction order must be obeyed even if the person to whom the order is directed considers that the order is irregular in law or onerous on the merits.[3] Likewise, an undertaking must be complied with even if the court would not have had jurisdiction to grant an injunction to the same effect. Want of jurisdiction in the making of an injunction or accepting an undertaking is no answer to an application for committal for a breach.

The court has a discretion not to entertain any application by a contemnor in the same proceedings in relation to which the contempt has been or is being committed, until the contemnor has purged his contempt.[4] The court which

---

1   [1998] 1 FLR 463.

2   FLA 1996, s 47(8), (9).

3   *Chuck v Cremer* (1846) 1 Coop temp Cott 338; *Hadkinson v Hadkinson* [1952] P 285, [1952] 2 All ER 567; *Isaacs v Robertson* [1985] AC 97, [1984] 3 All ER 140; *Johnson v Walton* [1990] 1 FLR 350.

4   *X Ltd v Morgan-Grampian (Publishers) Ltd and Others* [1991] 1 AC 1, [1990] 2 All ER 1; see also *Hadkinson v Hadkinson* [1952] P 285, [1952] 2 All ER 567.

granted an injunction will generally entertain an application by a contemnor where:

(a) the application is founded on argument that, on the true construction of the original injunction or undertaking, the conduct said to be a contempt did not amount to a contempt;[1]
(b) the application is grounded on an alleged lack of jurisdiction to have made the order;[2]
(c) the application is to purge or in mitigation of the contempt.[3]

An order made without notice is a provisional order and every judge who makes an order without notice expects that the merits will be reviewed by the court on the return day or upon application.[4] A person against whom an injunction has been granted without notice is entitled to a review by the court as a matter of urgency.[5]

Where it is contended that an injunction order granted on notice is irregular or oppressive, the proper course is to appeal.

Committal hearings

7.34 In general terms, hearings of committal proceedings are in many respects similar to hearings of criminal charges. Thus, the burden of proof rests on the person making the allegation of contempt; the standard of proof is the criminal standard; the respondent must be allowed to cross-examine witnesses and to call evidence; the respondent is entitled to submit that there is no case to answer; if a contempt is found proved, the contemnor must be allowed to address the court by way of mitigation or seeking to purge his contempt; and autrefois acquit and autrefois convict apply.

Since the coming into force of Part IV of the FLA 1996, the Court of Appeal has given guidance as to the proper approach when dealing with breaches of orders. Not all of these decisions are consistent and some cases, clearly, turn on their own facts. It has been held that:

(a) imprisonment is only appropriate in the most serious cases involving repeated breaches;[6]
(b) there is no principle that a first breach of an injunction is not to be visited with imprisonment, and the length of the sentence must reflect

---

1   *Hadkinson v Hadkinson* [1952] P 285, [1952] 2 All ER 567.
2   *X Ltd v Morgan-Grampian (Publishers) Ltd and Others* [1991] 1 AC 1, [1990] 2 All ER 1.
3   *Hadkinson v Hadkinson* [1952] P 285, [1952] 2 All ER 567.
4   *WEA Records Ltd v Visions Channel 4 Ltd* [1983] 2 All ER 589 at 593F–G; and see *R v R (Contempt of Court)* [1988] Fam Law 388.
5   *G v G (Ouster: Ex Parte Application)* [1990] 1 FLR 395.
6   *G v C (Residence Order: Committal)* [1998] 1 FLR 43, CA.

the fact that orders of the court must be obeyed;[1]

(c)   courts must take incidents of domestic violence very seriously and it is important as a matter of public policy that the court's jurisdiction be upheld (3 months substituted for 'wholly inadequate' 14 days after violent assault breaching undertaking).[2]

In *Rafiq v Muse*,[3] a son who had been in care terrorised his mother and ignored several non-molestation orders. The court took account of the terrifying effect on the mother, the gross interference with her way of life, the resolute defiance of court orders and the absence of remorse and upheld a sentence of 6 months' imprisonment.

7.35   It was no doubt in an effort to remove some ambiguities that the Court of Appeal set out some detailed guidelines in *Hale v Tanner*.[4] Without wishing to suggest that there was a general principle that the principles of sentencing in criminal cases applied in contempt proceedings, the court said that the following principles were applicable in family cases only.

(a)   Contempt of court cases had to come before the court on an application to commit. That was the procedure available. It was not surprising, therefore, that the court had to direct itself as to whether committal to prison was appropriate. However, it did not follow that prison was the automatic consequence of breach of an order, nor was there any principle that prison should not be imposed at the first occasion.[5]

(b)   Although the full range of sentencing options available in criminal cases was not available in contempt proceedings, there was a range of things the court might consider. It could make no order; it might adjourn, and in a case where the alleged contemnor had not attended court, depending on the reason for not doing so, that might be appropriate; it might fine or sequester assets, or a mental health order might be appropriate. Such alternatives might need to be considered, in particular, where no act of violence was proved.

(c)   If prison was appropriate, the length of committal should be determined without reference to whether it was to be suspended. A longer custodial period was not justified because it was suspended.

(d)   The length of committal had to depend on the court's objectives. In contempt proceedings there were always two objectives. One was to mark the court's disapproval of disobedience to its order; the other was to secure future compliance with the order. Thus, the seriousness of what had taken place had to be viewed in that light as well.

(e)   The period of imprisonment had to bear some reasonable relationship to

---

[1]   *Thorpe v Thorpe* [1998] 2 FLR 127, CA.
[2]   *Wilson v Webster* [1998] 1 FLR 1098, CA.
[3]   [2000] 1 FLR 820, CA.
[4]   [2000] 2 FLR 879.
[5]   See *Thorpe v Thorpe* [1998] 2 FLR 127, CA.

the maximum 2 years' imprisonment available.

(f) Suspension was available in a wider range of circumstances than in criminal cases. It was the first way of securing compliance.

(g) The length of suspension required separate consideration, although it was linked to the period of the underlying order.

(h) The court had to bear in mind the context, which might be aggravating or mitigating.

(i) In many cases, the court would have to bear in mind that there were concurrent proceedings in another court based on the same or some of the same facts. The court could not ignore those proceedings and might have to take the outcome into account in practical terms. Contempt proceedings had a different purpose and often the overlap was not exact, but the court would not want a contemnor to suffer the same punishment twice for the same events.

(j) It would usually be desirable for the court to explain briefly why it had made the choices it had made in a particular case. It was appropriate in most cases for a contemnor to know why he was being sent to prison, why for so long, and why the period was being suspended. It was an important part of the exercise that a contemnor understood the importance of keeping court orders and not breaking them and the consequences of breach.

7.36 Further important guidance has now been given in two decisions of the Court of Appeal. The first was *Carabott v Huxley* [2005] Law Soc Gazette 102, where it was held that a sentence of 18 months' imprisonment imposed under Part IV of FLA 1996 was not manifestly excessive in respect of persistent and serious breaches of a non-molestation order. The second case was *Robinson v Murray* [2005] *The Times* August 19. This was the first case in which the Lord Chief Justice exercised his newly acquired right to sit on appeals in any division – in this case of course, the Family Division.

Lord Woolf said that when sentencing for contempt for non-compliance with an order of the court, it was appropriate that the approach to sentencing should take into account the approach to sentencing in the Criminal Division. In that area, as in others, imprisonment needed to be reserved for those cases where it was necessary. Alternatives might be more appropriate. Unfortunately, the available alternatives in the case of proceedings under Part IV were limited. Courts could suspend sentences, which might be a constructive course, but the court had nothing like the alternatives that were available to the criminal courts. Nonetheless, the purposes of sentencing in criminal proceedings, set out in s 142(b) of the Criminal Justice Act 2003, could be seen as being very relevant in this area. Section 143, which set out factors relevant to considering the seriousness of the offence, could also be relevant, as could s 144, which dealt with the reduction of sentences for guilty pleas. It was desirable, as in criminal proceedings, that an offender who breached an order should show remorse and repentance. One way he could do that was by admitting his responsibility.

The result of the appeal was that the court dismissed an appeal against a sentence of 8 months' imprisonment for three breaches of a non-molestation and occupation order.

Application to purge contempt

7.37 A person committed to prison for disobedience of an injunction or breach of an undertaking is entitled to apply to purge his contempt and to be discharged from prison.[1]

Whenever a person is committed immediately to prison in judge courts, the court sends copies of the committal order in Form N79 and the application in Form N78 to the Official Solicitor, who reviews all cases where imprisonment is imposed.[2]

Warrant of possession for enforcing an occupation order requiring the respondent to vacate the family home

7.38 Where a respondent fails to obey an order that he shall vacate the family home, in a county court a warrant of possession is an appropriate means for procuring the removal of the respondent.[3]

Issue of a warrant of possession may be requested without notice under CCR Ord 26, r 17(2); the applicant is entitled to apply without giving notice.[4] However, it may be less likely to cause resentment if the respondent is warned by letter that an application for a warrant is being made.

---

[1] RSC Ord 52, r 8(1); CCR Ord 29, r 3(1); FPR 1991, r 7.2(2); FPC (MP etc) R 1991, r 20(15) and see Forms N79 and FL419
[2] *Notes for Guidance and Completion of N79 and LCD Court Business*, November 1996, B 3288.
[3] *Danchevsky v Danchevsky* [1975] Fam 17, [1974] 3 All ER 934; *Larkman v Lindsell* [1989] Fam Law 229; *C v C (Contempt: Committal)* [1989] Fam Law 477.
[4] *Leicester City Council v Aldwinkle* (1991) 24 HLR 40.

Applications for committal orders: checklists

7.39

Checklist 1 – Preparing an application for committal for disobedience of an injunctive order or breach of an undertaking

I.   FORM OF INJUNCTIVE ORDER OR DOCUMENT RECORDING AN UNDERTAKING

(1)   Was the order one which the court had jurisdiction to make?

If made in proceedings other than family proceedings, does the order support a legal right, eg forbid a recognised tort or harassment within s 1 of PHA 1997, or protect a legal or equitable interest?

If made in family proceedings (under FLA 1996, Part IV, the CA 1989, matrimonial proceedings begun by petition, or under the inherent jurisdiction of the High Court), was the order available as a non-molestation or occupation order? Or was the order available for the protection of family property? The High Court has further injunctive powers under the inherent jurisdiction.

An injunctive order or an undertaking must be obeyed, even if it is irregular, until it is discharged, but want of jurisdiction may affect the conduct of an application to commit and/or the approach to sentence for a contempt.

(2)   Was the instruction to the other party, or the undertaking, precise and explicit as to what the person was required to do or abstain from doing?

And, if the doing of an act was required, did the injunctive order specify when or by when the act was to be done, as required by RSC Ord 42, r 2(1), CCR Ord 22, r 3 or FPC (MP etc) R 1991, r 20(6)(b)? Or did the undertaking specify when or by when the act was to be done?

(3)

(a)   In the case of an injunctive order:

–   in the High Court, was there 'prominently displayed on the front', of the copy of the order for service, a warning (penal) notice, as required by RSC Ord 45, r 7(4) and CPR 1998, PD 40B – Judgments and Orders, para 9.1?

–   in a county court, was the injunctive order issued with a penal notice in Form
N77 indorsed or incorporated, as required by Ord 29, r 1(3) or FPR 1991,
r 3.9A(5) and by CPR 1998, PD 40B – Judgments and Orders, para 9.1? Was
it issued in prescribed Form FL404 or N16 or N138 or with Form N77 indorsed
or incorporated?

Note: A warning (penal) notice cannot be indorsed on or incorporated in an order
under s 8 of CA 1989 unless a judge has so directed: FPR 1991, r 4.21A.

–   in a family proceedings court, was the injunctive order issued in Form FL404
or was it issued with a penal notice indorsed or incorporated, as required by
FPC (MP etc) R 1991, r 20(7)?

(b)   In the case of an undertaking:

–   in the High Court or a county court, was the undertaking recorded in an order
or form of undertaking in which a penal notice was incorporated or endorsed
in accordance with PD 40B, paras 9.2 and 9.3, and in a county court as
required by CCR Ord 29, r 1A? And was it acknowledged by signature of the
giver upon the direction of the court under PD 40B, paras 9.3, 9.4? In a county
court, Form N117 should be used and, in the Family Division, practice Form
D787;

–   in a family proceedings court, was the undertaking recorded in Form FL422,
as required by FPC (MP etc) R 1991, r 20(14)?

II. SERVICE OF INJUNCTIVE ORDER OR RECORD OF UNDERTAKING

(a)   In the case of an injunctive order:

(i)   was personal service of the order, with a warning or penal notice prominently
displayed on the front of it (High Court) or indorsed on it or incorporated in it
(county or family proceedings court), effected?

Personal service is required by RSC Ord 45, r 7(2) or CCR Ord 29, r 1(2) or
FPC (MP etc) R 1991, r 20(11) unless (I) the order recites that personal
service was dispensed with, or (ii) the terms of the order are only prohibitory,
and do not require an act to be done and, pending service, have been
communicated to the other party.

(ii)   if the injunctive order required the other party to do an act, was the injunctive
order served personally before the expiration of the time within which he was
to do the act, as required by RSC Ord 45, r 7(2)(b), CCR Ord 29, r 1(2)(b) or
FPC (MP etc) R 1991, r 20(6)(b)?

Note *Davy International Ltd v Tazzyman* [1997] 3 All ER 183 and *Jolly v Hull; Jolly v Jolly* [2000] 2 FLR 69, as to the powers to dispense with service of the order at the hearing of a committal application, under RSC Ord 45, r 7(7) and CCR Ord 29, r 1(7).

(iii)   if served, is personal service proved?

Proof is usually by affidavit of service in judge courts and by Form FL415 in family proceedings courts.

(b)   In the case of an undertaking:

was the Form FL422, D787, or N117 or the order recording the undertaking delivered to or served on the giver of the undertaking?

Personal service of a document recording an undertaking is not necessary to render the undertaking enforceable because it is the giving of the undertaking which makes it effective. See *Hussain v Hussain* [1986] Fam 134. However, unless either the giver of the undertaking signed the Form FL422, D787 or N117 or the court papers, or a document recording the undertaking was delivered to or served upon the giver, difficulties may arise on an application to commit (see *Hussain v Hussain* (above), at 140 and 142).

In a county court, CCR Ord 29, r 1A requires delivery by the court to be recorded on the back of Form N117; alternatively, personal service is required. FPC (MP etc) R 1991, r 20(14) is to like effect.

III. FORM OF THE APPLICATION TO COMMIT AND THE REQUIREMENT OF AN AFFIDAVIT OR STATEMENT IN SUPPORT

(1)

(a)   In civil proceedings in the High Court and county courts, does the Claim Form N208 or Application Notice N244 give the essential information to the respondent and to the Court?

There is no separate prescribed form specific to committal applications. The prescribed requirements are in PD Committal, paras 2.2, 2.5 and 2.6. County court Form N78 is a useful guide.

(b)   In family proceedings, does the summons in the Family Division (FPR 1991, r 7.2(1), or the Form N78 in a county court, or the Form FL244 in a family proceedings court, give the essential information to the respondent and the court?

In particular (all courts: PD Committal, paras 2.5–2.6, CCR Ord 29, r 1(4A), FPC (MP etc) R 1991, r 20(9)):

(i)   does the application accurately identify the terms of the injunctive order or undertaking of which breach is alleged? (CCR Ord 29, r 1(4A)) and

(ii)   does the application 'list' (CCR Ord 29, r 1(4A)) or 'identify, separately and numerically, each alleged act of contempt'? (PD Committal, paras 2.5–2.6) and

(iii)   does the application clearly inform the respondent when and where he must attend to show reason why he should not be sent to prison?

Although there are no formal rules as to the way the allegations have to be framed, the ways in which the party alleged to be in contempt is alleged to have committed the contempt(s) must be sufficiently clear to inform him what case he has to meet.

(2)   Is the application supported by an affidavit as required by RSC Ord 52, r 4(1) and PD Committal, paras 2.5–2.6, 3.1 or CCR Ord 29, r 1(4A)?
or a statement signed and declared to be true as required by FPC (MP etc) R 1991, r 20(9)(c)?

IV. SERVICE OF THE APPLICATION TO COMMIT AND THE AFFIDAVIT OR STATEMENT IN SUPPORT

(1)   Is personal service of the application and the affidavit or statement proved (in judge courts usually by an affidavit of service in family proceedings courts by Form FL415) as required by RSC Ord 52, r 4(2), PD Committal, paras 2.5–2.6, CCR Ord 29, r 1(4), or FPC (MP etc) R, r 20(8), (9), unless the court has dispensed with service under RSC Ord 52, r 4(3) or CCR Ord 29, r 1(7) or FPC (MP etc) R 1991, r 20(12) or has provided for substituted service under RSC Ord 65, r 4(2), or CCR Ord 13, r (1) (substituted service is not available in magistrates' courts).

(2)   Was personal service achieved at least two days, not counting Saturdays, Sundays or bank holidays, before the hearing, as required by RSC Ord 8, r 2(2) or at least two court office business days as required by CCR Ord 13, r 1(2) and Ord 1, r 9(4), FPC (MP etc) R 1991, r 3A(5), unless the court has abridged time under RSC Ord 3, r 5(1), CCR Ord 13, r 4(1) or FPC (MP etc) R 1991, r 3A(6)?

V. EVIDENCE

(1)   Is there sufficient evidence to prove, to the criminal standard of proof, the alleged contempt(s)?

(2)   Is/are the witness(es) relied on available for cross-examination?

Checklist 2 – Preparing for hearing following an arrest under a power or warrant of arrest granted under s 47 of FLA 1996 or arrest under a warrant of arrest granted under s 3 of PHA 1997

INTRODUCTION: SUMMARY COMMITTAL FOLLOWING ARREST

Some practitioners and judges consider that, upon production in court of an arrested alleged contemnor, it is good practice to adjourn, to remand the respondent if the arrest was under FLA 1996, s 47, and to expect the applicant to issue an application for committal. However, FPR, r 3.9A(4) specifically authorises the established practice that, when a person is brought before the court following an arrest under FLA 1996, s 47, the court; 'may (a) determine whether the facts, and the circumstances which led to the arrest, amounted to disobedience of the order, or (b) adjourn the proceedings ...'. RSC Ord 94, r 16(5)(a) specifically authorises summary trial in the case of an arrest under PHA 1997, s 3. County court Form N79, for recording a finding of contempt, specifically provides for proceeding on the basis of the respondent being before the court upon an arrest without there having been served an application for committal in Form N78, in the case of an arrest under FLA 1996, s 47, or in a claim form, in the case of an arrest on a warrant under PHA 1997, s 3(5).

Where a person is arrested under either FLA 1996, s 47 or PHA 1997, s 3, and is brought before the court within the powers under the Acts, and there is sufficient evidence to proceed with a summary trial, and the arrested person is able to put his case adequately before the court, there clearly is power to proceed forthwith, without requiring preparation or service of a form of committal application. Further, there is no power to remand under PHA 1997. Where the court does proceed forthwith without a form of committal application being prepared, the arrested person is before the court only for the matter upon which he has been arrested, previous alleged contempts are not before the court, and the court must be clear about what the circumstances of the arrest and alleged contempt are. Summary disposal in this way is convenient particularly where the respondent admits the contempt. Where he denies the alleged contempt, and he may need witnesses to support his denial, an adjournment will be appropriate.

I. FORM OF INJUNCTIVE ORDER

Was the order one to which the court had jurisdiction to attach a power of arrest under s 47 of FLA 1996? (There is no power under the PHA 1997 to attach a power of arrest.)

In other words, was there evidence on which the court which granted the power could have concluded that the respondent had used or threatened violence against the applicant or a relevant child? If not, the arrest was unlawful and the respondent must be released.

In the case of arrest under a power of arrest, the 'relevant provisions', ie the arrestable provisions and no other clauses of the injunction, should have been delivered to the appropriate police station in prescribed Form FL406: FPR 1991, r 3.9A(1), FPC (MP etc) R 1991, r 20(1).

A power of arrest cannot be attached to an undertaking: it must be an order, non-molestation or occupation.

If the arrest was under a warrant of arrest, were there injunctive non-molestation or occupation provisions available as the foundation for a warrant, ie provisions to which no power of arrest had been attached?

II. SERVICE OF THE INJUNCTIVE ORDER

(a)   Is personal service proved, as required by RSC Ord 45, r 7(2)(a), CCR Ord 29, r 1(2)(a) or FPC (MP etc) R 1991, r 20(6)? Proof is usually by affidavit of service in judge courts and by Form FL415 in family proceedings courts. Note powers to dispense with service under RSC Ord 45, r 7(7) and CCR Ord 29, r 1(7), and see *Davy International Ltd v Tazzyman* [1997] 3 All ER 183 and *Jolly v Hull; Jolly v Jolly* [2000] 2 FLR 69.
    OR

(b)   Was the arrested person aware of the terms of the injunctive order either by being present when it was granted or by being notified of its terms? If so, under RSC Ord 45, r 7(6), CCR Ord 29, r 1(6) or FPC (MP etc) R 1991, r 20(11) he may be dealt with for the matter for which he was arrested if it was something he was forbidden to do. The arrested person cannot be dealt with unless he was aware of the terms, because contempt involves disobedience and unless the respondent was aware of the terms he cannot be guilty of contempt.

III. THE ARREST

In the case of arrest under a power of arrest under the Family Law Act 1996, s 47(6):

(1)   was the operative period of the power of arrest, as recited in the injunction and prescribed Form FL406, still running at the time of the arrest?

(2)   was the arrest by a constable who had 'reasonable cause for suspecting' the arrested person of being in breach of a provision of injunctive order to which the power of arrest was attached (FLA 1996, s 47(6))? If not, the arrest was unlawful and the arrested person must be released.

In the case of arrest under a warrant of arrest under FLA 1996, s 47(8), (9):

(1)   were there injunctive non-molestation or occupation provisions available as the foundation for a warrant, ie provisions to which a power of arrest had not been attached? And

(2)   was there evidence on oath before the court which granted the warrant on which it could have had reasonable grounds for believing that the respondent had failed to comply with the injunctive order? Or the undertaking? Note that there is doubt as to whether a warrant can be granted for breach of an undertaking given in proceedings under FLA 1996, Part IV.

In the case of a warrant of arrest under PHA 1997, s 3(3), (5), was there evidence on oath before the court which granted the warrant that could have raised reasonable grounds for believing that the defendant had failed to comply with the injunction? Note that a warrant cannot be granted for breach of an undertaking in proceedings under the PHA 1997.

IV. THE HEARING

In the case of arrest under a power of arrest under FLA 1996, s 47(6), will the hearing before the judge begin within the period of 24 hours beginning at the time of the arrest (no account being taken of Christmas Day, Good Friday or any Sunday) as required by s 47(7)(a) of FLA 1996? If not, the proceedings are ultra vires, there being no power to detain the arrested person beyond the statutory period, and the arrested person must be released.

However, the court may remand the arrested person (FLA 1996, s 47(7)(b)) and adjourn the hearing to be resumed within 14 days of the arrest: FPR 1991, r 3.9A(4)(b)(i), FPC (MP etc) R 1991, r 20(4)(b)(i). If the court does adjourn the hearing, the arrested person may be remanded (s 47(7)(b)) or released: FPR 1991, r 3.9A(4)(b), FPC (MP etc) R 1991, r 20(4)(b); where the court does adjourn, the arrested person must be dealt with within 14 days of the day on which he was arrested, whether by the same or another judge, and the person must be given not less than 2 days' notice of the adjourned hearing: FPR 1991, r 3.9A(4)(b)(ii), FPC (MP etc) R 1991, r 20(4)(b)(ii). Personal service of the notice of the adjourned hearing should be effected, unless the arrested person was given notice before being released: see *Chiltern DC v Keane* [1985] 1 WLR 619 at 622A.

If the arrested person is not dealt with within 14 days, FPR 1991, r 3.9A(4), FPC (MP etc) R 1991, r 20(4) permit the other party to request the issue of Notice to Show Good Reason under CCR Ord 29, r 1(4) or FPC (MP etc) R 1991, r 20(8).

Following any arrest, is there sufficient evidence to prove, to the criminal standard of proof, the alleged contempt?

Checklist 3 – Conduct of hearing of notice to show good reason or following arrest under a power or warrant of arrest

I. PRELIMINARY REQUIREMENTS

(1)   If the application is made (civil proceedings) by Claim Form N208 or Application Notice N244 or (High Court Family Division) by summons or issued (county court) in Form N78 or (family proceedings court) in FL418, is breach of a specific, explicit (not implied) direction in an injunctive order or a promise in an undertaking alleged?

OR if the respondent has been arrested upon a power of arrest or warrant of arrest and brought before the court, was he arrested for an arrestable disobedience and, where arrested under a power of arrest, has the hearing begun within 24 hours of the arrest? AND should the hearing proceed or should an adjournment be allowed to enable the case and evidence to be prepared? FPR 1991, r 3.9A(4) and FPC (MP etc) R 1991, r 20(4) and (under the PHA 1997) CCR Ord 49, r 15A(7) allow the court to deal forthwith with the matter upon which the respondent was arrested without service on him of a Notice to Show Good Reason or dispensation with this under CCR Ord 29, r 1(7) or FPC (MP etc) R 1991, r 20(12); alternatively the court may adjourn the proceedings for not more than 14 days. In proceedings under the FLA 1996, there is general power to remand in s 47(7)(b), (10) and power to remand for a medical report under s 48. There is no power under the PHA 1997 to remand.

(2)   Was the respondent a party in the proceedings to whom the injunctive direction was ordered? With few exceptions, an injunctive order cannot be made against someone who is not a party. Quaere whether a non-party can give an undertaking without becoming a party.

(3)   Was the injunctive order (with a warning notice prominently displayed on the front (High Court) or penal notice indorsed or incorporated (county court or family proceedings court)) personally served? Or if it was prohibitory (not mandatory), was the respondent present when the order was made? Or has he been notified of it? (RSC Ord 45, r 7(6); CCR Ord 29, r 1(6); FPC (MP etc) R 1991, r 20(11)).

OR was the undertaking recorded in county court Form N117, Principal Registry Form D787 or family proceedings court Form FL422 or, in the Chancery or Queen's Bench Divisions of the High Court, in a document in which the giver signed a statement to the effect that he understood the terms of his undertaking and the consequences of failure to comply with it in accordance with CPR PD40B, paras 9.3–9.4? Was that document delivered to or served on or acknowledged by signature of the respondent?

(4)   Was the direction or promise either:

    (a)   to do a specified act or specified acts at or before a specified time? If so, is the act one which the court has power to enforce by committal proceedings? Committal for contempt is not available, for example, for failure to attend a county court upon a witness summons (see County Courts Act 1984, s 55 and CCR Ord 34, r 2), to enforce payment of a money judgment (except where judgment summons is still available: see *Nwogbe v Nwogbe* [2000] 2 FLR 744, CA), or for a declaratory order such as a defined pattern of contact with a child. Also, was the order served before the time specified in the order for the act to be done, as required by RSC Ord 42, r 2(1), CCR Ord 22, r 3 or FPC (MP etc) R 1991, r 20(5)(b)? OR

    (b)   to abstain from doing a specified act or specified acts? Note the powers to dispense with service of the order under RSC Ord 45, r 7(6), (7) and CCR Ord 29, r 1(6), (7), and see *Davy International v Tazzyman* [1997] 3 All ER 183 and *Jolly v Hull; Jolly v Jolly* [2000] 2 FLR 69.

(5)   In the case of breach of an injunction granted under PHA 1997, s 3(5), has the person arrested already been convicted of an offence in respect of the alleged contempt? If so, he cannot be punished in contempt proceedings (s 3(7)).

II. TRIAL PROCEDURE

Preliminary procedural points

A. Is the court following normal criminal procedure?

If the court is embarking on a re-hearing after a previous hearing in the absence of the respondent, either because the court dispensed with service of notice on him or the court accepts that his absence was not his fault, the entire procedure must be followed. No short cuts are permissible. Note that on a review on notice of a committal ordered in the absence of the respondent, the sentence cannot be increased.

B. In the case of proceedings under the Family Law Act 1996, should the court remand, before or after deciding whether the contempt(s) is (are) proved, for a medical report under FLA 1996, s 48?

C. If the respondent is not legally represented, should a solicitor within the precincts of the court be invited to represent the respondent under Help at Court? (See Funding Code, Part 1, para 2.1.)

Conduct of hearing

(1)   In civil proceedings under CPR 1998, Part 8 and PD Committal, has the respondent filed affidavits giving any evidence in opposition to the committal application (PD Committal, paras 3.1–3.2)? But he does not need permission to adduce oral evidence if he has not filed affidavits (PD Committal, paras 3.3–3.4). In family proceedings also, it is good practice to file affidavits in opposition to a committal application.

(2)   Amendment of the committal application can be permitted by the court (PD Committal, para 2.6(3)).

(3)   Does the respondent admit the allegation(s) and, if so, precisely what does he admit? The exact finding(s) of contempt will have to be recorded in the committal order (A85, High Court; N79, county court; FL419, family proceedings court). Are the admissions adequate to enable the court to proceed to consideration of penalty without hearing evidence?

(4)   Burden of proof on applicant.

(5)   Normal sequence of evidence. Chief, affidavit or statement and/or oral; cross-examination; re-examination. Applicant and his witnesses first; respondent and his witnesses after. The alleged contemnor is not compellable as a witness at the instance of the applicant or the judge (*Comet Products UK Ltd v Hawkex Plastics Ltd* [1971] 2 QB 67) and cannot be directed to give information (PD Committal, paras 6, 7). The privilege against self-incrimination applies in civil contempt proceedings (*Memory Corp plc and another v Sidhu and another* [2000] 1 All ER 434).

(6)   Respondent entitled to submit 'no case'.

(7)   Actus reus and mens rea must be proved. Mens rea is knowledge of the injunctive direction plus deliberate conduct which in fact is a breach. Not necessary to prove that the respondent understood the nature of the court's procedures provided he knew what was forbidden (*P v P (Contempt of Court: Mental Incapacity)* [1999] 2 FLR 897, CA).

(8)   Criminal standard of proof.

(9)   Contempt(s) found proved must be specified and recorded in committal order (A85, High Court; N79 county court; FL419 family proceedings court.)

III. CONSIDERATION OF PENALTY

Range of powers and appropriate approach to choice of disposal

The disposal must be proportionate to the seriousness of the contempt, reflect the disapproval of the court and be designed to secure compliance in the future (*Hale v Tanner* [2000] 2 FLR 879, where the range of powers is summarised).

(1)   Does the contemnor wish to mitigate or attempt to purge his contempt?

(2)   In family cases, does the applicant wish to give her views?

(3)   Is the contemnor eligible for imprisonment being aged 21 or more? Or eligible for detention being aged 18 or over and less than 21? Or is no custodial sentence available, the contemnor being aged less than 18?

(4)   If available, is an immediate custodial sentence the only appropriate disposal? What alternatives are available? Note that there is no principle that 'a first breach [of an injunction] cannot result in a sentence of imprisonment'. Where the disobedience of an injunction or undertaking is serious an immediate custodial sentence may be imposed (*Jordan v Jordan* [1993] 1 FLR 169; *Thorpe v Thorpe* [1998] 2 FLR 127).

(5)   What penalty should be imposed for each separate contempt found proved? If more than one contempt, should penalties be consecutive or concurrent? Is the total appropriate? The maximum total imprisonment that can be imposed on one occasion is 2 years in a judge court, 2 months in a family proceedings court. Sentences can be consecutive, including an implemented suspended sentence, but the total cannot exceed the maximum of 2 years or 2 months.

(6)   Should imprisonment (of contemnor aged 21 or more) be suspended? Or should consideration of penalty be adjourned with liberty to restore? If so,

   (a)   for how long? and
   (b)   what conditions should be ordered to define the event(s) which would render the contemnor liable to implementation or imposition of a penalty?

The period of suspension or adjournment should be fixed, but an indefinite period can be valid (*Griffin v Griffin* [2000] 2 FLR 44, CA).

The power to remand an arrested person under FLA 1996, s 47(7), (10) is not available where the contemnor appeared in answer to a Notice to Show Good Reason, therefore the case-law which established that sentence could not be deferred by remand in custody, after finding contempt proved, should still apply.

IV. PREPARATION OF THE ORDER OF COMMITTAL OR OTHER DISPOSAL

(1)   What should be recorded in the order of committal (A85 High Court, N79 county court, FL419 family proceedings court)? In particular:

   (a)   what precise findings of contempt? and
   (b)   what precise terms of disposal have been ordered?

   Form N79 or FL419 should be checked and initialled by the judge or the chairman or bench of justices.

(2)   If an immediate custodial sentence is ordered, can the committal order be issued in time to be served when the respondent is detained upon the warrant of committal? In a county court, CCR Ord 29, r 1(5)(a) requires that the committal order be served when the warrant is executed, unless the warrant is signed by the judge; if the judge signs the warrant, 36 hours is permitted for preparation and service of the committal order (CCR Ord 29, r 1(5)(b)). FPC (MP etc) R 1991, r 20(10) permits the committal order to be served within 36 hours after execution of the warrant.

V. APPEAL

Where there has been a really substantial error leading to a demonstrable injustice to the victim of a contempt, the Court of Appeal can allow an appeal by the claimant and increase the sentence (*Manchester City Council v Worthington* [2000] 1 FLR 411, CA; *Wilson v Webster* [1998] 1 FLR 1097, CA). A contemnor contemplating an appeal should be warned that a sentence imposed for contempt can be increased.

APPENDIX 1

STATUTES

Children Act 1989[1]

****

Part IV

Care and Supervision

****

[38A Power to include exclusion requirement in interim care order

(1)   Where—

(a)   on being satisfied that there are reasonable grounds for believing that the circumstances with respect to a child are as mentioned in section 31(2)(a) and (b)(i), the court makes an interim care order with respect to a child, and

(b)   the conditions mentioned in subsection (2) are satisfied,

the court may include an exclusion requirement in the interim care order.

(2)   The conditions are—

(a)   that there is reasonable cause to believe that, if a person ('the relevant person') is excluded from a dwelling-house in which the child lives, the child will cease to suffer, or cease to be likely to suffer, significant harm, and

(b)   that another person living in the dwelling-house (whether a parent of the child or some other person)—

(i)   is able and willing to give to the child the care which it would be reasonable to expect a parent to give him, and

(ii)   consents to the inclusion of the exclusion requirement.

(3)   For the purposes of this section an exclusion requirement is any one or more of the following—

(a)   a provision requiring the relevant person to leave a dwelling-house in which he is living with the child,

(b)   a provision prohibiting the relevant person from entering a dwelling-house in which the child lives, and

[1]   Act reference: 1989 c 41.
Royal assent: 16 November 1989.
Long title: An Act to reform the law relating to children; to provide for local authority services for children in need and others; to amend the law with respect to children's homes, community homes, voluntary homes and voluntary organisations; to make provision with respect to fostering, child minding and day care for young children and adoption; and for connected purposes.

(c)   a provision excluding the relevant person from a defined area in which a dwelling-house in which the child lives is situated.

(4)   The court may provide that the exclusion requirement is to have effect for a shorter period than the other provisions of the interim care order.

(5)   Where the court makes an interim care order containing an exclusion requirement, the court may attach a power of arrest to the exclusion requirement.

(6)   Where the court attaches a power of arrest to an exclusion requirement of an interim care order, it may provide that the power of arrest is to have effect for a shorter period than the exclusion requirement.

(7)   Any period specified for the purposes of subsection (4) or (6) may be extended by the court (on one or more occasions) on an application to vary or discharge the interim care order.

(8)   Where a power of arrest is attached to an exclusion requirement of an interim care order by virtue of subsection (5), a constable may arrest without warrant any person whom he has reasonable cause to believe to be in breach of the requirement.

(9)   Sections 47(7), (11) and (12) and 48 of, and Schedule 5 to, the Family Law Act 1996 shall have effect in relation to a person arrested under subsection (8) of this section as they have effect in relation to a person arrested under section 47(6) of that Act.

(10)   If, while an interim care order containing an exclusion requirement is in force, the local authority have removed the child from the dwelling-house from which the relevant person is excluded to other accommodation for a continuous period of more than 24 hours, the interim care order shall cease to have effect in so far as it imposes the exclusion requirement.][2]

[38B   Undertakings relating to interim care orders

(1)   In any case where the court has power to include an exclusion requirement in an interim care order, the court may accept an undertaking from the relevant person.

(2)   No power of arrest may be attached to any undertaking given under subsection (1).

(3)   An undertaking given to a court under subsection (1)—

(a)   shall be enforceable as if it were an order of the court, and
(b)   shall cease to have effect if, while it is in force, the local authority have removed the child from the dwelling house from which the relevant person is excluded to other accommodation for a continuous period of more than 24 hours.

---

[2]   Amendment: Section inserted: Family Law Act 1996, s 52, Sch 6, para 1, with effect from 1 October 1997 (Family Law Act 1996 (Commencement No 2) Order 1997, SI 1997/1892).

(4)   This section has effect without prejudice to the powers of the High Court and county court apart from this section.

(5)   In this section 'exclusion requirement' and 'relevant person' have the same meaning as in section 38A.][3]

39[4]   Discharge and variation etc of care orders and supervision orders

(1)   A care order may be discharged by the court on the application of—

(a)   any person who has parental responsibility for the child;
(b)   the child himself; or
(c)   the local authority designated by the order.

(2)   A supervision order may be varied or discharged by the court on the application of—

(a)   any person who has parental responsibility for the child;
(b)   the child himself; or
(c)   the supervisor.

(3)   On the application of a person who is not entitled to apply for the order to be discharged, but who is a person with whom the child is living, a supervision order may be varied by the court in so far as it imposes a requirement which affects that person.

[(3A)   On the application of a person who is not entitled to apply for the order to be discharged, but who is a person to whom an exclusion requirement contained in the order applies, an interim care order may be varied or discharged by the court in so far as it imposes the exclusion requirement.

(3B)   Where a power of arrest has been attached to an exclusion requirement of an interim care order, the court may, on the application of any person entitled to apply for the discharge of the order so far as it imposes the exclusion requirement, vary or discharge the order in so far as it confers a power of arrest (whether or not any application has been made to vary or discharge any other provision of the order).][5]

(4)   Where a care order is in force with respect to a child the court may, on the application of any person entitled to apply for the order to be discharged, substitute a supervision order for the care order.

(5)   When a court is considering whether to substitute one order for another under subsection (4) any provision of this Act which would otherwise require section 31(2) to be satisfied at the time when the proposed order is substituted or made shall be disregarded.

---

3   Amendment: Section inserted: Family Law Act 1996, s 52, Sch 6, para 1, with effect from 1 October 1997 (Family Law Act 1996 (Commencement No 2) Order 1997, SI 1997/1892).
4   Commencement: 14 October 1991 (SI 1991/828).
5   Amendment: Subsections inserted: Family Law Act 1996, s 52, Sch 6, para 2, with effect from 1 October 1997 (Family Law Act 1996 (Commencement No 2) Order 1997, SI 1997/1892).

****

Part V

Protection of Children

****

[44A Power to include exclusion requirement in emergency protection order

(1)   Where—

(a)   on being satisfied as mentioned in section 44(1)(a), (b) or (c), the court makes an emergency protection order with respect to a child, and
(b)   the conditions mentioned in subsection (2) are satisfied,

the court may include an exclusion requirement in the emergency protection order.

(2)   The conditions are—

(a)   that there is reasonable cause to believe that, if a person ('the relevant person') is excluded from a dwelling-house in which the child lives, then—

(i)   in the case of an order made on the ground mentioned in section 44(1)(a), the child will not be likely to suffer significant harm, even though the child is not removed as mentioned in section 44(1)(a)(i) or does not remain as mentioned in section 44(1)(a)(ii), or
(ii)   in the case of an order made on the ground mentioned in paragraph (b) or (c) of section 44(1), the enquiries referred to in that paragraph will cease to be frustrated, and

(b)   that another person living in the dwelling-house (whether a parent of the child or some other person)—

(i)   is able and willing to give to the child the care which it would be reasonable to expect a parent to give him, and
(ii)   consents to the inclusion of the exclusion requirement.

(3)   For the purposes of this section an exclusion requirement is any one or more of the following—

(a)   a provision requiring the relevant person to leave a dwelling-house in which he is living with the child,
(b)   a provision prohibiting the relevant person from entering a dwelling-house in which the child lives, and
(c)   a provision excluding the relevant person from a defined area in which a dwelling-house in which the child lives is situated.

(4)   The court may provide that the exclusion requirement is to have effect for a shorter period than the other provisions of the order.

(5)   Where the court makes an emergency protection order containing an exclusion requirement, the court may attach a power of arrest to the exclusion requirement.

(6)   Where the court attaches a power of arrest to an exclusion requirement of an emergency protection order, it may provide that the power of arrest is to have effect for a shorter period than the exclusion requirement.

(7)   Any period specified for the purposes of subsection (4) or (6) may be extended by the court (on one or more occasions) on an application to vary or discharge the emergency protection order.

(8)   Where a power of arrest is attached to an exclusion requirement of an emergency protection order by virtue of subsection (5), a constable may arrest without warrant any person whom he has reasonable cause to believe to be in breach of the requirement.

(9)   Sections 47(7), (11) and (12) and 48 of, and Schedule 5 to, the Family Law Act 1996 shall have effect in relation to a person arrested under subsection (8) of this section as they have effect in relation to a person arrested under section 47(6) of that Act.

(10)   If, while an emergency protection order containing an exclusion requirement is in force, the applicant has removed the child from the dwelling-house from which the relevant person is excluded to other accommodation for a continuous period of more than 24 hours, the order shall cease to have effect in so far as it imposes the exclusion requirement.][6]

[44B   Undertakings relating to emergency protection orders

(1)   In any case where the court has power to include an exclusion requirement in an emergency protection order, the court may accept an undertaking from the relevant person.

(2)   No power of arrest may be attached to any undertaking given under subsection (1).

(3)   An undertaking given to a court under subsection (1)—

(a)   shall be enforceable as if it were an order of the court, and
(b)   shall cease to have effect if, while it is in force, the applicant has removed the child from the dwelling-house from which the relevant person is excluded to other accommodation for a continuous period of more than 24 hours.

(4)   This section has effect without prejudice to the powers of the High Court and county court apart from this section.

---

6   Amendment: Section inserted: Family Law Act 1996, s 52, Sch 6, para 3, with effect from 1 October 1997 (Family Law Act 1996 (Commencement No 2) Order 1997, SI 1997/1892).

(5)   In this section 'exclusion requirement' and 'relevant person' have the same meaning as in section 44A.][7]

45[8]   Duration of emergency protection orders and other supplemental provisions

(1)   An emergency protection order shall have effect for such period, not exceeding eight days, as may be specified in the order.

(2)   Where—

(a)   the court making an emergency protection order would, but for this subsection, specify a period of eight days as the period for which the order is to have effect; but

(b)   the last of those eight days is a public holiday (that is to say, Christmas Day, Good Friday, a bank holiday or a Sunday),

the court may specify a period which ends at noon on the first later day which is not such a holiday.

(3)   Where an emergency protection order is made on an application under section 46(7), the period of eight days mentioned in subsection (1) shall begin with the first day on which the child was taken into police protection under section 46.

(4)   Any person who—

(a)   has parental responsibility for a child as the result of an emergency protection order; and

(b)   is entitled to apply for a care order with respect to the child,

may apply to the court for the period during which the emergency protection order is to have effect to be extended.

(5)   On an application under subsection (4) the court may extend the period during which the order is to have effect by such period, not exceeding seven days, as it thinks fit, but may do so only if it has reasonable cause to believe that the child concerned is likely to suffer significant harm if the order is not extended.

(6)   An emergency protection order may only be extended once.

(7)   Regardless of any enactment or rule of law which would otherwise prevent it from doing so, a court hearing an application for, or with respect to, an emergency protection order may take account of—

(a)   any statement contained in any report made to the court in the course of, or in connection with, the hearing; or

(b)   any evidence given during the hearing,

---

[7]   Amendment: Section inserted: Family Law Act 1996, s 52, Sch 6, para 3, with effect from 1 October 1997 (Family Law Act 1996 (Commencement No 2) Order 1997, SI 1997/1892).

[8]   Commencement: 14 October 1991 (SI 1991/828).

which is, in the opinion of the court, relevant to the application.

(8)   Any of the following may apply to the court for an emergency protection order to be discharged—

(a)   the child;

(b)   a parent of his;

(c)   any person who is not a parent of his but who has parental responsibility for him; or

(d)   any person with whom he was living immediately before the making of the order.

[(8A)   On the application of a person who is not entitled to apply for the order to be discharged, but who is a person to whom an exclusion requirement contained in the order applies, an emergency protection order may be varied or discharged by the court in so far as it imposes the exclusion requirement.

(8B)   Where a power of arrest has been attached to an exclusion requirement of an emergency protection order, the court may, on the application of any person entitled to apply for the discharge of the order so far as it imposes the exclusion requirement, vary or discharge the order in so far as it confers a power of arrest (whether or not any application has been made to vary or discharge any other provision of the order).][9]

(9)   No application for the discharge of an emergency protection order shall be heard by the court before the expiry of the period of 72 hours beginning with the making of the order.

[(10)   No appeal may be made against—

(a)   the making of, or refusal to make, an emergency protection order;

(b)   the extension of, or refusal to extend, the period during which such an order is to have effect;

(c)   the discharge of, or refusal to discharge, such an order; or

(d)   the giving of, or refusal to give, any direction in connection with such an order.][10]

(11)   Subsection (8) does not apply—

(a)   where the person who would otherwise be entitled to apply for the emergency protection order to be discharged—

(i)   was given notice (in accordance with rules of court) of the hearing at which the order was made; and

(ii)   was present at that hearing; or

---

[9]   Amendment: Subsections inserted: Family Law Act 1996, s 52, Sch 6, para 4, with effect from 1 October 1997 (Family Law Act 1996 (Commencement No 2) Order 1997, SI 1997/1892).

[10]   Amendment: Subsection substituted: Courts and Legal Services Act 1990, s 116, Sch 16, para 19, with effect from 14 October 1991 (Courts and Legal Services Act 1990 (Commencement No 6) Order 1991, SI 1991/1883).

(b)   to any emergency protection order the effective period of which has been extended under subsection (5).

(12)   A court making an emergency protection order may direct that the applicant may in exercising any powers which he has by virtue of the order, be accompanied by a registered medical practitioner, registered nurse or [registered midwife][11], if he so chooses.

[(13)   The reference in subsection (12) to a registered midwife is to such a midwife who is also registered in the Specialist Community Public Health Nurses' Part of the register maintained under article 5 of the Nursing and Midwifery Order 2001.][12]

---

[11]   Amendment: Words substituted: Nursing and Midwifery Order 2001, SI 2002/253, with effect from 1 August 2004: see the London Gazette, 21 July 2004; for transitional provisions see SI 2002/253, Sch 2.
[12]   Amendment: Sub-section inserted: Health Act 1999 (Consequential Amendments) (Nursing and Midwifery) Order 2004, SI 2004/1771, with effect from 1 August 2004.

Family Law Act 1996[13]

****

Part IV

Family Homes and Domestic Violence

Rights to occupy matrimonial [or civil partnership][14] home

30[15] Rights concerning [home where one spouse or civil partner][16] has no estate, etc

(1) This section applies if—

(a) one spouse [or civil partner ('A')][17] is entitled to occupy a dwelling-house by virtue of—

(i) a beneficial estate or interest or contract; or

(ii) any enactment giving [A][18] the right to remain in occupation; and

(b) the other spouse [or civil partner ('B')][19] is not so entitled.

---

[13] Act reference: 1996 c 27.
Royal assent: 4 July 1996.
Long title: An Act to make provision with respect to: divorce and separation; legal aid in connection with mediation in disputes relating to family matters; proceedings in cases where marriages have broken down; rights of occupation of certain domestic premises; prevention of molestation; the inclusion in certain orders under the Children Act 1989 of provisions about the occupation of a dwelling-house; the transfer of tenancies between spouses and persons who have lived together as husband and wife; and for connected purposes.

[14] Amendment: Words inserted: Civil Partnership Act 2004, s 82, Sch 9, Pt 1, para 1(1), (11), with effect from 5 December 2005; for transitional provisions see Civil Partnership Act 2004, s 82, Sch 9, Pt 3.

[15] Commencement: 1 October 1997 (SI 1997/1892).

[16] Amendment: Words substituted: Civil Partnership Act 2004, s 82, Sch 9, Pt 1, para 1(1), (11), with effect from 5 December 2005; for transitional provisions see Civil Partnership Act 2004, s 82, Sch 9, Pt 3.

[17] Amendment: Words inserted: Civil Partnership Act 2004, s 82, Sch 9, Pt 1, para 1(1), (2)(a)(i), with effect from 5 December 2005; for transitional provisions see Civil Partnership Act 2004, s 82, Sch 9, Pt 3.

[18] Amendment: Words substituted: Civil Partnership Act 2004, s 82, Sch 9, Pt 1, para 1(1), (2)(a)(ii), with effect from 5 December 2005; for transitional provisions see Civil Partnership Act 2004, s 82, Sch 9, Pt 3.

[19] Amendment: Words inserted: Civil Partnership Act 2004, s 82, Sch 9, Pt 1, para 1(1), (2)(b), with effect from 5 December 2005; for transitional provisions see Civil Partnership Act 2004, s 82, Sch 9, Pt 3.

(2) Subject to the provisions of this Part, [B][20] has the following rights [('home rights')][21]—

(a) if in occupation, a right not to be evicted or excluded from the dwelling-house or any part of it by [A][22] except with the leave of the court given by an order under section 33;

(b) if not in occupation, a right with the leave of the court so given to enter into and occupy the dwelling-house.

(3) If [B][23] is entitled under this section to occupy a dwelling-house or any part of a dwelling-house, any payment or tender made or other thing done by [B][24] in or towards satisfaction of any liability of [A][25] in respect of rent, mortgage payments or other outgoings affecting the dwelling-house shall, whether or not it is made or done in pursuance of an order under section 40, be as good as if made or done by [A][26].

(4) [B's][27] occupation by virtue of this section—

(a) is to be treated, for the purposes of the Rent (Agriculture) Act 1976 and the Rent Act 1977 (other than Part V and sections 103 to 106 of that Act), as occupation [by A as A's][28] residence, and

---

[20] Amendment: Words substituted: Civil Partnership Act 2004, s 82, Sch 9, Pt 1, para 1(1), (3)(a), with effect from 5 December 2005; for transitional provisions see Civil Partnership Act 2004, s 82, Sch 9, Pt 3.

[21] Amendment: Words substituted: Civil Partnership Act 2004, s 82, Sch 9, Pt 1, para 1(1), (3)(b), with effect from 5 December 2005; for transitional provisions see Civil Partnership Act 2004, s 82, Sch 9, Pt 3.

[22] Amendment: Words substituted: Civil Partnership Act 2004, s 82, Sch 9, Pt 1, para 1(1), (3)(c), with effect from 5 December 2005; for transitional provisions see Civil Partnership Act 2004, s 82, Sch 9, Pt 3.

[23] Amendment: Words substituted: Civil Partnership Act 2004, s 82, Sch 9, Pt 1, para 1(1), (4)(a), with effect from 5 December 2005; for transitional provisions see Civil Partnership Act 2004, s 82, Sch 9, Pt 3.

[24] Amendment: Words substituted: Civil Partnership Act 2004, s 82, Sch 9, Pt 1, para 1(1), (4)(a), with effect from 5 December 2005; for transitional provisions see Civil Partnership Act 2004, s 82, Sch 9, Pt 3.

[25] Amendment: Words substituted: Civil Partnership Act 2004, s 82, Sch 9, Pt 1, para 1(1), (4)(b), with effect from 5 December 2005; for transitional provisions see Civil Partnership Act 2004, s 82, Sch 9, Pt 3.

[26] Amendment: Words substituted: Civil Partnership Act 2004, s 82, Sch 9, Pt 1, para 1(1), (4)(b), with effect from 5 December 2005; for transitional provisions see Civil Partnership Act 2004, s 82, Sch 9, Pt 3.

[27] Amendment: Words substituted: Civil Partnership Act 2004, s 82, Sch 9, Pt 1, para 1(1), (5)(a), with effect from 5 December 2005; for transitional provisions see Civil Partnership Act 2004, s 82, Sch 9, Pt 3.

[28] Amendment: Words substituted: Civil Partnership Act 2004, s 82, Sch 9, Pt 1, para 1(1), (5)(b), with effect from 5 December 2005; for transitional provisions see Civil Partnership Act 2004, s 82, Sch 9, Pt 3.

(b) if [B occupies the dwelling-house as B's][29] only or principal home, is to be treated, for the purposes of the Housing Act 1985[, Part I of the Housing Act 1988 and Chapter I of Part V of the Housing Act 1996][30], as occupation [by A as A's][31] only or principal home.

(5) If [B][32]—

(a) is entitled under this section to occupy a dwelling-house or any part of a dwelling-house, and

(b) makes any payment in or towards satisfaction of any liability of [A][33] in respect of mortgage payments affecting the dwelling-house,

the person to whom the payment is made may treat it as having been made by [A][34], but the fact that that person has treated any such payment as having been so made does not affect any claim of [B against A][35] to an interest in the dwelling-house by virtue of the payment.

(6) If [B][36] is entitled under this section to occupy a dwelling-house or part of a dwelling-house by reason of an interest of [A][37] under a trust, all the provisions of subsections (3) to (5) apply in relation to the trustees as they apply in relation to [A][38].

(7) This section does not apply to a dwelling-house [which—

---

[29] Amendment: Words substituted: Civil Partnership Act 2004, s 82, Sch 9, Pt 1, para 1(1), (5)(c)(i), with effect from 5 December 2005; for transitional provisions see Civil Partnership Act 2004, s 82, Sch 9, Pt 3.

[30] Amendment: Words substituted: Housing Act 1996 (Consequential Amendments) Order 1997, SI 1997/74, with effect from 12 February 1997.

[31] Amendment: Words substituted: Civil Partnership Act 2004, s 82, Sch 9, Pt 1, para 1(1), (5)(c)(ii), with effect from 5 December 2005; for transitional provisions see Civil Partnership Act 2004, s 82, Sch 9, Pt 3.

[32] Amendment: Words substituted: Civil Partnership Act 2004, s 82, Sch 9, Pt 1, para 1(1), (6)(a), with effect from 5 December 2005; for transitional provisions see Civil Partnership Act 2004, s 82, Sch 9, Pt 3.

[33] Amendment: Words substituted: Civil Partnership Act 2004, s 82, Sch 9, Pt 1, para 1(1), (6)(b), with effect from 5 December 2005; for transitional provisions see Civil Partnership Act 2004, s 82, Sch 9, Pt 3.

[34] Amendment: Words substituted: Civil Partnership Act 2004, s 82, Sch 9, Pt 1, para 1(1), (6)(c), with effect from 5 December 2005; for transitional provisions see Civil Partnership Act 2004, s 82, Sch 9, Pt 3.

[35] Amendment: Words substituted: Civil Partnership Act 2004, s 82, Sch 9, Pt 1, para 1(1), (6)(d), with effect from 5 December 2005; for transitional provisions see Civil Partnership Act 2004, s 82, Sch 9, Pt 3.

[36] Amendment: Words substituted: Civil Partnership Act 2004, s 82, Sch 9, Pt 1, para 1(1), (7)(a), with effect from 5 December 2005; for transitional provisions see Civil Partnership Act 2004, s 82, Sch 9, Pt 3.

[37] Amendment: Words substituted: Civil Partnership Act 2004, s 82, Sch 9, Pt 1, para 1(1), (7)(b), with effect from 5 December 2005; for transitional provisions see Civil Partnership Act 2004, s 82, Sch 9, Pt 3.

[38] Amendment: Words substituted: Civil Partnership Act 2004, s 82, Sch 9, Pt 1, para 1(1), (7)(b), with effect from 5 December 2005; for transitional provisions see Civil Partnership Act 2004, s 82, Sch 9, Pt 3.

(a)   in the case of spouses, has at no time been, and was at no time intended by them to be, a matrimonial home of theirs; and

(b)   in the case ofcivil partners, has at no time been, and was at no time intended by them to be, a civil partnership home of theirs][39].

(8)   [B's home rights][40] continue—

(a)   only so long as the marriage [or civil partnership][41] subsists, except to the extent that an order under section 33(5) otherwise provides; and

(b)   only so long as [A][42] is entitled as mentioned in subsection (1) to occupy the dwelling-house, except where provision is made by section 31 for those rights to be a charge on an estate or interest in the dwelling-house.

(9)   It is hereby declared that [a person][43]—

(a)   who has an equitable interest in a dwelling-house or in its proceeds of sale, but

(b)   is not [a person][44] in whom there is vested (whether solely or as joint tenant) a legal estate in fee simple or a legal term of years absolute in the dwelling-house,

is to be treated, only for the purpose of determining whether he has [home rights][45], as not being entitled to occupy the dwelling-house by virtue of that interest.

31[46]   Effect of [home rights][47] as charge on dwelling-house

(1)   Subsections (2) and (3) apply if, at any time during a [marriage or civil partnership, A][48] is entitled to occupy a dwelling-house by virtue of a beneficial estate or interest.

---

[39]   Amendment: Word and subsequent sub-paragraphs substituted: Civil Partnership Act 2004, s 82, Sch 9, Pt 1, para 1(1), (8), with effect from 5 December 2005; for transitional provisions see Civil Partnership Act 2004, s 82, Sch 9, Pt 3.

[40]   Amendment: Words substituted: Civil Partnership Act 2004, s 82, Sch 9, Pt 1, para 1(1), (9)(a), with effect from 5 December 2005; for transitional provisions see Civil Partnership Act 2004, s 82, Sch 9, Pt 3.

[41]   Amendment: Words inserted: Civil Partnership Act 2004, s 82, Sch 9, Pt 1, para 1(1), (9)(b), with effect from 5 December 2005; for transitional provisions see Civil Partnership Act 2004, s 82, Sch 9, Pt 3.

[42]   Amendment: Words substituted: Civil Partnership Act 2004, s 82, Sch 9, Pt 1, para 1(1), (9)(c), with effect from 5 December 2005; for transitional provisions see Civil Partnership Act 2004, s 82, Sch 9, Pt 3.

[43]   Amendment: Words substituted: Civil Partnership Act 2004, s 82, Sch 9, Pt 1, para 1(1), (10)(a), with effect from 5 December 2005; for transitional provisions see Civil Partnership Act 2004, s 82, Sch 9, Pt 3.

[44]   Amendment: Words substituted: Civil Partnership Act 2004, s 82, Sch 9, Pt 1, para 1(1), (10)(a), with effect from 5 December 2005; for transitional provisions see Civil Partnership Act 2004, s 82, Sch 9, Pt 3.

[45]   Amendment: Words substituted: Civil Partnership Act 2004, s 82, Sch 9, Pt 1, para 1(1), (10)(b), with effect from 5 December 2005; for transitional provisions see Civil Partnership Act 2004, s 82, Sch 9, Pt 3.

[46]   Commencement: 1 October 1997 (SI 1997/1892).

[47]   Amendment: Words substituted: Civil Partnership Act 2004, s 82, Sch 9, Pt 1, para 2(1), (12), with effect from 5 December 2005; for transitional provisions see Civil Partnership Act 2004, s 82, Sch 9, Pt 3.

[48]   Amendment: Words substituted: Civil Partnership Act 2004, s 82, Sch 9, Pt 1, para 2(1), (2), with effect from 5 December 2005; for transitional provisions see Civil Partnership Act 2004, s 82, Sch 9, Pt 3.

(2)　[B's home rights][49] are a charge on the estate or interest.

(3)　The charge created by subsection (2) has the same priority as if it were an equitable interest created at whichever is the latest of the following dates—

(a)　the date on which [A][50] acquires the estate or interest;

(b)　the date of the marriage [or of the formation of the civil partnership][51]; and

(c)　1st January 1968 (the commencement date of the Matrimonial Homes Act 1967).

(4)　Subsections (5) and (6) apply if, at any time when [B's home rights][52] are a charge on an interest of [A][53] under a trust, there are, apart from [A or B][54], no persons, living or unborn, who are or could become beneficiaries under the trust.

(5)　The rights are a charge also on the estate or interest of the trustees for [A][55].

(6)　The charge created by subsection (5) has the same priority as if it were an equitable interest created (under powers overriding the trusts) on the date when it arises.

(7)　In determining for the purposes of subsection (4) whether there are any persons who are not, but could become, beneficiaries under the trust, there is to be disregarded any potential exercise of a general power of appointment exercisable by either or both of [A and B][56] alone (whether or not the exercise of it requires the consent of another person).

(8)　Even though [B's home rights][57] are a charge on an estate or interest in the dwelling-house, those rights are brought to an end by—

---

[49]　Amendment: Words substituted: Civil Partnership Act 2004, s 82, Sch 9, Pt 1, para 2(1), (3), with effect from 5 December 2005; for transitional provisions see Civil Partnership Act 2004, s 82, Sch 9, Pt 3.

[50]　Amendment: Words substituted: Civil Partnership Act 2004, s 82, Sch 9, Pt 1, para 2(1), (4)(a), with effect from 5 December 2005; for transitional provisions see Civil Partnership Act 2004, s 82, Sch 9, Pt 3.

[51]　Amendment: Words inserted: Civil Partnership Act 2004, s 82, Sch 9, Pt 1, para 2(1), (4)(b), with effect from 5 December 2005; for transitional provisions see Civil Partnership Act 2004, s 82, Sch 9, Pt 3.

[52]　Amendment: Words substituted: Civil Partnership Act 2004, s 82, Sch 9, Pt 1, para 2(1), (5)(a), with effect from 5 December 2005; for transitional provisions see Civil Partnership Act 2004, s 82, Sch 9, Pt 3.

[53]　Amendment: Words substituted: Civil Partnership Act 2004, s 82, Sch 9, Pt 1, para 2(1), (5)(b), with effect from 5 December 2005; for transitional provisions see Civil Partnership Act 2004, s 82, Sch 9, Pt 3.

[54]　Amendment: Words substituted: Civil Partnership Act 2004, s 82, Sch 9, Pt 1, para 2(1), (5)(c), with effect from 5 December 2005; for transitional provisions see Civil Partnership Act 2004, s 82, Sch 9, Pt 3.

[55]　Amendment: Words substituted: Civil Partnership Act 2004, s 82, Sch 9, Pt 1, para 2(1), (6), with effect from 5 December 2005; for transitional provisions see Civil Partnership Act 2004, s 82, Sch 9, Pt 3.

[56]　Amendment: Words substituted: Civil Partnership Act 2004, s 82, Sch 9, Pt 1, para 2(1), (7), with effect from 5 December 2005; for transitional provisions see Civil Partnership Act 2004, s 82, Sch 9, Pt 3.

[57]　Amendment: Words substituted: Civil Partnership Act 2004, s 82, Sch 9, Pt 1, para 2(1), (8)(a), with effect from 5 December 2005; for transitional provisions see Civil Partnership Act 2004, s 82, Sch 9, Pt 3.

(a)   the death of [A]⁵⁸, or

(b)   the termination (otherwise than by death) of the marriage [or civil partnership]⁵⁹,

unless the court directs otherwise by an order made under section 33(5).

(9)   If—

(a)   [B's home rights]⁶⁰ are a charge on an estate or interest in the dwelling-house, and

(b)   that estate or interest is surrendered to merge in some other estate or interest expectant on it in such circumstances that, but for the merger, the person taking the estate or interest would be bound by the charge,

the surrender has effect subject to the charge and the persons thereafter entitled to the other estate or interest are, for so long as the estate or interest surrendered would have endured if not so surrendered, to be treated for all purposes of this Part as deriving title to the other estate or interest under the [A]⁶¹ or, as the case may be, under the trustees for [A]⁶², by virtue of the surrender.

(10)   If the title to the legal estate by virtue of which [A]⁶³ is entitled to occupy a dwelling-house (including any legal estate held by trustees for [A]⁶⁴) is registered under the [Land Registration Act 2002]⁶⁵ or any enactment replaced by that Act—

(a)   registration of a land charge affecting the dwelling-house by virtue of this Part is to be effected by registering a notice under that Act; and

(b)   [B's home rights]⁶⁶[are not to be capable of falling within paragraph 2 of Schedule 1 or 3 to that Act]⁶⁷

---

⁵⁸   Amendment: Words substituted: Civil Partnership Act 2004, s 82, Sch 9, Pt 1, para 2(1), (8)(b), with effect from 5 December 2005; for transitional provisions see Civil Partnership Act 2004, s 82, Sch 9, Pt 3.

⁵⁹   Amendment: Words inserted: Civil Partnership Act 2004, s 82, Sch 9, Pt 1, para 2(1), (8)(c), with effect from 5 December 2005; for transitional provisions see Civil Partnership Act 2004, s 82, Sch 9, Pt 3.

⁶⁰   Amendment: Words inserted: Civil Partnership Act 2004, s 82, Sch 9, Pt 1, para 2(1), (9)(a), with effect from 5 December 2005; for transitional provisions see Civil Partnership Act 2004, s 82, Sch 9, Pt 3.

⁶¹   Amendment: Words substituted: Civil Partnership Act 2004, s 82, Sch 9, Pt 1, para 2(1), (9)(b), with effect from 5 December 2005; for transitional provisions see Civil Partnership Act 2004, s 82, Sch 9, Pt 3.

⁶²   Amendment: Words substituted: Civil Partnership Act 2004, s 82, Sch 9, Pt 1, para 2(1), (9)(b), with effect from 5 December 2005; for transitional provisions see Civil Partnership Act 2004, s 82, Sch 9, Pt 3.

⁶³   Amendment: Words substituted: Civil Partnership Act 2004, s 82, Sch 9, Pt 1, para 2(1), (10)(a), with effect from 5 December 2005; for transitional provisions see Civil Partnership Act 2004, s 82, Sch 9, Pt 3.

⁶⁴   Amendment: Words substituted: Civil Partnership Act 2004, s 82, Sch 9, Pt 1, para 2(1), (10)(a), with effect from 5 December 2005; for transitional provisions see Civil Partnership Act 2004, s 82, Sch 9, Pt 3.

⁶⁵   Amendment: Words substituted: Land Registration Act 2002, s 133, Sch 11, para 34(1), (2)(a), with effect from 13 October 2003.

⁶⁶   Amendment: Words substituted: Civil Partnership Act 2004, s 82, Sch 9, Pt 1, para 2(1), (10)(b), with effect from 5 December 2005; for transitional provisions see Civil Partnership Act 2004, s 82, Sch 9, Pt 3.

⁶⁷   Amendment: Sub-paragraph substituted: Land Registration Act 2002, s 133, Sch 11, para 34(1), (2)(b), with effect from 13 October 2003.

(11) ...[68]

(12) If—

[(a)   B's home rights are a charge on the estate of A or of trustees of A, and][69]
(b)   that estate is the subject of a mortgage,

then if, after the date of the creation of the mortgage ('the first mortgage'), the charge is registered under section 2 of the Land Charges Act 1972, the charge is, for the purposes of section 94 of the Law of Property Act 1925 (which regulates the rights of mortgagees to make further advances ranking in priority to subsequent mortgages), to be deemed to be a mortgage subsequent in date to the first mortgage.

(13)   It is hereby declared that a charge under subsection (2) or (5) is not registrable under subsection (10) or under section 2 of the Land Charges Act 1972 unless it is a charge on a legal estate.

[32[70]   Further provisions relating to home rights

Schedule 4 (provisions supplementary to sections 30 and 31) has effect.][71]

Occupation orders

33[72]   Occupation orders where applicant has estate or interest etc or has [home rights][73]

(1)   If—

(a)   a person ('the person entitled')—

   (i)   is entitled to occupy a dwelling-house by virtue of a beneficial estate or interest or contract or by virtue of any enactment giving him the right to remain in occupation, or
   (ii)   has [home rights][74] in relation to a dwelling-house, and

(b)   the dwelling-house—

   (i)   is or at any time has been the home of the person entitled and of another person with whom he is associated, or

---

[68]   Amendment: Paragraph repealed: Land Registration Act 2002, s 135, Sch 13, with effect from 13 October 2003.
[69]   Amendment: Sub-paragraph substituted: Civil Partnership Act 2004, s 82, Sch 9, Pt 1, para 2(1), (11), with effect from 5 December 2005; for transitional provisions see Civil Partnership Act 2004, s 82, Sch 9, Pt 3.
[70]   Commencement: 1 October 1997 (SI 1997/1892).
[71]   Amendment: Provision substituted: Civil Partnership Act 2004, s 82, Sch 9, Pt 1, para 3, with effect from 5 December 2005; for transitional provisions see Civil Partnership Act 2004, s 82, Sch 9, Pt 3.
[72]   Commencement: 1 October 1997 (SI 1997/1892).
[73]   Amendment: Words substituted: Civil Partnership Act 2004, s 82, Sch 9, Pt 1, para 4(1), (7), with effect from 5 December 2005; for transitional provisions see Civil Partnership Act 2004, s 82, Sch 9, Pt 3.
[74]   Amendment: Words substituted: Civil Partnership Act 2004, s 82, Sch 9, Pt 1, para 4(1), (2), with effect from 5 December 2005; for transitional provisions see Civil Partnership Act 2004, s 82, Sch 9, Pt 3.

(ii)   was at any time intended by the person entitled and any such other person to be their home,

the person entitled may apply to the court for an order containing any of the provisions specified in subsections (3), (4) and (5).

(2)   If an agreement to marry is terminated, no application under this section may be made by virtue of section 62(3)(e) by reference to that agreement after the end of the period of three years beginning with the date on which it is terminated.

[(2A)   If a civil partnership agreement (as defined by section 73 of the Civil Partnership Act 2004) is terminated, no application under this section may be made by virtue of section 62(3)(eza) by reference to that agreement after the end of the period of three years beginning with the day on which it is terminated.][75]

(3)   An order under this section may—

(a)   enforce the applicant's entitlement to remain in occupation as against the other person ('the respondent');
(b)   require the respondent to permit the applicant to enter and remain in the dwelling-house or part of the dwelling-house;
(c)   regulate the occupation of the dwelling-house by either or both parties;
(d)   if the respondent is entitled as mentioned in subsection (1)(a)(i), prohibit, suspend or restrict the exercise by him of his right to occupy the dwelling-house;
(e)   if the respondent has [home rights][76] in relation to the dwelling-house and the applicant is the other spouse [or civil partner][77], restrict or terminate those rights;
(f)   require the respondent to leave the dwelling-house or part of the dwelling-house; or
(g)   exclude the respondent from a defined area in which the dwelling-house is included.

(4)   An order under this section may declare that the applicant is entitled as mentioned in subsection (1)(a)(i) or has [home rights][78].

(5)   If the applicant has [home rights][79] and the respondent is the other spouse [or civil partner][80], an order under this section made during the marriage [or civil

---

[75]   Amendment: Paragraph inserted: Civil Partnership Act 2004, s 82, Sch 9, Pt 1, para 4(1), (3), with effect from 5 December 2005; for transitional provisions see Civil Partnership Act 2004, s 82, Sch 9, Pt 3.

[76]   Amendment: Words substituted: Civil Partnership Act 2004, s 82, Sch 9, Pt 1, para 4(1), (4)(a), with effect from 5 December 2005; for transitional provisions see Civil Partnership Act 2004, s 82, Sch 9, Pt 3.

[77]   Amendment: Words inserted: Civil Partnership Act 2004, s 82, Sch 9, Pt 1, para 4(1), (4)(b), with effect from 5 December 2005; for transitional provisions see Civil Partnership Act 2004, s 82, Sch 9, Pt 3.

[78]   Amendment: Words substituted: Civil Partnership Act 2004, s 82, Sch 9, Pt 1, para 4(1), (5), with effect from 5 December 2005; for transitional provisions see Civil Partnership Act 2004, s 82, Sch 9, Pt 3.

[79]   Amendment: Words substituted: Civil Partnership Act 2004, s 82, Sch 9, Pt 1, para 4(1), (6)(a), with effect from 5 December 2005; for transitional provisions see Civil Partnership Act 2004, s 82, Sch 9, Pt 3.

[80]   Amendment: Words inserted: Civil Partnership Act 2004, s 82, Sch 9, Pt 1, para 4(1), (6)(b), with effect from 5 December 2005; for transitional provisions see Civil Partnership Act 2004, s 82, Sch 9, Pt 3.

partnership][81] may provide that those rights are not brought to an end by—

(a)   the death of the other spouse [or civil partner][82]; or

(b)   the termination (otherwise than by death) of the marriage [or civil partnership][83].

(6)   In deciding whether to exercise its powers under subsection (3) and (if so) in what manner, the court shall have regard to all the circumstances including—

(a)   the housing needs and housing resources of each of the parties and of any relevant child;

(b)   the financial resources of the parties;

(c)   the likely effect of any order, or of any decision by the court not to exercise its powers under subsection (3), on the health, safety or well-being of the parties and of any relevant child; and

(d)   the conduct of the parties in relation to each other and otherwise.

(7)   If it appears to the court that the applicant or any relevant child is likely to suffer significant harm attributable to conduct of the respondent if an order under this section containing one or more of the provisions mentioned in subsection (3) is not made, the court shall make the order unless it appears to the court that—

(a)   the respondent or any relevant child is likely to suffer significant harm if the order is made; and

(b)   the harm likely to be suffered by the respondent or child in that event is as great as, or greater than, the harm attributable to conduct of the respondent which is likely to be suffered by the applicant or child if the order is not made.

(8)   The court may exercise its powers under subsection (5) in any case where it considers that in all the circumstances it is just and reasonable to do so.

(9)   An order under this section—

(a)   may not be made after the death of either of the parties mentioned in subsection (1); and

(b)   except in the case of an order made by virtue of subsection (5)(a), ceases to have effect on the death of either party.

(10) An order under this section may, in so far as it has continuing effect, be made for a specified period, until the occurrence of a specified event or until further order.

---

[81]   Amendment: Words inserted: Civil Partnership Act 2004, s 82, Sch 9, Pt 1, para 4(1), (6)(c), with effect from 5 December 2005; for transitional provisions see Civil Partnership Act 2004, s 82, Sch 9, Pt 3.

[82]   Amendment: Words inserted: Civil Partnership Act 2004, s 82, Sch 9, Pt 1, para 4(1), (6)(d), with effect from 5 December 2005; for transitional provisions see Civil Partnership Act 2004, s 82, Sch 9, Pt 3.

[83]   Amendment: Words inserted: Civil Partnership Act 2004, s 82, Sch 9, Pt 1, para 4(1), (6)(e), with effect from 5 December 2005; for transitional provisions see Civil Partnership Act 2004, s 82, Sch 9, Pt 3.

34[84]   Effect of order under s 33 where rights are charge on dwelling-house

(1)   If [B's home rights][85] are a charge on the estate or interest of [A][86] or of trustees for [A][87]—

(a)   an order under section 33 against [A][88] has, except so far as a contrary intention appears, the same effect against persons deriving title under [A][89] or under the trustees and affected by the charge, and

(b)   sections 33(1), (3), (4) and (10) and 30(3) to (6) apply in relation to any person deriving title under [A][90] or under the trustees and affected by the charge as they apply in relation to [A][91].

(2)   The court may make an order under section 33 by virtue of subsection (1)(b) if it considers that in all the circumstances it is just and reasonable to do so.

35[92]   One former spouse [or former civil partner][93] with no existing right to occupy

(1)   This section applies if—

(a)   one former spouse [or former civil partner][94] is entitled to occupy a dwelling-house by virtue of a beneficial estate or interest or contract, or by virtue of any enactment giving him the right to remain in occupation;

(b)   the other former spouse [or former civil partner][95] is not so entitled; and

[(c)   the dwelling-house—

    (i)   in the case of former spouses, was at any time their matrimonial home or was at any time intended by them to be their matrimonial home, or

---

84   Commencement: 1 October 1997 (SI 1997/1892).

85   Amendment: Words substituted: Civil Partnership Act 2004, s 82, Sch 9, Pt 1, para 5(a), with effect from 5 December 2005; for transitional provisions see Civil Partnership Act 2004, s 82, Sch 9, Pt 3.

86   Amendment: Words substituted: Civil Partnership Act 2004, s 82, Sch 9, Pt 1, para 5(b), with effect from 5 December 2005; for transitional provisions see Civil Partnership Act 2004, s 82, Sch 9, Pt 3.

87   Amendment: Words substituted: Civil Partnership Act 2004, s 82, Sch 9, Pt 1, para 5(b), with effect from 5 December 2005; for transitional provisions see Civil Partnership Act 2004, s 82, Sch 9, Pt 3.

88   Amendment: Words substituted: Civil Partnership Act 2004, s 82, Sch 9, Pt 1, para 5(b), with effect from 5 December 2005; for transitional provisions see Civil Partnership Act 2004, s 82, Sch 9, Pt 3.

89   Amendment: Words substituted: Civil Partnership Act 2004, s 82, Sch 9, Pt 1, para 5(b), with effect from 5 December 2005; for transitional provisions see Civil Partnership Act 2004, s 82, Sch 9, Pt 3.

90   Amendment: Words substituted: Civil Partnership Act 2004, s 82, Sch 9, Pt 1, para 5(b), with effect from 5 December 2005; for transitional provisions see Civil Partnership Act 2004, s 82, Sch 9, Pt 3.

91   Amendment: Words substituted: Civil Partnership Act 2004, s 82, Sch 9, Pt 1, para 5(b), with effect from 5 December 2005; for transitional provisions see Civil Partnership Act 2004, s 82, Sch 9, Pt 3.

92   Commencement: 1 October 1997 (SI 1997/1892).

93   Amendment: Words inserted: Civil Partnership Act 2004, s 82, Sch 9, Pt 1, para 6(1), (10), with effect from 5 December 2005; for transitional provisions see Civil Partnership Act 2004, s 82, Sch 9, Pt 3.

94   Amendment: Words inserted: Civil Partnership Act 2004, s 82, Sch 9, Pt 1, para 6(1), (2), with effect from 5 December 2005; for transitional provisions see Civil Partnership Act 2004, s 82, Sch 9, Pt 3.

95   Amendment: Words inserted: Civil Partnership Act 2004, s 82, Sch 9, Pt 1, para 6(1), (2), with effect from 5 December 2005; for transitional provisions see Civil Partnership Act 2004, s 82, Sch 9, Pt 3.

(ii)   in the case of former civil partners, was at any time their civil partnership home or was at any time intended by them to be their civil partnership home.][96]

(2)   The former spouse [or former civil partner][97] not so entitled may apply to the court for an order under this section against the other former spouse [or former civil partner][98] ('the respondent').

(3)   If the applicant is in occupation, an order under this section must contain provision—

(a)   giving the applicant the right not to be evicted or excluded from the dwelling-house or any part of it by the respondent for the period specified in the order; and

(b)   prohibiting the respondent from evicting or excluding the applicant during that period.

(4) If the applicant is not in occupation, an order under this section must contain provision—

(a)   giving the applicant the right to enter into and occupy the dwelling-house for the period specified in the order; and

(b)   requiring the respondent to permit the exercise of that right.

(5)   An order under this section may also—

(a)   regulate the occupation of the dwelling-house by either or both of the parties;

(b)   prohibit, suspend or restrict the exercise by the respondent of his right to occupy the dwelling-house;

(c)   require the respondent to leave the dwelling-house or part of the dwelling-house; or

(d)   exclude the respondent from a defined area in which the dwelling-house is included.

(6)   In deciding whether to make an order under this section containing provision of the kind mentioned in subsection (3) or (4) and (if so) in what manner, the court shall have regard to all the circumstances including—

(a)   the housing needs and housing resources of each of the parties and of any relevant child;

(b)   the financial resources of each of the parties;

(c)   the likely effect of any order, or of any decision by the court not to exercise its powers under subsection (3) or (4), on the health, safety or well-being of the parties and of any relevant child;

---

[96]   Amendment: Sub-paragraph substituted: Civil Partnership Act 2004, s 82, Sch 9, Pt 1, para 6(1), (3), with effect from 5 December 2005; for transitional provisions see Civil Partnership Act 2004, s 82, Sch 9, Pt 3.

[97]   Amendment: Words inserted: Civil Partnership Act 2004, s 82, Sch 9, Pt 1, para 6(1), (4), with effect from 5 December 2005; for transitional provisions see Civil Partnership Act 2004, s 82, Sch 9, Pt 3.

[98]   Amendment: Words inserted: Civil Partnership Act 2004, s 82, Sch 9, Pt 1, para 6(1), (4), with effect from 5 December 2005; for transitional provisions see Civil Partnership Act 2004, s 82, Sch 9, Pt 3.

(d)   the conduct of the parties in relation to each other and otherwise;

(e)   the length of time that has elapsed since the parties ceased to live together;

(f)   the length of time that has elapsed since the marriage [or civil partnership][99] was dissolved or annulled; and

(g)   the existence of any pending proceedings between the parties—

> (i)   for an order under section 23A or 24 of the Matrimonial Causes Act 1973 (property adjustment orders in connection with divorce proceedings etc);
>
> [(ia)   for a property adjustment order under Part 2 of Schedule 5 to the Civil Partnership Act 2004;][100]
>
> (ii)   for an order under paragraph 1(2)(d) or (e) of Schedule 1 to the Children Act 1989 (orders for financial relief against parents); or
>
> (iii)   relating to the legal or beneficial ownership of the dwelling-house.

(7)   In deciding whether to exercise its power to include one or more of the provisions referred to in subsection (5) ('a subsection (5) provision') and (if so) in what manner, the court shall have regard to all the circumstances including the matters mentioned in subsection (6)(a) to (e).

(8)   If the court decides to make an order under this section and it appears to it that, if the order does not include a subsection (5) provision, the applicant or any relevant child is likely to suffer significant harm attributable to conduct of the respondent, the court shall include the subsection (5) provision in the order unless it appears to the court that—

(a)   the respondent or any relevant child is likely to suffer significant harm if the provision is included in the order; and

(b)   the harm likely to be suffered by the respondent or child in that event is as great as or greater than the harm attributable to conduct of the respondent which is likely to be suffered by the applicant or child if the provision is not included.

(9)   An order under this section—

(a)   may not be made after the death of either of the former spouses [or former civil partners][101]; and

(b)   ceases to have effect on the death of either of them.

(10)   An order under this section must be limited so as to have effect for a specified period not exceeding six months, but may be extended on one or more occasions for a further specified period not exceeding six months.

---

[99]   Amendment: Words inserted: Civil Partnership Act 2004, s 82, Sch 9, Pt 1, para 6(1), (5), with effect from 5 December 2005; for transitional provisions see Civil Partnership Act 2004, s 82, Sch 9, Pt 3.

[100]   Amendment: Sub-paragraph inserted: Civil Partnership Act 2004, s 82, Sch 9, Pt 1, para 6(1), (6), with effect from 5 December 2005; for transitional provisions see Civil Partnership Act 2004, s 82, Sch 9, Pt 3.

[101]   Amendment: Words inserted: Civil Partnership Act 2004, s 82, Sch 9, Pt 1, para 6(1), (7), with effect from 5 December 2005; for transitional provisions see Civil Partnership Act 2004, s 82, Sch 9, Pt 3.

(11)   A former spouse [or former civil partner][102] who has an equitable interest in the dwelling-house or in the proceeds of sale of the dwelling-house but in whom there is not vested (whether solely or as joint tenant) a legal estate in fee simple or a legal term of years absolute in the dwelling-house is to be treated (but only for the purpose of determining whether he is eligible to apply under this section) as not being entitled to occupy the dwelling-house by virtue of that interest.

(12)   Subsection (11) does not prejudice any right of such a former spouse [or former civil partner][103] to apply for an order under section 33.

(13)   So long as an order under this section remains in force, subsections (3) to (6) of section 30 apply in relation to the applicant—

[(a)   as if he were B (the person entitled to occupy the dwelling-house by virtue of that section); and

(b)   as if the respondent were A (the person entitled as mentioned in subsection (1)(a) of that section)][104].

36[105]   One cohabitant or former cohabitant with no existing right to occupy

(1)   This section applies if—

(a)   one cohabitant or former cohabitant is entitled to occupy a dwelling-house by virtue of a beneficial estate or interest or contract or by virtue of any enactment giving him the right to remain in occupation;

(b)   the other cohabitant or former cohabitant is not so entitled; and

(c)   that dwelling-house is the home in which they [cohabit or a home in which they at any time cohabited or intended to cohabit][106]

(2)   The cohabitant or former cohabitant not so entitled may apply to the court for an order under this section against the other cohabitant or former cohabitant ('the respondent').

(3)   If the applicant is in occupation, an order under this section must contain provision—

(a)   giving the applicant the right not to be evicted or excluded from the dwelling-house or any part of it by the respondent for the period specified in the order, and

(b)   prohibiting the respondent from evicting or excluding the applicant during that period.

---

102   Amendment: Words inserted: Civil Partnership Act 2004, s 82, Sch 9, Pt 1, para 6(1), (8), with effect from 5 December 2005; for transitional provisions see Civil Partnership Act 2004, s 82, Sch 9, Pt 3.

103   Amendment: Words inserted: Civil Partnership Act 2004, s 82, Sch 9, Pt 1, para 6(1), (8), with effect from 5 December 2005; for transitional provisions see Civil Partnership Act 2004, s 82, Sch 9, Pt 3.

104   Amendment: Sub-paragraph substituted: Civil Partnership Act 2004, s 82, Sch 9, Pt 1, para 6(1), (9), with effect from 5 December 2005; for transitional provisions see Civil Partnership Act 2004, s 82, Sch 9, Pt 3.

105   Commencement: 1 October 1997 (SI 1997/1892).

106   Amendment: Words substituted: Domestic Violence, Crime and Victims Act 2004, s 58(1), Sch 10, para 34(1), (2), with effect from 5 December 2005.

(4) If the applicant is not in occupation, an order under this section must contain provision—

(a) giving the applicant the right to enter into and occupy the dwelling-house for the period specified in the order; and
(b) requiring the respondent to permit the exercise of that right.

(5) An order under this section may also—

(a) regulate the occupation of the dwelling-house by either or both of the parties;
(b) prohibit, suspend or restrict the exercise by the respondent of his right to occupy the dwelling-house;
(c) require the respondent to leave the dwelling-house or part of the dwelling-house; or
(d) exclude the respondent from a defined area in which the dwelling-house is included.

(6) In deciding whether to make an order under this section containing provision of the kind mentioned in subsection (3) or (4) and (if so) in what manner, the court shall have regard to all the circumstances including—

(a) the housing needs and housing resources of each of the parties and of any relevant child;
(b) the financial resources of each of the parties;
(c) the likely effect of any order, or of any decision by the court not to exercise its powers under subsection (3) or (4), on the health, safety or well-being of the parties and of any relevant child;
(d) the conduct of the parties in relation to each other and otherwise;
(e) the nature of the parties' relationship [and in particular the level of commitment involved in it][107];
(f) the length of time during which they have [cohabited][108];
(g) whether there are or have been any children who are children of both parties or for whom both parties have or have had parental responsibility;
(h) the length of time that has elapsed since the parties ceased to live together; and
(i) the existence of any pending proceedings between the parties—

　　(i) for an order under paragraph 1(2)(d) or (e) of Schedule 1 to the Children Act 1989 (orders for financial relief against parents), or
　　(ii) relating to the legal or beneficial ownership of the dwelling-house.

(7) In deciding whether to exercise its powers to include one or more of the provisions referred to in subsection (5) ('a subsection (5) provision') and (if so) in what manner, the court shall have regard to all the circumstances including—

(a) the matters mentioned in subsection (6)(a) to (d); and
(b) the questions mentioned in subsection (8).

---

[107] Amendment: Words inserted: Domestic Violence, Crime and Victims Act 2004, s 2(2), with effect from 5 December 2005.
[108] Amendment: Word substituted: Domestic Violence, Crime and Victims Act 2004, s 58(1), Sch 10, para 34(1), (3), with effect from 5 December 2005.

(8)   The questions are—

(a)   whether the applicant or any relevant child is likely to suffer significant harm attributable to conduct of the respondent if the subsection (5) provision is not included in the order; and

(b)   whether the harm likely to be suffered by the respondent or child if the provision is included is as great as or greater than the harm attributable to conduct of the respondent which is likely to be suffered by the applicant or child if the provision is not included.

(9)   An order under this section—

(a)   may not be made after the death of either of the parties; and

(b)   ceases to have effect on the death of either of them.

(10)   An order under this section must be limited so as to have effect for a specified period not exceeding six months, but may be extended on one occasion for a further specified period not exceeding six months.

(11)   A person who has an equitable interest in the dwelling-house or in the proceeds of sale of the dwelling-house but in whom there is not vested (whether solely or as joint tenant) a legal estate in fee simple or a legal term of years absolute in the dwelling-house is to be treated (but only for the purpose of determining whether he is eligible to apply under this section) as not being entitled to occupy the dwelling-house by virtue of that interest.

(12)   Subsection (11) does not prejudice any right of such a person to apply for an order under section 33.

(13)   So long as the order remains in force, subsections (3) to (6) of section 30 apply in relation to the applicant—

[(a)   as if he were B (the person entitled to occupy the dwelling-house by virtue of that section); and

(b)   as if the respondent were A (the person entitled as mentioned in subsection (1)(a) of that section)][109].

37[110]   Neither spouse [or civil partner][111] entitled to occupy

(1)   This section applies if—

(a)   one spouse or former spouse and the other spouse or former spouse occupy a dwelling-house which is or was the matrimonial home; but

(b)   neither of them is entitled to remain in occupation—

---

[109]   Amendment: Sub-paragraphs substituted: Civil Partnership Act 2004, s 82, Sch 9, Pt 1, para 7, with effect from 5 December 2005; for transitional provisions see Civil Partnership Act 2004, s 82, Sch 9, Pt 3.

[110]   Commencement: 1 October 1997 (SI 1997/1892).

[111]   Amendment: Words inserted: Civil Partnership Act 2004, s 82, Sch 9, Pt 1, para 8(1), (4), with effect from 5 December 2005; for transitional provisions see Civil Partnership Act 2004, s 82, Sch 9, Pt 3.

(i)   by virtue of a beneficial estate or interest or contract; or

(ii)   by virtue of any enactment giving him the right to remain in occupation.]

[(1A)   This section also applies if—

(a)   one civil partner or former civil partner and the other civil partner or former civil partner occupy a dwelling-house which is or was the civil partnership home; but

(b)   neither of them is entitled to remain in occupation—

(i)   by virtue of a beneficial estate or interest or contract; or

(ii)   by virtue of any enactment giving him the right to remain in occupation.][112]

(2)   Either of the parties may apply to the court for an order against the other under this section.

(3)   An order under this section may—

(a)   require the respondent to permit the applicant to enter and remain in the dwelling-house or part of the dwelling-house;

(b)   regulate the occupation of the dwelling-house by either or both of the [parties][113];

(c)   require the respondent to leave the dwelling-house or part of the dwelling-house; or

(d)   exclude the respondent from a defined area in which the dwelling-house is included.

(4)   Subsections (6) and (7) of section 33 apply to the exercise by the court of its powers under this section as they apply to the exercise by the court of its powers under subsection (3) of that section.

(5)   An order under this section must be limited so as to have effect for a specified period not exceeding six months, but may be extended on one or more occasions for a further specified period not exceeding six months.

38[114]   Neither cohabitant or former cohabitant entitled to occupy

(1)   This section applies if—

(a)   one cohabitant or former cohabitant and the other cohabitant or former cohabitant occupy a dwelling-house which is the home in which they [cohabit or cohabited][115]; but

---

[112] Amendment: Paragraph inserted: Civil Partnership Act 2004, s 82, Sch 9, Pt 1, para 8(1), (2), with effect from 5 December 2005; for transitional provisions see Civil Partnership Act 2004, s 82, Sch 9, Pt 3.

[113] Amendment: Word substituted: Civil Partnership Act 2004, s 82, Sch 9, Pt 1, para 8(1), (3), with effect from 5 December 2005; for transitional provisions see Civil Partnership Act 2004, s 82, Sch 9, Pt 3.

[114] Commencement: 1 October 1997 (SI 1997/1892).

[115] Amendment: Words substituted: Domestic Violence, Crime and Victims Act 2004, s 58(1), Sch 10, para 35, with effect from 5 December 2005.

(b)   neither of them is entitled to remain in occupation—

    (i)   by virtue of a beneficial estate or interest or contract; or

    (ii)   by virtue of any enactment giving him the right to remain in occupation.

(2)   Either of the parties may apply to the court for an order against the other under this section.

(3)   An order under this section may—

(a)   require the respondent to permit the applicant to enter and remain in the dwelling-house or part of the dwelling-house;

(b)   regulate the occupation of the dwelling-house by either or both of the parties;

(c)   require the respondent to leave the dwelling-house or part of the dwelling-house; or

(d)   exclude the respondent from a defined area in which the dwelling-house is included.

(4)   In deciding whether to exercise its powers to include one or more of the provisions referred to in subsection (3) ('a subsection (3) provision') and (if so) in what manner, the court shall have regard to all the circumstances including—

(a)   the housing needs and housing resources of each of the parties and of any relevant child;

(b)   the financial resources of each of the parties;

(c)   the likely effect of any order, or of any decision by the court not to exercise its powers under subsection (3), on the health, safety or well-being of the parties and of any relevant child;

(d)   the conduct of the parties in relation to each other and otherwise; and

(e)   the questions mentioned in subsection (5).

(5)   The questions are—

(a)   whether the applicant or any relevant child is likely to suffer significant harm attributable to conduct of the respondent if the subsection (3) provision is not included in the order; and

(b)   whether the harm likely to be suffered by the respondent or child if the provision is included is as great as or greater than the harm attributable to conduct of the respondent which is likely to be suffered by the applicant or child if the provision is not included.

(6)   An order under this section shall be limited so as to have effect for a specified period not exceeding six months, but may be extended on one occasion for a further specified period not exceeding six months.

39[116] Supplementary provisions

(1)   In this Part an 'occupation order' means an order under section 33, 35, 36, 37 or 38.

---

[116] Commencement: 1 October 1997 (SI 1997/1892).

(2)   An application for an occupation order may be made in other family proceedings or without any other family proceedings being instituted.

(3)   If—

(a)   an application for an occupation order is made under section 33, 35, 36, 37 or 38, and

(b)   the court considers that it has no power to make the order under the section concerned, but that it has power to make an order under one of the other sections,

the court may make an order under that other section.

(4)   The fact that a person has applied for an occupation order under sections 35 to 38, or that an occupation order has been made, does not affect the right of any person to claim a legal or equitable interest in any property in any subsequent proceedings (including subsequent proceedings under this Part).

40[117]   Additional provisions that may be included in certain occupation orders

(1)   The court may on, or at any time after, making an occupation order under section 33, 35 or 36—

(a)   impose on either party obligations as to—

(i)   the repair and maintenance of the dwelling-house; or
(ii)   the discharge of rent, mortgage payments or other outgoings affecting the dwelling-house;

(b)   order a party occupying the dwelling-house or any part of it (including a party who is entitled to do so by virtue of a beneficial estate or interest or contract or by virtue of any enactment giving him the right to remain in occupation) to make periodical payments to the other party in respect of the accommodation, if the other party would (but for the order) be entitled to occupy the dwelling-house by virtue of a beneficial estate or interest or contract or by virtue of any such enactment;

(c)   grant either party possession or use of furniture or other contents of the dwelling-house;

(d)   order either party to take reasonable care of any furniture or other contents of the dwelling-house;

(e)   order either party to take reasonable steps to keep the dwelling-house and any furniture or other contents secure.

(2)   In deciding whether and, if so, how to exercise its powers under this section, the court shall have regard to all the circumstances of the case including—

(a)   the financial needs and financial resources of the parties; and

(b)   the financial obligations which they have, or are likely to have in the foreseeable future, including financial obligations to each other and to any relevant child.

---

[117]   Commencement: 1 October 1997 (SI 1997/1892).

(3)   An order under this section ceases to have effect when the occupation order to which it relates ceases to have effect.

41   ...[118]

Non-molestation orders

42[119]   Non-molestation orders

(1)   In this Part a 'non-molestation order' means an order containing either or both of the following provisions—

(a)   provision prohibiting a person ('the respondent') from molesting another person who is associated with the respondent;

(b)   provision prohibiting the respondent from molesting a relevant child.

(2)   The court may make a non-molestation order—

(a)   if an application for the order has been made (whether in other family proceedings or without any other family proceedings being instituted) by a person who is associated with the respondent; or

(b)   if in any family proceedings to which the respondent is a party the court considers that the order should be made for the benefit of any other party to the proceedings or any relevant child even though no such application has been made.

(3)   In subsection (2) 'family proceedings' includes proceedings in which the court has made an emergency protection order under section 44 of the Children Act 1989 which includes an exclusion requirement (as defined in section 44A(3) of that Act).

(4)   Where an agreement to marry is terminated, no application under subsection (2)(a) may be made by virtue of section 62(3)(e) by reference to that agreement after the end of the period of three years beginning with the day on which it is terminated.

[(4ZA) If a civil partnership agreement (as defined by section 73 of the Civil Partnership Act 2004) is terminated, no application under this section may be made by virtue of section 62(3)(eza) by reference to that agreement after the end of the period of three years beginning with the day on which it is terminated.][120]

[(4A)   A court considering whether to make an occupation order shall also consider whether to exercise the power conferred by subsection (2)(b).

---

[118]   Amendment: Provision repealed: Domestic Violence, Crime and Victims Act 2004, ss 2(1), 58(2), Sch 11, with effect from 5 December 2005.

[119]   Commencement: 1 October 1997 (SI 1997/1892).

[120]   Prospective Amendment: Paragraph prospectively inserted: Civil Partnership Act 2004, s 82, Sch 9, Pt 1, para 9, from a date to be appointed.

(4B) In this Part "the applicant", in relation to a non-molestation order, includes (where the context permits) the person for whose benefit such an order would be or is made in exercise of the power conferred by subsection (2)(b).][121]

(5)   In deciding whether to exercise its powers under this section and, if so, in what manner, the court shall have regard to all the circumstances including the need to secure the health, safety and well-being—

(a)   of the applicant [or, in a case falling within subsection (2)(b), the person for whose benefit the order would be made] …[122]; and

(b)   of any relevant child.

(6)   A non-molestation order may be expressed so as to refer to molestation in general, to particular acts of molestation, or to both.

(7)   A non-molestation order may be made for a specified period or until further order.

(8)   A non-molestation order which is made in other family proceedings ceases to have effect if those proceedings are withdrawn or dismissed.

[42A   *Offence of breaching non-molestation order*]

[(1) A person who without reasonable excuse does anything that he is prohibited from doing by a non-molestation order is guilty of an offence.

(2)   In the case of a non-molestation order made by virtue of section 45(1), a person can be guilty of an offence under this section only in respect of conduct engaged in at a time when he was aware of the existence of the order.

(3)   Where a person is convicted of an offence under this section in respect of any conduct, that conduct is not punishable as a contempt of court.

(4)   A person cannot be convicted of an offence under this section in respect of any conduct which has been punished as a contempt of court.

(5)   A person guilty of an offence under this section is liable—

(a)   on conviction on indictment, to imprisonment for a term not exceeding five years, or a fine, or both;

(b)   on summary conviction, to imprisonment for a term not exceeding 12 months, or a fine not exceeding the statutory maximum, or both.

---

[121]   Prospective Amendment: Paragraphs prospectively inserted: Domestic Violence, Crime and Victims Act 2004, s 58(1), Sch 10, para 36(1), (2), from a date to be appointed.

[122]   Prospective Amendment: Words prospectively repealed: Domestic Violence, Crime and Victims Act 2004, s 58(1), (2), Sch 10, para 36(1), (3), Sch 11, from a date to be appointed.

(6)   *A reference in any enactment to proceedings under this Part, or to an order under this Part, does not include a reference to proceedings for an offence under this section or to an order made in such proceedings.*

'Enactment' includes an enactment contained in subordinate legislation within the meaning of the Interpretation Act 1978 (c 30).][123]

Further provisions relating to occupation and non-molestation orders

43[124]   Leave of court required for applications by children under sixteen

(1)   A child under the age of sixteen may not apply for an occupation order or a non-molestation order except with the leave of the court.

(2)   The court may grant leave for the purposes of subsection (1) only if it is satisfied that the child has sufficient understanding to make the proposed application for the occupation order or non-molestation order.

44[125]   Evidence of agreement to marry [or form a civil partnership][126]

(1)   Subject to subsection (2), the court shall not make an order under section 33 or 42 by virtue of section 62(3)(e) unless there is produced to it evidence in writing of the existence of the agreement to marry.

(2)   Subsection (1) does not apply if the court is satisfied that the agreement to marry was evidenced by—

(a)   the gift of an engagement ring by one party to the agreement to the other in contemplation of their marriage, or

(b)   a ceremony entered into by the parties in the presence of one or more other persons assembled for the purpose of witnessing the ceremony.

[(3)   Subject to subsection (4), the court shall not make an order under section 33 or 42 by virtue of section 62(3)(eza) unless there is produced to it evidence in writing of the existence of the civil partnership agreement (as defined by section 73 of the Civil Partnership Act 2004)

(4)   Subsection (3) does not apply if the court is satisfied that the civil partnership agreement was evidenced by—

(a)   a gift by one party to the agreement to the other as a token of the agreement, or

---

[123]   Prospective Amendment: Provision prospectively inserted: Domestic Violence, Crime and Victims Act 2004, s 1, from a date to be appointed; for transitional and transitory provisions see s 59, Sch 12, para 1.

[124]   Commencement: 1 October 1997 (SI 1997/1892).

[125]   Commencement: 1 October 1997 (SI 1997/1892).

[126]   Amendment: Words inserted: Civil Partnership Act 2004, s 82, Sch 9, Pt 1, para 10(2), with effect from 5 December 2005; for transitional provisions see Civil Partnership Act 2004, s 82, Sch 9, Pt 3.

(b) a ceremony entered into by the parties in the presence of one or more other persons assembled for the purpose of witnessing the ceremony.][127]

45[128]   Ex parte orders

(1) The court may, in any case where it considers that it is just and convenient to do so, make an occupation order or a non-molestation order even though the respondent has not been given such notice of the proceedings as would otherwise be required by rules of court.

(2) In determining whether to exercise its powers under subsection (1), the court shall have regard to all the circumstances including—

(a) any risk of significant harm to the applicant or a relevant child, attributable to conduct of the respondent, if the order is not made immediately;

(b) whether it is likely that the applicant will be deterred or prevented from pursuing the application if an order is not made immediately; and

(c) whether there is reason to believe that the respondent is aware of the proceedings but is deliberately evading service and that the applicant or a relevant child will be seriously prejudiced by the delay involved—

    (i) where the court is a magistrates' court, in effecting service of proceedings; or

    (ii) in any other case, in effecting substituted service.

(3) If the court makes an order by virtue of subsection (1) it must afford the respondent an opportunity to make representations relating to the order as soon as just and convenient at a full hearing.

(4) If, at a full hearing, the court makes an occupation order ('the full order'), then—

(a) for the purposes of calculating the maximum period for which the full order may be made to have effect, the relevant section is to apply as if the period for which the full order will have effect began on the date on which the initial order first had effect; and

(b) the provisions of section 36(10) or 38(6) as to the extension of orders are to apply as if the full order and the initial order were a single order.

(5) In this section—

'full hearing' means a hearing of which notice has been given to all the parties in accordance with rules of court;
'initial order' means an occupation order made by virtue of subsection (1); and
'relevant section' means section 33(10), 35(10), 36(10), 37(5) or 38(6).

---

[127] Amendment: Paragraphs inserted: Civil Partnership Act 2004, s 82, Sch 9, Pt 1, para 10(1), with effect from 5 December 2005; for transitional provisions see Civil Partnership Act 2004, s 82, Sch 9, Pt 3.
[128] Commencement: 1 October 1997 (SI 1997/1892).

46¹²⁹ Undertakings

(1)   In any case where the court has power to make an occupation order or non-molestation order, the court may accept an undertaking from any party to the proceedings.

(2)   No power of arrest may be attached to any undertaking given under subsection (1).

(3)   The court shall not accept an undertaking under subsection (1) [*instead of making an occupation order*]¹³⁰ in any case where apart from this section a power of arrest would be attached to the order.

[*(3A) The court shall not accept an undertaking under subsection (1) instead of making a non-molestation order in any case where it appears to the court that—*
(a)   the respondent has used or threatened violence against the applicant or a relevant child; and
(b)   for the protection of the applicant or child it is necessary to make a non-molestation order so that any breach may be punishable under section 42A.]¹³¹

(4)   An undertaking given to a court under subsection (1) is enforceable as if [it were an order of the court] [*the court had made an occupation order or a non-molestation order in terms corresponding to those of the undertaking*]¹³².

(5)   This section has effect without prejudice to the powers of the High Court and the county court apart from this section.

47¹³³   Arrest for breach of order

[(1)   *In this section 'a relevant order' means an occupation order or a non-molestation order.*]¹³⁴

(2)   If—

(a)   the court makes [a relevant order] [*an occupation order*]¹³⁵; and

---

129   Commencement: 1 October 1997 (SI 1997/1892).
130   Prospective Amendment: Words prospectively inserted: Domestic Violence, Crime and Victims Act 2004, s 58(1), Sch 10, para 37(1), (2), from a date to be appointed; for transitional and transitory provisions see s 59, Sch 12, para 1(1).
131   Prospective Amendment: Paragraph prospectively inserted: Domestic Violence, Crime and Victims Act 2004, s 58(1), Sch 10, para 37(1), (3), from a date to be appointed; for transitional and transitory provisions see s 59, Sch 12, para 1(1).
132   Prospective Amendment: Words prospectively substituted: Domestic Violence, Crime and Victims Act 2004, s 58(1), Sch 10, para 37(1), (4), from a date to be appointed; for transitional and transitory provisions see s 59, Sch 12, para 1(1).
133   Commencement: 1 October 1997 (SI 1997/1892).
134   Prospective Amendment: Paragraph prospectively repealed: Domestic Violence, Crime and Victims Act 2004, s 58(1), (2), Sch 10, para 38(1), (2), Sch 11, from a date to be appointed; for transitional and transitory provisions see s 59, Sch 12, para 1(1).
135   Prospective Amendment: Words prospectively substituted: Domestic Violence, Crime and Victims Act 2004, s 58(1), Sch 10, para 38(1), (3), from a date to be appointed; for transitional and transitory provisions see s 59, Sch 12, para 1(1).

(b)   it appears to the court that the respondent has used or threatened violence against the applicant or a relevant child,

it shall attach a power of arrest to one or more provisions of the order unless the court is satisfied that in all the circumstances of the case the applicant or child will be adequately protected without such a power of arrest.

(3)   Subsection (2) does not apply in any case where [the relevant order]*[the occupation order]*[136] is made by virtue of section 45(1), but in such a case the court may attach a power of arrest to one or more provisions of the order if it appears to it—

(a)   that the respondent has used or threatened violence against the applicant or a relevant child; and

(b)   that there is a risk of significant harm to the applicant or child, attributable to conduct of the respondent, if the power of arrest is not attached to those provisions immediately.

(4)   If, by virtue of subsection (3), the court attaches a power of arrest to any provisions of [a relevant order]*[an occupation order]*[137], it may provide that the power of arrest is to have effect for a shorter period than the other provisions of the order.

(5)   Any period specified for the purposes of subsection (4) may be extended by the court (on one or more occasions) on an application to vary or discharge [the relevant order]*[the occupation order]*[138].

(6)   If, by virtue of subsection (2) or (3), a power of arrest is attached to certain provisions of an order, a constable may arrest without warrant a person whom he has reasonable cause for suspecting to be in breach of any such provision.

(7)   If a power of arrest is attached under subsection (2) or (3) to certain provisions of the order and the respondent is arrested under subsection (6)—

(a)   he must be brought before the relevant judicial authority within the period of 24 hours beginning at the time of his arrest; and

(b)   if the matter is not then disposed of forthwith, the relevant judicial authority before whom he is brought may remand him.

In reckoning for the purposes of this subsection any period of 24 hours, no account is to be taken of Christmas Day, Good Friday or any Sunday.

[(8)   If the court has made a relevant order but—

---

[136]   Prospective Amendment: Words prospectively substituted: Domestic Violence, Crime and Victims Act 2004, s 58(1), Sch 10, para 38(1), (4), from a date to be appointed; for transitional and transitory provisions see s 59, Sch 12, para 1(1).

[137]   Prospective Amendment: Words prospectively substituted: Domestic Violence, Crime and Victims Act 2004, s 58(1), Sch 10, para 38(1), (3), from a date to be appointed; for transitional and transitory provisions see s 59, Sch 12, para 1(1).

[138]   Prospective Amendment: Words prospectively substituted: Domestic Violence, Crime and Victims Act 2004, s 58(1), Sch 10, para 38(1), (4), from a date to be appointed; for transitional and transitory provisions see s 59, Sch 12, para 1(1).

(a)   has not attached a power of arrest under subsection (2) or (3) to any provisions of the order, or

(b)   has attached that power only to certain provisions of the order,]

[(8)   *If the court—*

(a)   has made a non-molestation order, or

(b)   has made an occupation order but has not attached a power of arrest under subsection (2) or (3) to any provision of the order, or has attached that power only to certain provisions of the order,][139]

then, if at any time the applicant considers that the respondent has failed to comply with the order, he may apply to the relevant judicial authority for the issue of a warrant for the arrest of the respondent.

(9)   The relevant judicial authority shall not issue a warrant on an application under subsection (8) unless—

(a)   the application is substantiated on oath; and

(b)   the relevant judicial authority has reasonable grounds for believing that the respondent has failed to comply with the order.

(10)   If a person is brought before a court by virtue of a warrant issued under subsection (9) and the court does not dispose of the matter forthwith, the court may remand him.

(11)   Schedule 5 (which makes provision corresponding to that applying in magistrates' courts in civil cases under sections 128 and 129 of the Magistrates' Courts Act 1980) has effect in relation to the powers of the High Court and a county court to remand a person by virtue of this section.

(12)   If a person remanded under this section is granted bail (whether in the High Court or a county court under Schedule 5 or in a magistrates' court under section 128 or 129 of the Magistrates' Courts Act 1980), he may be required by the relevant judicial authority to comply, before release on bail or later, with such requirements as appear to that authority to be necessary to secure that he does not interfere with witnesses or otherwise obstruct the course of justice.

48[140]   Remand for medical examination and report

(1)   If the relevant judicial authority has reason to consider that a medical report will be required, any power to remand a person under section 47(7)(b) or (10) may be exercised for the purpose of enabling a medical examination and report to be made.

(2)   If such a power is so exercised, the adjournment must not be for more than 4 weeks at a time unless the relevant judicial authority remands the accused in custody.

---

[139]   Prospective Amendment: Sub-paragraph prospectively substituted: Domestic Violence, Crime and Victims Act 2004, s 58(1), Sch 10, para 38(1), (5), from a date to be appointed; for transitional and transitory provisions see s 59, Sch 12, para 1(1).

[140]   Commencement: 1 October 1997 (SI 1997/1892).

(3)   If the relevant judicial authority so remands the accused, the adjournment must not be for more than 3 weeks at a time.

(4)   If there is reason to suspect that a person who has been arrested—

(a)   under section 47(6), or

(b)   under a warrant issued on an application made under section 47(8),

is suffering from mental illness or severe mental impairment, the relevant judicial authority has the same power to make an order under section 35 of the Mental Health Act 1983 (remand for report on accused's mental condition) as the Crown Court has under section 35 of the Act of 1983 in the case of an accused person within the meaning of that section.

49[141]   Variation and discharge of orders

(1)   An occupation order or non-molestation order may be varied or discharged by the court on an application by—

(a)   the respondent, or

(b)   the person on whose application the order was made.

(2)   In the case of a non-molestation order made by virtue of section 42(2)(b), the order may be varied or discharged by the court even though no such application has been made.

(3)   If [B's home rights are, under section 31][142] a charge on the estate or interest of the other spouse or of trustees for [A][143], an order under section 33 against [A][144] may also be varied or discharged by the court on an application by any person deriving title under [A][145] or under the trustees and affected by the charge.

(4)   If, by virtue of section 47(3), a power of arrest has been attached to certain provisions of an occupation order [*or non-molestation order*][146], the court may vary or discharge the order under subsection (1) in so far as it confers a power of arrest (whether or not any application has been made to vary or discharge any other provision of the order).

---

[141]   Commencement: 1 October 1997 (SI 1997/1892).

[142]   Amendment: Words substituted: Civil Partnership Act 2004, s 82, Sch 9, Pt 1, para 11(a), with effect from 5 December 2005; for transitional provisions see Civil Partnership Act 2004, s 82, Sch 9, Pt 3.

[143]   Amendment: Reference substituted: Civil Partnership Act 2004, s 82, Sch 9, Pt 1, para 11(b), with effect from 5 December 2005; for transitional provisions see Civil Partnership Act 2004, s 82, Sch 9, Pt 3.

[144]   Amendment: Reference number substituted: Civil Partnership Act 2004, s 82, Sch 9, Pt 1, para 11(b), with effect from 5 December 2005; for transitional provisions see Civil Partnership Act 2004, s 82, Sch 9, Pt 3.

[145]   Amendment: Reference number substituted: Civil Partnership Act 2004, s 82, Sch 9, Pt 1, para 11(b), with effect from 5 December 2005; for transitional provisions see Civil Partnership Act 2004, s 82, Sch 9, Pt 3.

[146]   Prospective Amendment: Words prospectively repealed: Domestic Violence, Crime and Victims Act 2004, s 58(1), (2), Sch 10, para 39, Sch 11, from a date to be appointed; for transitional and transitory provisions see s 59, Sch 12, para 1(1).

Enforcement powers of magistrates' courts

50[147] Power of magistrates' court to suspend execution of committal order

(1) If, under section 63(3) of the Magistrates' Courts Act 1980, a magistrates' court has power to commit a person to custody for breach of a relevant requirement, the court may by order direct that the execution of the order of committal is to be suspended for such period or on such terms and conditions as it may specify.

(2) In subsection (1) 'a relevant requirement' means—

(a) an occupation order or non-molestation order;
(b) an exclusion requirement included by virtue of section 38A of the Children Act 1989 in an interim care order made under section 38 of that Act; or
(c) an exclusion requirement included by virtue of section 44A of the Children Act 1989 in an emergency protection order under section 44 of that Act.

51[148] Power of magistrates' court to order hospital admission or guardianship

(1) A magistrates' court shall have the same power to make a hospital order or guardianship order under section 37 of the Mental Health Act 1983 or an interim hospital order under section 38 of that Act in the case of a person suffering from mental illness or severe mental impairment who could otherwise be committed to custody for breach of a relevant requirement as a magistrates' court has under those sections in the case of a person convicted of an offence punishable on summary conviction with imprisonment.

(2) In subsection (1) 'a relevant requirement' has the meaning given by section 50(2).

Interim care orders and emergency protection orders

52[149] Amendments of Children Act 1989

Schedule 6 makes amendments of the provisions of the Children Act 1989 relating to interim care orders and emergency protection orders.

Transfer of tenancies

53[150] Transfer of certain tenancies

Schedule 7 makes provision in relation to the transfer of certain tenancies on divorce etc or on separation of cohabitants.

Dwelling-house subject to mortgage

---

[147] Commencement: 1 October 1997 (SI 1997/1892).
[148] Commencement: 1 October 1997 (SI 1997/1892).
[149] Commencement: 1 October 1997 (SI 1997/1892).
[150] Commencement: 1 October 1997 (SI 1997/1892).

54[151]   **Dwelling-house subject to mortgage**

(1)   In determining for the purposes of this Part whether a person is entitled to occupy a dwelling-house by virtue of an estate or interest, any right to possession of the dwelling-house conferred on a mortgagee of the dwelling-house under or by virtue of his mortgage is to be disregarded.

(2)   Subsection (1) applies whether or not the mortgagee is in possession.

(3)   Where a person ('A') is entitled to occupy a dwelling-house by virtue of an estate or interest, a connected person does not by virtue of—

(a)   any [home rights][152] conferred by section 30, or
(b)   any rights conferred by an order under section 35 or 36,

have any larger right against the mortgagee to occupy the dwelling-house than A has by virtue of his estate or interest and of any contract with the mortgagee.

(4)   Subsection (3) does not apply, in the case of [home rights][153], if under section 31 those rights are a charge, affecting the mortgagee, on the estate or interest mortgaged.

(5)   In this section 'connected person', in relation to any person, means that person's spouse, former spouse[, civil partner, former civil partner][154], cohabitant or former cohabitant.

55[155]   **Actions by mortgagees: joining connected persons as parties**

(1)   This section applies if a mortgagee of land which consists of or includes a dwelling-house brings an action in any court for the enforcement of his security.

(2)   A connected person who is not already a party to the action is entitled to be made a party in the circumstances mentioned in subsection (3).

(3)   The circumstances are that—

(a)   the connected person is enabled by section 30(3) or (6) (or by section 30(3) or (6) as applied by section 35(13) or 36(13)), to meet the mortgagor's liabilities under the mortgage;
(b)   he has applied to the court before the action is finally disposed of in that court; and

---

[151]   Commencement: 1 October 1997 (SI 1997/1892).
[152]   Amendment: Words substituted: Civil Partnership Act 2004, s 82, Sch 9, Pt 1, para 12(1), (2), with effect from 5 December 2005; for transitional provisions see Civil Partnership Act 2004, s 82, Sch 9, Pt 3.
[153]   Amendment: Words substituted: Civil Partnership Act 2004, s 82, Sch 9, Pt 1, para 12(1), (2), with effect from 5 December 2005; for transitional provisions see Civil Partnership Act 2004, s 82, Sch 9, Pt 3.
[154]   Amendment: Words inserted: Civil Partnership Act 2004, s 82, Sch 9, Pt 1, para 12(1), (3), with effect from 5 December 2005; for transitional provisions see Civil Partnership Act 2004, s 82, Sch 9, Pt 3.
[155]   Commencement: 1 October 1997 (SI 1997/1892).

(c)   the court sees no special reason against his being made a party to the action and is satisfied—

    (i)   that he may be expected to make such payments or do such other things in or towards satisfaction of the mortgagor's liabilities or obligations as might affect the outcome of the proceedings; or

    (ii)   that the expectation of it should be considered under section 36 of the Administration of Justice Act 1970.

(4)   In this section 'connected person' has the same meaning as in section 54.

56[156]   Actions by mortgagees: service of notice on certain persons

(1)   This section applies if a mortgagee of land which consists, or substantially consists, of a dwelling-house brings an action for the enforcement of his security, and at the relevant time there is—

(a)   in the case of unregistered land, a land charge of Class F registered against the person who is the estate owner at the relevant time or any person who, where the estate owner is a trustee, preceded him as trustee during the subsistence of the mortgage; or

(b)   in the case of registered land, a subsisting registration of—

    (i)   a notice under section 31(10);

    (ii)   a notice under section 2(8) of the Matrimonial Homes Act 1983; or

    (iii)   a notice or caution under section 2(7) of the Matrimonial Homes Act 1967.

(2)   If the person on whose behalf—

(a)   the land charge is registered, or

(b)   the notice or caution is entered,

is not a party to the action, the mortgagee must serve notice of the action on him.

(3)   If—

(a)   an official search has been made on behalf of the mortgagee which would disclose any land charge of Class F, notice or caution within subsection (1)(a) or (b),

(b)   a certificate of the result of the search has been issued, and

(c)   the action is commenced within the priority period,

the relevant time is the date of the certificate.

(4)   In any other case the relevant time is the time when the action is commenced.

(5)   The priority period is, for both registered and unregistered land, the period for which, in accordance with section 11(5) and (6) of the Land Charges Act 1972, a certificate on an official search operates in favour of a purchaser.

---

[156]   Commencement: 1 October 1997 (SI 1997/1892).

Jurisdiction and procedure etc

57[157] Jurisdiction of courts

(1)   For the purposes of this Act 'the court' means the High Court, a county court or a magistrates' court.

(2)   Subsection (1) above is subject to the provision made by or under the following provisions of this section, to section 59 and to any express provision as to the jurisdiction of any court made by any other provision of this Part.

(3)   The Lord Chancellor may, *[after consulting the Lord Chief Justice,]*[158] by order specify proceedings under this Act which may only be commenced in—

(a)   a specified level of court;
(b)   a court which falls within a specified class of court; or
(c)   a particular court determined in accordance with, or specified in, the order.

(4)   The Lord Chancellor may, *[after consulting the Lord Chief Justice,]*[159] by order specify circumstances in which specified proceedings under this Part may only be commenced in—

(a)   a specified level of court;
(b)   a court which falls within a specified class of court; or
(c)   a particular court determined in accordance with, or specified in, the order.

(5)   The Lord Chancellor may, *[after consulting the Lord Chief Justice,]*[160] by order provide that in specified circumstances the whole, or any specified part of any specified proceedings under this Part shall be transferred to—

(a)   a specified level of court;
(b)   a court which falls within a specified class of court; or
(c)   a particular court determined in accordance with, or specified in, the order.

(6)   An order under subsection (5) may provide for the transfer to be made at any stage, or specified stage, of the proceedings and whether or not the proceedings, or any part of them, have already been transferred.

(7)   An order under subsection (5) may make provision as the Lord Chancellor thinks appropriate, *[after consulting the Lord Chief Justice]*[161] for excluding specified proceedings from the operation of section 38 or 39 of the Matrimonial and Family

---

[157]   Commencement: 28 July 1997 (SI 1997/1892).
[158]   Prospective amendment: Words prospectively inserted: Constitutional Reform Act 2005, s 15(1), Sch 4, Pt 1, paras 252, 253(1), (2), from a date to be appointed.
[159]   Prospective amendment: Words prospectively inserted: Constitutional Reform Act 2005, s 15(1), Sch 4, Pt 1, paras 252, 253(1), (2), from a date to be appointed.
[160]   Prospective amendment: Words prospectively inserted: Constitutional Reform Act 2005, s 15(1), Sch 4, Pt 1, paras 252, 253(1), (2), from a date to be appointed.
[161]   Prospective amendment: Words prospectively inserted: Constitutional Reform Act 2005, s 15(1), Sch 4, Pt 1, paras 252, 253(1), (3), from a date to be appointed.

Proceedings Act 1984 (transfer of family proceedings) or any other enactment which would otherwise govern the transfer of those proceedings, or any part of them.

(8)   For the purposes of subsections (3), (4) and (5), there are three levels of court—

(a)   the High Court;
(b)   any county court; and
(c)   any magistrates' court.

(9)   The Lord Chancellor may, [*after consulting the Lord Chief Justice,*]162 by order make provision for the principal registry of the Family Division of the High Court to be treated as if it were a county court for specified purposes of this Part, or of any provision made under this Part.

(10)   Any order under subsection (9) may make such provision as the Lord Chancellor thinks expedient, [*after consulting the Lord Chief Justice,*]163 for the purpose of applying (with or without modifications) provisions which apply in relation to the procedure in county courts to the principal registry when it acts as if it were a county court.

(11)   In this section 'specified' means specified by an order under this section.

[*(12)   The Lord Chief Justice may nominate a judicial office holder (as defined in section 109(4) of the Constitutional Reform Act 2005) to exercise his functions under this section.*]164

58165   Contempt proceedings

The powers of the court in relation to contempt of court arising out of a person's failure to comply with an order under this Part may be exercised by the relevant judicial authority.

59166   Magistrates' courts

(1)   A magistrates' court shall not be competent to entertain any application, or make any order, involving any disputed question as to a party's entitlement to occupy any property by virtue of a beneficial estate or interest or contract or by virtue of any enactment giving him the right to remain in occupation, unless it is unnecessary to determine the question in order to deal with the application or make the order.

(2)   A magistrates' court may decline jurisdiction in any proceedings under this Part if it considers that the case can more conveniently be dealt with by another court.

---

162   Prospective amendment: Words prospectively inserted: Constitutional Reform Act 2005, s 15(1), Sch 4, Pt 1, paras 252, 253(1), (4), from a date to be appointed.
163   Prospective amendment: Words prospectively inserted: Constitutional Reform Act 2005, s 15(1), Sch 4, Pt 1, paras 252, 253(1), (5), from a date to be appointed.
164   Prospective amendment: Sub-paragraph prospectively inserted: Constitutional Reform Act 2005, s 15(1), Sch 4, Pt 1, paras 252, 253(1), (6), from a date to be appointed.
165   Commencement: 1 October 1997 (SI 1997/1892).
166   Commencement: 1 October 1997 (SI 1997/1892).

(3)   The powers of a magistrates' court under section 63(2) of the Magistrates' Courts Act 1980 to suspend or rescind orders shall not apply in relation to any order made under this Part.

60[167]   **Provision for third parties to act on behalf of victims of domestic violence**

(1)   Rules of court may provide for a prescribed person, or any person in a prescribed category, ('a representative') to act on behalf of another in relation to proceedings to which this Part applies.

(2)   Rules made under this section may, in particular, authorise a representative to apply for an occupation order or for a non-molestation order for which the person on whose behalf the representative is acting could have applied.

(3)   Rules made under this section may prescribe—

(a)   conditions to be satisfied before a representative may make an application to the court on behalf of another; and

(b)   considerations to be taken into account by the court in determining whether, and if so how, to exercise any of its powers under this Part when a representative is acting on behalf of another.

(4)   Any rules made under this section may be made so as to have effect for a specified period and may make consequential or transitional provision with respect to the expiry of the specified period.

(5)   Any such rules may be replaced by further rules made under this section.

61[168]   **Appeals**

(1)   An appeal shall lie to the High Court against—

(a)   the making by a magistrates' court of any order under this Part, or

(b)   any refusal by a magistrates' court to make such an order,

but no appeal shall lie against any exercise by a magistrates' court of the power conferred by section 59(2).

(2)   On an appeal under this section, the High Court may make such orders as may be necessary to give effect to its determination of the appeal.

(3)   Where an order is made under subsection (2), the High Court may also make such incidental or consequential orders as appear to it to be just.

---

[167]   Commencement: Not yet in force.
[168]   Commencement: 1 October 1997 (SI 1997/1892).

(4) Any order of the High Court made on an appeal under this section (other than one directing that an application be re-heard by a magistrates' court) shall, for the purposes—

(a) of the enforcement of the order, and

(b) of any power to vary, revive or discharge orders,

be treated as if it were an order of the magistrates' court from which the appeal was brought and not an order of the High Court.

(5) The Lord Chancellor may, [*after consulting the Lord Chief Justice,*][169] by order make provision as to the circumstances in which appeals may be made against decisions taken by courts on questions arising in connection with the transfer, or proposed transfer, of proceedings by virtue of any order under section 57(5).

(6) Except to the extent provided for in any order made under subsection (5), no appeal may be made against any decision of a kind mentioned in that subsection.

[*(7) The Lord Chief Justice may nominate a judicial office holder (as defined in section 109(4) of the Constitutional Reform Act 2005) to exercise his functions under this section.*][170]

General

62[171] Meaning of 'cohabitants', 'relevant child' and 'associated persons'

(1) For the purposes of this Part—

(a) 'cohabitants' are [[two persons who are neither married to each other nor civil partners of each other but are living together as husband and wife or as if they were civil partners;][172] and][173]

(b) ['cohabit' and 'former cohabitants' are to be read accordingly, but the latter expression][174] does not include cohabitants who have subsequently married each other [or become civil partners of each other][175].

(2) In this Part, 'relevant child', in relation to any proceedings under this Part, means—

---

[169] Prospective amendment: Words prospectively inserted: Constitutional Reform Act 2005, s 15(1), Sch 4, Pt 1, paras 252, 254(1), (2), from a date to be appointed.

[170] Prospective amendment: Sub-paragraph prospectively inserted: Constitutional Reform Act 2005, s 15(1), Sch 4, Pt 1, paras 252, 254(1), (3), from a date to be appointed.

[171] Commencement: 1 October 1997 (SI 1997/1892).

[172] Amendment: Words substituted: Civil Partnership Act 2004, s 82, Sch 9, Pt 1, para 13(1), (2)(a), with effect from 5 December 2005; for transitional provisions see Civil Partnership Act 2004, s 82, Sch 9, Pt 3.

[173] Amendment: Words substituted: Domestic Violence, Crime and Victims Act 2004, s 3, with effect from 5 December 2005.

[174] Amendment: Words substituted: Domestic Violence, Crime and Victims Act 2004, s 58(1), Sch 10, para 40, with effect from 5 December 2005.

[175] Amendment: Words inserted: Civil Partnership Act 2004, s 82, Sch 9, Pt 1, para 13(1), (2)(b), with effect from 5 December 2005; for transitional provisions see Civil Partnership Act 2004, s 82, Sch 9, Pt 3.

(a)　any child who is living with or might reasonably be expected to live with either party to the proceedings;

(b)　any child in relation to whom an order under the Adoption Act 1976[, the Adoption and Children Act 2002][176] or the Children Act 1989 is in question in the proceedings; and

(c)　any other child whose interests the court considers relevant.

(3)　For the purposes of this Part, a person is associated with another person if—

(a)　they are or have been married to each other;

[(aa)　they are or have been civil partners of each other;][177]

(b)　they are cohabitants or former cohabitants;

(c)　they live or have lived in the same household, otherwise than merely by reason of one of them being the other's employee, tenant, lodger or boarder;

(d)　they are relatives;

(e)　they have agreed to marry one another (whether or not that agreement has been terminated);

[(eza)　they have entered into a civil partnership agreement (as defined by section 73 of the Civil Partnership Act 2004) (whether or not that agreement has been terminated);][178]

[*(ea)　they have or have had an intimate personal relationship with each other which is or was of significant duration;*][179]

(f)　in relation to any child, they are both persons falling within subsection (4); or

(g)　they are parties to the same family proceedings (other than proceedings under this Part).

(4)　A person falls within this subsection in relation to a child if—

(a)　he is a parent of the child; or

(b)　he has or has had parental responsibility for the child.

(5)　If a child has been adopted or [falls within subsection (7)][180], two persons are also associated with each other for the purpose of this Part if—

(a)　one is a natural parent of the child or a parent of such a natural parent; and

(b)　the other is the child or any person—

(i)　who had become a parent of the child by virtue of an adoption order or has applied for an adoption order, or

---

[176]　Amendment: Words inserted: Adoption and Children Act 2002, s 139(1), Sch 3, paras 85, 86(a), with effect from 30 December 2005.

[177]　Amendment: Sub-paragraph inserted: Civil Partnership Act 2004, s 82, Sch 9, Pt 1, para 13(1), (3), with effect from 5 December 2005; for transitional provisions see Civil Partnership Act 2004, s 82, Sch 9, Pt 3.

[178]　Amendment: Sub-paragraph inserted: Civil Partnership Act 2004, s 82, Sch 9, Pt 1, para 13(1), (4), with effect from 5 December 2005; for transitional provisions see Civil Partnership Act 2004, s 82, Sch 9, Pt 3.

[179]　Prospective amendment: Sub-paragraph prospectively inserted: Domestic Violence, Crime and Victims Act 2004, s 4, from a date to be appointed.

[180]　Amendment: Words substituted: Adoption and Children Act 2002, s 139(1), Sch 3, paras 85, 86(b), with effect from 30 December 2005.

(ii) with whom the child has at any time been placed for adoption.

(6) A body corporate and another person are not, by virtue of subsection (3)(f) or (g), to be regarded for the purposes of this Part as associated with each other.

[(7) A child falls within this subsection if—

(a) an adoption agency, within the meaning of section 2 of the Adoption and Children Act 2002, has power to place him for adoption under section 19 of that Act (placing children with parental consent) or he has become the subject of an order under section 21 of that Act (placement orders), or

(b) he is freed for adoption by virtue of an order made—

(i) in England and Wales, under section 18 of the Adoption Act 1976,

(ii) in Scotland, under section 18 of the Adoption (Scotland) Act 1978, or

(iii) in Northern Ireland, under Article 17(1) or 18(1) of the Adoption (Northern Ireland) Order 1987.][181]

63[182] Interpretation of Part IV

(1) In this Part—

['adoption order' means an adoption order within the meaning of section 72(1) of the Adoption Act 1976 or section 46(1) of the Adoption and Children Act 2002;][183]
'associated', in relation to a person, is to be read with section 62(3) to (6);
'child' means a person under the age of eighteen years;
['cohabit',][184] 'cohabitant' and 'former cohabitant' have the meaning given by section 62(1);
'the court' is to be read with section 57;
'development' means physical, intellectual, emotional, social or behavioural development;
'dwelling-house' includes (subject to subsection (4))—

(a) any building or part of a building which is occupied as a dwelling,

(b) any caravan, house-boat or structure which is occupied as a dwelling,

and any yard, garden, garage or outhouse belonging to it and occupied with it;
'family proceedings' means any proceedings—

(a) under the inherent jurisdiction of the High Court in relation to children; or

(b) under the enactments mentioned in subsection (2);

'harm'—

---

[181] Amendment: Paragraph inserted: Adoption and Children Act 2002, s 139(1), Sch 3, paras 85, 87, with effect from 30 December 2005.

[182] Commencement: 1 October 1997 (SI 1997/1892).

[183] Amendment: Definition 'adoption order' substituted: Adoption and Children Act 2002, s 139(1), Sch 3, paras 85, 88(a), with effect from 30 December 2005.

[184] Amendment: Word inserted: Domestic Violence, Crime and Victims Act 2004, s 58(1), Sch 10, para 41(1), (2), with effect from 5 December 2005.

(a)   in relation to a person who has reached the age of eighteen years, means ill-treatment or the impairment of health; and

(b)   in relation to a child, means ill-treatment or the impairment of health or development;

'health' includes physical or mental health;

'home rights' has the meaning given by section 30;][185]

'ill-treatment' includes forms of ill-treatment which are not physical and, in relation to a child, includes sexual abuse;

...[186]

'mortgage', 'mortgagor' and 'mortgagee' have the same meaning as in the Law of Property Act 1925;

'mortgage payments' includes any payments which, under the terms of the mortgage, the mortgagor is required to make to any person;

'non-molestation order' has the meaning given by section 42(1);

'occupation order' has the meaning given by section 39;

'parental responsibility' has the same meaning as in the Children Act 1989;

'relative', in relation to a person, means—

(a)   the father, mother, stepfather, stepmother, son, daughter, stepson, stepdaughter, grandmother, grandfather, grandson or granddaughter of that person or of that person's [spouse, former spouse, civil partner or former civil partner][187], or

(b)   the brother, sister, uncle, aunt, niece[, nephew or first cousin][188] (whether of the full blood or of the half blood or [by marriage or civil partnership)][189] of that person or of that person's [spouse, former spouse, civil partner or former civil partner][190],

and includes, in relation to a person who [is cohabiting or has cohabited with another person][191], any person who would fall within paragraph (a) or (b) if the parties were married to each other [or were civil partners of each other][192];

---

[185]   Amendment: Definition 'home rights' inserted: Civil Partnership Act 2004, s 82, Sch 9, Pt 1, para 14(1), (2), with effect from 5 December 2005; for transitional provisions see Civil Partnership Act 2004, s 82, Sch 9, Pt 3.

[186]   Amendment: Definition 'matrimonial home rights' repealed: Civil Partnership Act 2004, ss 82, 261(4), Sch 9, Pt 1, para 14(1), (3), Sch 30, with effect from 5 December 2005; for transitional provisions see Civil Partnership Act 2004, s 82, Sch 9, Pt 3.

[187]   Amendment: Words substituted: Civil Partnership Act 2004, s 82, Sch 9, Pt 1, para 14(1), (4)(a), with effect from 5 December 2005; for transitional provisions see Civil Partnership Act 2004, s 82, Sch 9, Pt 3.

[188]   Amendment: Word substituted: Domestic Violence, Crime and Victims Act 2004, s 58(1), Sch 10, para 41(1), (3)(a), with effect from 5 December 2005.

[189]   Amendment: Words substituted: Civil Partnership Act 2004, s 82, Sch 9, Pt 1, para 14(1), (4)(b), with effect from 5 December 2005; for transitional provisions see Civil Partnership Act 2004, s 82, Sch 9, Pt 3.

[190]   Amendment: Words substituted: Civil Partnership Act 2004, s 82, Sch 9, Pt 1, para 14(1), (4)(a), with effect from 5 December 2005; for transitional provisions see Civil Partnership Act 2004, s 82, Sch 9, Pt 3.

[191]   Amendment: Word substituted: Domestic Violence, Crime and Victims Act 2004, s 58(1), Sch 10, para 41(1), (3)(b), with effect from 5 December 2005.

[192]   Amendment: Words substituted: Civil Partnership Act 2004, s 82, Sch 9, Pt 1, para 14(1), (4)(c), with effect from 5 December 2005; for transitional provisions see Civil Partnership Act 2004, s 82, Sch 9, Pt 3.

'relevant child', in relation to any proceedings under this Part, has the meaning given by section 62(2);

'the relevant judicial authority', in relation to any order under this Part, means—

(a) where the order was made by the High Court, a judge of that court;

(b) where the order was made by a county court, a judge or district judge of that or any other county court; or

(c) where the order was made by a magistrates' court, any magistrates' court.

(2) The enactments referred to in the definition of 'family proceedings' are—

(a) Part II;

(b) this Part;

(c) the Matrimonial Causes Act 1973;

(d) the Adoption Act 1976;

(e) the Domestic Proceedings and Magistrates' Court Act 1978;

(f) Part III of the Matrimonial and Family Proceedings Act 1984;

(g) Parts I, II and IV of the Children Act 1989;

(h) section 30 of the Human Fertilisation and Embryology Act 1990;

[(i) the Adoption and Children Act 2002][193];

[(j) Schedules 5 to 7 to the Civil Partnership Act 2004][194].

(3) Where the question of whether harm suffered by a child is significant turns on the child's health or development, his health or development shall be compared with that which could reasonably be expected of a similar child.

(4) For the purposes of sections 31, 32, 53 and 54 and such other provisions of this Part (if any) as may be prescribed, this Part is to have effect as if paragraph (b) of the definition of 'dwelling-house' were omitted.

(5) It is hereby declared that this Part applies as between the parties to a marriage even though either of them is, or has at any time during the marriage been, married to more than one person.

Part V

Supplemental

64[195] Provision for separate representation for children

(1) The Lord Chancellor may by regulation provide for the separate representation of children in proceedings in England and Wales which relate to any matter in respect of which a question has arisen, or may arise, under—

---

[193] Amendment: Sub-paragraph inserted: Adoption and Children Act 2002, s 139(1), Sch 3, paras 85, 88(b), with effect from 30 December 2005.

[194] Amendment: Sub-paragraph inserted: Civil Partnership Act 2004, s 82, Sch 9, Pt 1, para 14(1), (5), with effect from 5 December 2005; for transitional provisions see Civil Partnership Act 2004, s 82, Sch 9, Pt 3.

[195] Commencement: Not yet in force.

(a) Part II;
(b) Part IV;
(c) the 1973 Act; [...][196]
(d) the Domestic Proceedings and Magistrates' Courts Act 1978[; or][197]
[(e) Schedule 5 or 6 to the Civil Partnership Act 2004][198].

(2) The regulations may provide for such representation only in specified circumstances.

65[199] Rules, regulations and orders

(1) Any power to make rules, orders or regulations which is conferred by this Act is exercisable by statutory instrument.

(2) Any statutory instrument made under this Act may—

(a) contain such incidental, supplemental, consequential and transitional provision as the Lord Chancellor considers appropriate; and
(b) make different provision for different purposes.

(3) Any statutory instrument containing an order, rules or regulations made under this Act, other than an order made under section 5(8) or 67(3), shall be subject to annulment by a resolution of either House of Parliament.

(4) No order shall be made under section 5(8) unless a draft of the order has been laid before, and approved by a resolution of, each House of Parliament.

(5) This section does not apply [*to rules made under section 12 or*][200] to rules of court made, or any power to make rules of court, for the purposes of this Act.

66[201] Consequential amendments, transitional provisions and repeals

(1) Schedule 8 makes minor and consequential amendments.

(2) Schedule 9 provides for the making of other modifications consequential on provisions of this Act, makes transitional provisions and provides for savings.

(3) Schedule 10 repeals certain enactments.

---

[196] Amendment: Words repealed: Civil Partnership Act 2004, s 261(1), (4), Sch 27, para 152(1), (2), Sch 30, with effect from 5 December 2005.

[197] Amendment: Word inserted: Civil Partnership Act 2004, s 261(1), Sch 27, para 152(1), (3), with effect from 5 December 2005.

[198] Amendment: Sub-paragraph inserted: Civil Partnership Act 2004, s 261(1), Sch 27, para 152(1), (3), with effect from 5 December 2005.

[199] Commencement: 4 July 1996 (s 67(2)).

[200] Prospective amendment: Words prospectively inserted: Constitutional Reform Act 2005, s 12(2), Sch 1, Pt 2, paras 22, 24, from a date to be appointed.

[201] Commencement: (in relation to subs (2)) see Sch 9 below.

67²⁰² Short title, commencement and extent

(1)   This Act may be cited as the Family Law Act 1996.

(2)   Section 65 and this section come into force on the passing of this Act.

(3)   The other provisions of this Act come into force on such day as the Lord Chancellor may by order appoint; and different days may be appointed for different purposes.

(4)   This Act, other than section 17, extends only to England and Wales, except that—

(a)   in Schedule 8—

    (i)   the amendments of section 38 of the Family Law Act 1986 extend also to Northern Ireland;

    (ii)   the amendments of the Judicial Proceedings (Regulation of Reports) Act 1926 extend also to Scotland; and

    (iii)   the amendments of the Maintenance Orders Act 1950, the Civil Jurisdiction and Judgments Act 1982, the Finance Act 1985 and sections 42 and 51 of the Family Law Act 1986 extend also to both Northern Ireland and Scotland; and

(b)   in Schedule 10, the repeal of section 2(1)(b) of the Domestic and Appellate Proceedings (Restriction of Publicity) Act 1968 extends also to Scotland.

****

Schedule 4

Provisions Supplementary to Sections 30 and 31

Section 32

1²⁰³   Interpretation

(1)   In this Schedule—

(a)   any reference to a solicitor includes a reference to a licensed conveyancer or a recognised body, and

(b)   any reference to a person's solicitor includes a reference to a licensed conveyancer or recognised body acting for that person.

(2)   In sub-paragraph (1)—

'licensed conveyancer' has the meaning given by section 11(2) of the Administration of Justice Act 1985;

---

202   Commencement: 4 July 1996 (s 67(2)).
203   Commencement: 1 October 1997 (SI 1997/1892).

'recognised body' means a body corporate for the time being recognised under section 9 (incorporated practices) or section 32 (provision of conveyancing by recognised bodies) of that Act.

2[204]   Restriction on registration where spouse [or civil partner][205] entitled to more than one charge

Where one spouse [or civil partner][206] is entitled by virtue of section 31 to a registrable charge in respect of each of two or more dwelling-houses, only one of the charges to which that spouse [or civil partner][207] is so entitled shall be registered under section 31(10) or under section 2 of the Land Charges Act 1972 at any one time, and if any of those charges is registered under either of those provisions the Chief Land Registrar, on being satisfied that any other of them is so registered, shall cancel the registration of the charge first registered.

3[208]   Contract for sale of house affected by registered charge to include term requiring cancellation of registration before completion

(1)   Where one spouse [or civil partner][209] is entitled by virtue of section 31 to a charge on an estate in a dwelling-house and the charge is registered under section 31(10) or section 2 of the Land Charges Act 1972, it shall be a term of any contract for the sale of that estate whereby the vendor agrees to give vacant possession of the dwelling-house on completion of the contract that the vendor will before such completion procure the cancellation of the registration of the charge at his expense.

(2)   Sub-paragraph (1) shall not apply to any such contract made by a vendor who is entitled to sell the estate in the dwelling-house freed from any such charge.

(3)   If, on the completion of such a contract as is referred to in sub-paragraph (1), there is delivered to the purchaser or his solicitor an application by the spouse [or civil partner][210] entitled to the charge for the cancellation of the registration of that charge, the term of the contract for which sub-paragraph (1) provides shall be deemed to have been performed.

(4)   This paragraph applies only if and so far as a contrary intention is not expressed in the contract.

---

[204] Commencement: 1 October 1997 (SI 1997/1892).

[205] Amendment: Words inserted: Civil Partnership Act 2004, s 82, Sch 9, Pt 1, para 15(1), (2), with effect from 5 December 2005; for transitional provisions see Civil Partnership Act 2004, s 82, Sch 9, Pt 3.

[206] Amendment: Words inserted: Civil Partnership Act 2004, s 82, Sch 9, Pt 1, para 15(1), (2), with effect from 5 December 2005; for transitional provisions see Civil Partnership Act 2004, s 82, Sch 9, Pt 3.

[207] Amendment: Words inserted: Civil Partnership Act 2004, s 82, Sch 9, Pt 1, para 15(1), (2), with effect from 5 December 2005; for transitional provisions see Civil Partnership Act 2004, s 82, Sch 9, Pt 3.

[208] Commencement: 1 October 1997 (SI 1997/1892).

[209] Amendment: Words inserted: Civil Partnership Act 2004, s 82, Sch 9, Pt 1, para 15(1), (3), with effect from 5 December 2005; for transitional provisions see Civil Partnership Act 2004, s 82, Sch 9, Pt 3.

[210] Amendment: Words inserted: Civil Partnership Act 2004, s 82, Sch 9, Pt 1, para 15(1), (3), with effect from 5 December 2005; for transitional provisions see Civil Partnership Act 2004, s 82, Sch 9, Pt 3.

(5)   This paragraph shall apply to a contract for exchange as it applies to a contract for sale.

(6)   This paragraph shall, with the necessary modifications, apply to a contract for the grant of a lease or underlease of a dwelling-house as it applies to a contract for the sale of an estate in a dwelling-house.

4[211]   Cancellation of registration after termination of marriage [or civil partnership][212], etc

(1)   Where a [spouse's or civil partner's home rights][213] are a charge on an estate in the dwelling-house and the charge is registered under section 31(10) or under section 2 of the Land Charges Act 1972, the Chief Land Registrar shall, subject to sub-paragraph (2), cancel the registration of the charge if he is satisfied—

[(a)   in the case of a marriage—

   (i)   by the production of a certificate or other sufficient evidence, that either spouse is dead,

   (ii)   by the production of an official copy of a decree or order of a court, that the marriage has been terminated otherwise than by death, or

   (iii)   by the production of an order of the court, that the spouse's home rights constituting the charge have been terminated by the order, and

(b)   in the case of a civil partnership—

   (i)   by the production of a certificate or other sufficient evidence, that either civil partner is dead,

   (ii)   by the production of an official copy of an order or decree of a court, that the civil partnership has been terminated otherwise than by death, or

   (iii)   by the production of an order of the court, that the civil partner's home rights constituting the charge have been terminated by the order][214].

(2)   Where—

(a)   the marriage [or civil partnership][215] in question has been terminated by the death of the spouse [or civil partner][216] entitled to an estate in the dwelling-house or otherwise than by death, and

---

[211]   Commencement: 1 October 1997 (SI 1997/1892).

[212]   Amendment: Words inserted: Civil Partnership Act 2004, s 82, Sch 9, Pt 1, para 15(1), (8), with effect from 5 December 2005; for transitional provisions see Civil Partnership Act 2004, s 82, Sch 9, Pt 3.

[213]   Amendment: Words substituted: Civil Partnership Act 2004, s 82, Sch 9, Pt 1, para 15(1), (4), with effect from 5 December 2005; for transitional provisions see Civil Partnership Act 2004, s 82, Sch 9, Pt 3.

[214]   Amendment: Sub-paragraphs substituted: Civil Partnership Act 2004, s 82, Sch 9, Pt 1, para 15(1), (5), with effect from 5 December 2005; for transitional provisions see Civil Partnership Act 2004, s 82, Sch 9, Pt 3.

[215]   Amendment: Words inserted: Civil Partnership Act 2004, s 82, Sch 9, Pt 1, para 15(1), (6)(a), with effect from 5 December 2005; for transitional provisions see Civil Partnership Act 2004, s 82, Sch 9, Pt 3.

[216]   Amendment: Words inserted: Civil Partnership Act 2004, s 82, Sch 9, Pt 1, para 15(1), (6)(a), with effect from 5 December 2005; for transitional provisions see Civil Partnership Act 2004, s 82, Sch 9, Pt 3.

(b)   an order affecting the charge of the spouse [or civil partner][217] not so entitled
        had been made under section 33(5),

then if, after the making of the order, registration of the charge was renewed or the
charge registered in pursuance of sub-paragraph (3), the Chief Land Registrar shall not
cancel the registration of the charge in accordance with sub-paragraph (1) unless he is
also satisfied that the order has ceased to have effect.

(3)   Where such an order has been made, then, for the purposes of sub-paragraph
(2), the spouse [or civil partner][218] entitled to the charge affected by the order may—

(a)   if before the date of the order the charge was registered under section 31(10) or
        under section 2 of the Land Charges Act 1972, renew the registration of the
        charge, and
(b)   if before the said date the charge was not so registered, register the charge under
        section 31(10) or under section 2 of the Land Charges Act 1972.

(4)   Renewal of the registration of a charge in pursuance of sub-paragraph (3) shall
be effected in such manner as may be prescribed, and an application for such renewal
or for registration of a charge in pursuance of that sub-paragraph shall contain such
particulars of any order affecting the charge made under section 33(5) as may be
prescribed.

(5)   The renewal in pursuance of sub-paragraph (3) of the registration of a charge
shall not affect the priority of the charge.

(6)   In this paragraph 'prescribed' means prescribed by rules made under section 16
of the Land Charges Act 1972 or [by land registration rules under the Land
Registration Act 2002][219], as the circumstances of the case require.

5[220]   Release of [home rights][221]

(1)   A [spouse or civil partner entitled to home rights][222] may by a release in writing
release those rights or release them as respects part only of the dwelling-house
affected by them.

---

[217] Amendment: Words inserted: Civil Partnership Act 2004, s 82, Sch 9, Pt 1, para 15(1), (6)(b), with
        effect from 5 December 2005; for transitional provisions see Civil Partnership Act 2004, s 82, Sch 9,
        Pt 3.
[218] Amendment: Words inserted: Civil Partnership Act 2004, s 82, Sch 9, Pt 1, para 15(1), (7), with effect
        from 5 December 2005; for transitional provisions see Civil Partnership Act 2004, s 82, Sch 9, Pt 3.
[219] Amendment: Words substituted: Land Registration Act 2002, s 133, Sch 11, para 34(1), (3); with effect
        from 13 October 2003.
[220] Commencement: 1 October 1997 (SI 1997/1892).
[221] Amendment: Words substituted: Civil Partnership Act 2004, s 82, Sch 9, Pt 1, para 15(1), (11), with
        effect from 5 December 2005; for transitional provisions see Civil Partnership Act 2004, s 82, Sch 9,
        Pt 3.
[222] Amendment: Words substituted: Civil Partnership Act 2004, s 82, Sch 9, Pt 1, para 15(1), (9), with
        effect from 5 December 2005; for transitional provisions see Civil Partnership Act 2004, s 82, Sch 9,
        Pt 3.

(2)   Where a contract is made for the sale of an estate or interest in a dwelling-house, or for the grant of a lease or underlease of a dwelling-house, being (in either case) a dwelling-house affected by a charge registered under section 31(10) or under section 2 of the Land Charges Act 1972, then, without prejudice to sub-paragraph (1), the [home rights][223] constituting the charge shall be deemed to have been released on the happening of whichever of the following events first occurs—

(a)   the delivery to the purchaser or lessee, as the case may be, or his solicitor on completion of the contract of an application by the spouse [or civil partner][224] entitled to the charge for the cancellation of the registration of the charge; or

(b)   the lodging of such an application at Her Majesty's Land Registry.

6[225] Postponement of priority of charge

A spouse [or civil partner][226] entitled by virtue of section 31 to a charge on an estate or interest may agree in writing that any other charge on, or interest in, that estate or interest shall rank in priority to the charge to which that spouse [or civil partner][227] is so entitled.

Schedule 5

Powers of High Court and County Court to Remand

Section 47(11)

1[228] Interpretation

In this Schedule 'the court' means the High Court or a county court and includes—

(a)   in relation to the High Court, a judge of that court, and

(b)   in relation to a county court, a judge or district judge of that court.

2[229] Remand in custody or on bail

(1)   Where a court has power to remand a person under section 47, the court may—

---

[223] Amendment: Words substituted: Civil Partnership Act 2004, s 82, Sch 9, Pt 1, para 15(1), (10)(a), with effect from 5 December 2005; for transitional provisions see Civil Partnership Act 2004, s 82, Sch 9, Pt 3.

[224] Amendment: Words inserted: Civil Partnership Act 2004, s 82, Sch 9, Pt 1, para 15(1), (10)(b), with effect from 5 December 2005; for transitional provisions see Civil Partnership Act 2004, s 82, Sch 9, Pt 3.

[225] Commencement: 1 October 1997 (SI 1997/1892).

[226] Amendment: Words inserted: Civil Partnership Act 2004, s 82, Sch 9, Pt 1, para 15(1), (12), with effect from 5 December 2005; for transitional provisions see Civil Partnership Act 2004, s 82, Sch 9, Pt 3.

[227] Amendment: Words inserted: Civil Partnership Act 2004, s 82, Sch 9, Pt 1, para 15(1), (12), with effect from 5 December 2005; for transitional provisions see Civil Partnership Act 2004, s 82, Sch 9, Pt 3.

[228] Commencement: 1 October 1997 (SI 1997/1892).

[229] Commencement: 1 October 1997 (SI 1997/1892).

(a)   remand him in custody, that is to say, commit him to custody to be brought before the court at the end of the period of remand or at such earlier time as the court may require, or

(b)   remand him on bail—

    (i)   by taking from him a recognizance (with or without sureties) conditioned as provided in sub-paragraph (3), or

    (ii)   by fixing the amount of the recognizances with a view to their being taken subsequently in accordance with paragraph 4 and in the meantime committing the person to custody in accordance with paragraph (a).

(2)   Where a person is brought before the court after remand, the court may further remand him.

(3)   Where a person is remanded on bail under sub-paragraph (1), the court may direct that his recognizance be conditioned for his appearance—

(a)   before that court at the end of the period of remand, or

(b)   at every time and place to which during the course of the proceedings the hearing may from time to time be adjourned.

(4)   Where a recognizance is conditioned for a person's appearance in accordance with sub-paragraph (1)(b), the fixing of any time for him next to appear shall be deemed to be a remand, but nothing in this sub-paragraph or sub-paragraph (3) shall deprive the court of power at any subsequent hearing to remand him afresh.

(5)   Subject to paragraph 3, the court shall not remand a person under this paragraph for a period exceeding 8 clear days, except that—

(a)   if the court remands him on bail, it may remand him for a longer period if he and the other party consent, and

(b)   if the court adjourns a case under section 48(1), the court may remand him for the period of the adjournment.

(6)   Where the court has power under this paragraph to remand a person in custody it may, if the remand is for a period not exceeding 3 clear days, commit him to the custody of a constable.

3[230]   Further remand

(1)   If the court is satisfied that any person who has been remanded under paragraph 2 is unable by reason of illness or accident to appear or be brought before the court at the expiration of the period for which he was remanded, the court may, in his absence, remand him for a further time; and paragraph 2(5) shall not apply.

(2)   Notwithstanding anything in paragraph 2(1), the power of the court under sub-paragraph (1) to remand a person on bail for a further time may be exercised by enlarging his recognizance and those of any sureties for him to a later time.

---

[230]   Commencement: 1 October 1997 (SI 1997/1892).

(3)   Where a person remanded on bail under paragraph 2 is bound to appear before the court at any time and the court has no power to remand him under sub-paragraph (1), the court may in his absence enlarge his recognizance and those of any sureties for him to a later time; and the enlargement of his recognizance shall be deemed to be a further remand.

4[231]   Postponement of taking of recognizance

Where under paragraph 2(1)(b)(ii) the court fixes the amount in which the principal and his sureties, if any, are to be bound, the recognizance may thereafter be taken by such person as may be prescribed by rules of court, and the same consequences shall follow as if it had been entered into before the court.

****

Schedule 7

Transfer of Certain Tenancies on Divorce etc or on Separation of Cohabitants

Section 53

Part I

General

1[232]   Interpretation

In this Schedule—

['civil partner', except in paragraph 2, includes (where the context requires) former civil partner;][233]
'cohabitant', except in paragraph 3, includes (where the context requires) former cohabitant;
'the court' does not include a magistrates' court,
'landlord' includes—

(a)   any person from time to time deriving title under the original landlord; and

(b)   in relation to any dwelling-house, any person other than the tenant who is, or (but for Part VII of the Rent Act 1977 or Part II of the Rent (Agriculture) Act 1976) would be, entitled to possession of the dwelling-house;

'Part II order' means an order under Part II of this Schedule;
'a relevant tenancy' means—

---

[231]   Commencement: 1 October 1997 (SI 1997/1892).
[232]   Commencement: 1 October 1997 (SI 1997/1892).
[233]   Amendment: Definition 'civil partner' inserted: Civil Partnership Act 2004, s 82, Sch 9, Pt 1, para 16(1), (2), with effect from 5 December 2005; for transitional provisions see the Civil Partnership Act 2004, s 82, Sch 9, Pt 3.

(a)   a protected tenancy or statutory tenancy within the meaning of the Rent Act 1977;

(b)   a statutory tenancy within the meaning of the Rent (Agriculture) Act 1976;

(c)   a secure tenancy within the meaning of section 79 of the Housing Act 1985; …[234]

(d)   an assured tenancy or assured agricultural occupancy within the meaning of Part I of the Housing Act 1988; [or

(e)   an introductory tenancy within the meaning of Chapter I of Part V of the Housing Act 1996;][235]

'spouse', except in paragraph 2, includes (where the context requires) former spouse; and

'tenancy' includes sub-tenancy.

Cases in which the court may make an order

2[236]

(1)   This paragraph applies if one spouse [or civil partner][237] is entitled, either in his own right or jointly with the other spouse [or civil partner][238], to occupy a dwelling-house by virtue of a relevant tenancy.

[(2)   The court may make a Part II order—

(a)   on granting a decree of divorce, a decree of nullity of marriage or a decree of judicial separation or at any time thereafter (whether, in the case of a decree of divorce or nullity of marriage, before or after the decree is made absolute), or

(b)   at any time when it has power to make a property adjustment order under Part 2 of Schedule 5 to the Civil Partnership Act 2004 with respect to the civil partnership.][239]

3[240]

(1)   This paragraph applies if one cohabitant is entitled, either in his own right or jointly with the other cohabitant, to occupy a dwelling-house by virtue of a relevant tenancy.

---

[234]   Amendment: Word repealed: Housing Act 1996 (Consequential Amendments) Order 1997, SI 1997/74, with effect from 12 February 1997.

[235]   Amendment: Paragraph and preceding word inserted: Housing Act 1996 (Consequential Amendments) Order 1997, SI 1997/74, with effect from 12 February 1997.

[236]   Commencement: 1 October 1997 (SI 1997/1892).

[237]   Amendment: Words inserted: Civil Partnership Act 2004, s 82, Sch 9, Pt 1, para 16(1), (3), with effect from 5 December 2005; for transitional provisions see Civil Partnership Act 2004, s 82, Sch 9, Pt 3.

[238]   Amendment: Words inserted: Civil Partnership Act 2004, s 82, Sch 9, Pt 1, para 16(1), (3), with effect from 5 December 2005; for transitional provisions see Civil Partnership Act 2004, s 82, Sch 9, Pt 3.

[239]   Amendment: Sub-paragraph substituted: Civil Partnership Act 2004, s 82, Sch 9, Pt 1, para 16(1), (4), with effect from 5 December 2005; for transitional provisions see Civil Partnership Act 2004, s 82, Sch 9, Pt 3.

[240]   Commencement: 1 October 1997 (SI 1997/1892).

(2)   If the cohabitants cease [to cohabit][241], the court may make a Part II order.

4[242]

The court shall not make a Part II order unless the dwelling-house is or was—

(a)   in the case of spouses, a matrimonial home; …[243]
[(aa)   in the case of civil partners, a civil partnership home; or][244]
(b)   in the case of cohabitants, a home in which they [cohabited][245].

5[246] **Matters to which the court must have regard**

In determining whether to exercise its powers under Part II of this Schedule and, if so, in what manner, the court shall have regard to all the circumstances of the case including—

(a)   the circumstances in which the tenancy was granted to either or both of the spouses[, civil partners][247] or cohabitants or, as the case requires, the circumstances in which either or both of them became tenant under the tenancy;
(b)   the matters mentioned in section 33(6)(a), (b) and (c) and, where the parties are cohabitants and only one of them is entitled to occupy the dwelling-house by virtue of the relevant tenancy, the further matters mentioned in section 36(6)(e), (f), (g) and (h); and
(c)   the suitability of the parties as tenants.

Part II

Orders that may be made

6[248]   **References to entitlement to occupy**

References in this Part of this Schedule to a spouse[, a civil partner][249] or a cohabitant being entitled to occupy a dwelling-house by virtue of a relevant tenancy apply

---

[241]   Amendment: Words substituted: Domestic Violence, Crime and Victims Act 2004, s 58(1), Sch 10, para 42(1), (2), with effect from 5 December 2005.

[242]   Commencement: 1 October 1997 (SI 1997/1892).

[243]   Amendment: Words repealed: Civil Partnership Act 2004, ss 82, 261(4), Sch 9, Pt 1, para 16(1), (5), Sch 30, with effect from 5 December 2005; for transitional provisions see Civil Partnership Act 2004, s 82, Sch 9, Pt 3.

[244]   Amendment: Sub-paragraph inserted: Civil Partnership Act 2004, s 82, Sch 9, Pt 1, para 16(1), (5), with effect from 5 December 2005; for transitional provisions see Civil Partnership Act 2004, s 82, Sch 9, Pt 3.

[245]   Amendment: Words substituted: Domestic Violence, Crime and Victims Act 2004, s 58(1), Sch 10, para 42(1), (3), with effect from 5 December 2005.

[246]   Commencement: 1 October 1997 (SI 1997/1892).

[247]   Amendment: Words inserted: Civil Partnership Act 2004, s 82, Sch 9, Pt 1, para 16(1), (6), with effect from 5 December 2005; for transitional provisions see Civil Partnership Act 2004, s 82, Sch 9, Pt 3.

[248]   Commencement: 1 October 1997 (SI 1997/1892).

[249]   Amendment: Words inserted: Civil Partnership Act 2004, s 82, Sch 9, Pt 1, para 16(1), (7), with effect from 5 December 2005; for transitional provisions see Civil Partnership Act 2004, s 82, Sch 9, Pt 3.

whether that entitlement is in his own right or jointly with the other spouse[, civil partner][250] or cohabitant.

7[251]   Protected, secure or assured tenancy or assured agricultural occupancy

(1)   If a spouse[, civil partner][252] or cohabitant is entitled to occupy the dwelling-house by virtue of a protected tenancy within the meaning of the Rent Act 1977, a secure tenancy within the meaning of the Housing Act 1985[, an assured tenancy][253] or assured agricultural occupancy within the meaning of Part I of the Housing Act 1988 [or an introductory tenancy within the meaning of Chapter I of Part V of the Housing Act 1996][254], the court may by order direct that, as from such date as may be specified in the order, there shall, by virtue of the order and without further assurance, be transferred to, and vested in, the other spouse[, civil partner][255] or cohabitant—

(a)   the estate or interest which the spouse[, civil partner][256] or cohabitant so entitled had in the dwelling-house immediately before that date by virtue of the lease or agreement creating the tenancy and any assignment of that lease or agreement, with all rights, privileges and appurtenances attaching to that estate or interest but subject to all covenants, obligations, liabilities and incumbrances to which it is subject; and

(b)   where the spouse[, civil partner][257] or cohabitant so entitled is an assignee of such lease or agreement, the liability of that spouse[, civil partner][258] or cohabitant under any covenant of indemnity by the assignee express or implied in the assignment of the lease or agreement to that spouse[, civil partner][259] or cohabitant.

(2)   If an order is made under this paragraph, any liability or obligation to which the spouse[, civil partner][260] or cohabitant so entitled is subject under any covenant having reference to the dwelling-house in the lease or agreement, being a liability or

---

[250]   Amendment: Words inserted: Civil Partnership Act 2004, s 82, Sch 9, Pt 1, para 16(1), (7), with effect from 5 December 2005; for transitional provisions see Civil Partnership Act 2004, s 82, Sch 9, Pt 3.

[251]   Commencement: 1 October 1997 (SI 1997/1892).

[252]   Amendment: Words inserted: Civil Partnership Act 2004, s 82, Sch 9, Pt 1, para 16(1), (8), with effect from 5 December 2005; for transitional provisions see Civil Partnership Act 2004, s 82, Sch 9, Pt 3.

[253]   Amendment: Words substituted: Housing Act 1996 (Consequential Amendments) Order 1997, SI 1997/74, with effect from 12 February 1997.

[254]   Amendment: Words inserted: Housing Act 1996 (Consequential Amendments) Order 1997, SI 1997/74, with effect from 12 February 1997.

[255]   Amendment: Words inserted: Civil Partnership Act 2004, s 82, Sch 9, Pt 1, para 16(1), (8), with effect from 5 December 2005; for transitional provisions see Civil Partnership Act 2004, s 82, Sch 9, Pt 3.

[256]   Amendment: Words inserted: Civil Partnership Act 2004, s 82, Sch 9, Pt 1, para 16(1), (8), with effect from 5 December 2005; for transitional provisions see Civil Partnership Act 2004, s 82, Sch 9, Pt 3.

[257]   Amendment: Words inserted: Civil Partnership Act 2004, s 82, Sch 9, Pt 1, para 16(1), (8), with effect from 5 December 2005; for transitional provisions see Civil Partnership Act 2004, s 82, Sch 9, Pt 3.

[258]   Amendment: Words inserted: Civil Partnership Act 2004, s 82, Sch 9, Pt 1, para 16(1), (8), with effect from 5 December 2005; for transitional provisions see Civil Partnership Act 2004, s 82, Sch 9, Pt 3.

[259]   Amendment: Words inserted: Civil Partnership Act 2004, s 82, Sch 9, Pt 1, para 16(1), (8), with effect from 5 December 2005; for transitional provisions see Civil Partnership Act 2004, s 82, Sch 9, Pt 3.

[260]   Amendment: Words inserted: Civil Partnership Act 2004, s 82, Sch 9, Pt 1, para 16(1), (8), with effect from 5 December 2005; for transitional provisions see Civil Partnership Act 2004, s 82, Sch 9, Pt 3.

obligation falling due to be discharged or performed on or after the date so specified, shall not be enforceable against that spouse[, civil partner][261] or cohabitant.

[(3) If the spouse, civil partner or cohabitant so entitled is a successor within the meaning of Part 4 of the Housing Act 1985—

(a)   his former spouse (or, in the case of judicial separation, his spouse),
(b)   his former civil partner (or, if a separation order is in force, his civil partner), or
(c)   his former cohabitant,

is to be deemed also to be a successor within the meaning of that Part.] [262]

[(3A) If the spouse, civil partner or cohabitant so entitled is a successor within the meaning of section 132 of the Housing Act 1996—

(a)   his former spouse (or, in the case of judicial separation, his spouse),
(b)   his former civil partner (or, if a separation order is in force, his civil partner), or
(c)   his former cohabitant,

is to be deemed also to be a successor within the meaning of that section.][263]

[(4) If the spouse, civil partner or cohabitant so entitled is for the purposes of section 17 of the Housing Act 1988 a successor in relation to the tenancy or occupancy—

(a)   his former spouse (or, in the case of judicial separation, his spouse),
(b)   his former civil partner (or, if a separation order is in force, his civil partner), or
(c)   his former cohabitant,

is to be deemed to be a successor in relation to the tenancy or occupancy for the purposes of that section.][264]

(5)   If the transfer under sub-paragraph (1) is of an assured agricultural occupancy, then, for the purposes of Chapter III of Part I of the Housing Act 1988—

(a)   the agricultural worker condition is fulfilled with respect to the dwelling-house while the spouse[, civil partner][265] or cohabitant to whom the assured agricultural occupancy is transferred continues to be the occupier under that occupancy, and
(b)   that condition is to be treated as so fulfilled by virtue of the same paragraph of Schedule 3 to the Housing Act 1988 as was applicable before the transfer.

---

[261]   Amendment: Words inserted: Civil Partnership Act 2004, s 82, Sch 9, Pt 1, para 16(1), (8), with effect from 5 December 2005; for transitional provisions see Civil Partnership Act 2004, s 82, Sch 9, Pt 3.
[262]   Amendment: Sub-paragraph substituted: Civil Partnership Act 2004, s 82, Sch 9, Pt 1, para 16(1), (9), with effect from 5 December 2005; for transitional provisions see Civil Partnership Act 2004, s 82, Sch 9, Pt 3.
[263]   Amendment: Sub-paragraph substituted: Civil Partnership Act 2004, s 82, Sch 9, Pt 1, para 16(1), (9), with effect from 5 December 2005; for transitional provisions see Civil Partnership Act 2004, s 82, Sch 9, Pt 3.
[264]   Amendment: Sub-paragraph substituted: Civil Partnership Act 2004, s 82, Sch 9, Pt 1, para 16(1), (9), with effect from 5 December 2005; for transitional provisions see Civil Partnership Act 2004, s 82, Sch 9, Pt 3.
[265]   Amendment: Words inserted: Civil Partnership Act 2004, s 82, Sch 9, Pt 1, para 16(1), (10), with effect from 5 December 2005; for transitional provisions see Civil Partnership Act 2004, s 82, Sch 9, Pt 3.

(6)   ...[266]

8[267]   Statutory tenancy within the meaning of the Rent Act 1977

(1)   This paragraph applies if the spouse[, civil partner][268] or cohabitant is entitled to occupy the dwelling-house by virtue of a statutory tenancy within the meaning of the Rent Act 1977.

(2)   The court may by order direct that, as from the date specified in the order—

(a)   that spouse[, civil partner][269] or cohabitant is to cease to be entitled to occupy the dwelling-house; and

(b)   the other spouse[, civil partner][270] or cohabitant is to be deemed to be the tenant or, as the case may be, the sole tenant under that statutory tenancy.

(3)   The question whether the provisions of paragraphs 1 to 3, or (as the case may be) paragraphs 5 to 7 of Schedule 1 to the Rent Act 1977, as to the succession by the surviving spouse [or surviving civil partner][271] of a deceased tenant, or by a member of the deceased tenant's family, to the right to retain possession are capable of having effect in the event of the death of the person deemed by an order under this paragraph to be the tenant or sole tenant under the statutory tenancy is to be determined according as those provisions have or have not already had effect in relation to the statutory tenancy.

9[272]   Statutory tenancy within the meaning of the Rent (Agriculture) Act 1976

(1)   This paragraph applies if the spouse[, civil partner][273] or cohabitant is entitled to occupy the dwelling-house by virtue of a statutory tenancy within the meaning of the Rent (Agriculture) Act 1976.

(2)   The court may by order direct that, as from such date as may be specified in the order—

---

[266] Amendment: Sub-paragraph repealed: Civil Partnership Act 2004, s 82, Sch 9, Pt 1, para 16(1), (11), with effect from 5 December 2005; for transitional provisions see Civil Partnership Act 2004, s 82, Sch 9, Pt 3.

[267] Commencement: 1 October 1997 (SI 1997/1892).

[268] Amendment: Words inserted: Civil Partnership Act 2004, s 82, Sch 9, Pt 1, para 16(1), (12), with effect from 5 December 2005; for transitional provisions see Civil Partnership Act 2004, s 82, Sch 9, Pt 3.

[269] Amendment: Words inserted: Civil Partnership Act 2004, s 82, Sch 9, Pt 1, para 16(1), (12), with effect from 5 December 2005; for transitional provisions see Civil Partnership Act 2004, s 82, Sch 9, Pt 3.

[270] Amendment: Words inserted: Civil Partnership Act 2004, s 82, Sch 9, Pt 1, para 16(1), (12), with effect from 5 December 2005; for transitional provisions see Civil Partnership Act 2004, s 82, Sch 9, Pt 3.

[271] Amendment: Words inserted: Civil Partnership Act 2004, s 82, Sch 9, Pt 1, para 16(1), (13), with effect from 5 December 2005; for transitional provisions see Civil Partnership Act 2004, s 82, Sch 9, Pt 3.

[272] Commencement: 1 October 1997 (SI 1997/1892).

[273] Amendment: Words inserted: Civil Partnership Act 2004, s 82, Sch 9, Pt 1, para 16(1), (14), with effect from 5 December 2005; for transitional provisions see Civil Partnership Act 2004, s 82, Sch 9, Pt 3.

(a) that spouse[, civil partner][274] or cohabitant is to cease to be entitled to occupy the dwelling-house; and

(b) the other spouse[, civil partner][275] or cohabitant is to be deemed to be the tenant or, as the case may be, the sole tenant under that statutory tenancy.

(3) A spouse[, civil partner][276] or cohabitant who is deemed under this paragraph to be the tenant under a statutory tenancy is (within the meaning of that Act) a statutory tenant in his own right, or a statutory tenant by succession, according as the other spouse[, civil partner][277] or cohabitant was a statutory tenant in his own right or a statutory tenant by succession.

Part III

Supplementary Provisions

10[278] **Compensation**

(1) If the court makes a Part II order, it may by the order direct the making of a payment by the spouse[, civil partner][279] or cohabitant to whom the tenancy is transferred ('the transferee') to the other spouse[, civil partner][280] or cohabitant ('the transferor').

(2) Without prejudice to that, the court may, on making an order by virtue of sub-paragraph (1) for the payment of a sum—

(a) direct that payment of that sum or any part of it is to be deferred until a specified date or until the occurrence of a specified event, or

(b) direct that that sum or any part of it is to be paid by instalments.

(3) Where an order has been made by virtue of sub-paragraph (1), the court may, on the application of the transferee or the transferor—

(a) exercise its powers under sub-paragraph (2), or

(b) vary any direction previously given under that sub-paragraph,

at any time before the sum whose payment is required by the order is paid in full.

---

274 Amendment: Words inserted: Civil Partnership Act 2004, s 82, Sch 9, Pt 1, para 16(1), (14), with effect from 5 December 2005; for transitional provisions see Civil Partnership Act 2004, s 82, Sch 9, Pt 3.

275 Amendment: Words inserted: Civil Partnership Act 2004, s 82, Sch 9, Pt 1, para 16(1), (14), with effect from 5 December 2005; for transitional provisions see Civil Partnership Act 2004, s 82, Sch 9, Pt 3.

276 Amendment: Words inserted: Civil Partnership Act 2004, s 82, Sch 9, Pt 1, para 16(1), (14), with effect from 5 December 2005; for transitional provisions see Civil Partnership Act 2004, s 82, Sch 9, Pt 3.

277 Amendment: Words inserted: Civil Partnership Act 2004, s 82, Sch 9, Pt 1, para 16(1), (14), with effect from 5 December 2005; for transitional provisions see Civil Partnership Act 2004, s 82, Sch 9, Pt 3.

278 Commencement: 1 October 1997 (SI 1997/1892).

279 Amendment: Words inserted: Civil Partnership Act 2004, s 82, Sch 9, Pt 1, para 16(1), (14), with effect from 5 December 2005; for transitional provisions see Civil Partnership Act 2004, s 82, Sch 9, Pt 3.

280 Amendment: Words inserted: Civil Partnership Act 2004, s 82, Sch 9, Pt 1, para 16(1), (14), with effect from 5 December 2005; for transitional provisions see Civil Partnership Act 2004, s 82, Sch 9, Pt 3.

(4)   In deciding whether to exercise its powers under this paragraph and, if so, in what manner, the court shall have regard to all the circumstances including—

(a)   the financial loss that would otherwise be suffered by the transferor as a result of the order;

(b)   the financial needs and financial resources of the parties; and

(c)   the financial obligations which the parties have, or are likely to have in the foreseeable future, including financial obligations to each other and to any relevant child.

(5)   The court shall not give any direction under sub-paragraph (2) unless it appears to it that immediate payment of the sum required by the order would cause the transferee financial hardship which is greater than any financial hardship that would be caused to the transferor if the direction were given.

11[281]   Liabilities and obligations in respect of the dwelling-house

(1)   If the court makes a Part II order, it may by the order direct that both spouses[, civil partners][282] or cohabitants are to be jointly and severally liable to discharge or perform any or all of the liabilities and obligations in respect of the dwelling-house (whether arising under the tenancy or otherwise) which—

(a)   have at the date of the order fallen due to be discharged or performed by one only of them; or

(b)   but for the direction, would before the date specified as the date on which the order is to take effect fall due to be discharged or performed by one only of them.

(2)   If the court gives such a direction, it may further direct that either spouse[, civil partner][283] or cohabitant is to be liable to indemnify the other in whole or in part against any payment made or expenses incurred by the other in discharging or performing any such liability or obligation.

[12[284]   Date when order made between spouses or civil partners is to take effect

The date specified in a Part II order as the date on which the order is to take effect must not be earlier than—

(a)   in the case of a marriage in respect of which a decree of divorce or nullity has been granted, the date on which the decree is made absolute;

---

281   Commencement: 1 October 1997 (SI 1997/1892).

282   Amendment: Words inserted: Civil Partnership Act 2004, s 82, Sch 9, Pt 1, para 16(1), (15), with effect from 5 December 2005; for transitional provisions see Civil Partnership Act 2004, s 82, Sch 9, Pt 3.

283   Amendment: Words inserted: Civil Partnership Act 2004, s 82, Sch 9, Pt 1, para 16(1), (16), with effect from 5 December 2005; for transitional provisions see Civil Partnership Act 2004, s 82, Sch 9, Pt 3.

284   Commencement: 1 October 1997 (SI 1997/1892).

(b)   in the case of a civil partnership in respect of which a dissolution or nullity order has been made, the date on which the order is made final.][285]

[13[286]   Effect of remarriage or subsequent civil partnership

(1) If after the grant of a decree dissolving or annulling a marriage either spouse remarries or forms a civil partnership, that spouse is not entitled to apply, by reference to the grant of that decree, for a Part II order.

(2) If after the making of a dissolution or nullity order either civil partner forms a subsequent civil partnership or marries, that civil partner is not entitled to apply, by reference to the making of that order, for a Part II order.

(3) In sub-paragraphs (1) and (2)—

(a)   the references to remarrying and marrying include references to cases where the marriage is by law void or voidable, and
(b)   the references to forming a civil partnership include references to cases where the civil partnership is by law void or voidable.][287]

14[288]   Rules of court

(1)   Rules of court shall be made requiring the court, before it makes an order under this Schedule, to give the landlord of the dwelling-house to which the order will relate an opportunity of being heard.

(2)   Rules of court may provide that an application for a Part II order by reference to an order or decree may not, without the leave of the court by which that order was made or decree was granted, be made after the expiration of such period from the order or grant as may be prescribed by the rules.

15[289]   Saving for other provisions of Act

(1) If a spouse [or civil partner][290] is entitled to occupy a dwelling-house by virtue of a tenancy, this Schedule does not affect the operation of sections 30 and 31 in relation

---

[285]   Amendment: Paragraph substituted: Civil Partnership Act 2004, s 82, Sch 9, Pt 1, para 16(1), (17), with effect from 5 December 2005; for transitional provisions see Civil Partnership Act 2004, s 82, Sch 9, Pt 3.

[286]   Commencement: 1 October 1997 (SI 1997/1892).

[287]   Amendment: Paragraph substituted: Civil Partnership Act 2004, s 82, Sch 9, Pt 1, para 16(1), (18), with effect from 5 December 2005; for transitional provisions see Civil Partnership Act 2004, s 82, Sch 9, Pt 3.

[288]   Commencement: 1 October 1997 (SI 1997/1892).

[289]   Commencement: 1 October 1997 (SI 1997/1892).

[290]   Amendment: Words inserted: Civil Partnership Act 2004, s 82, Sch 9, Pt 1, para 16(1), (19)(a), with effect from 5 December 2005; for transitional provisions see Civil Partnership Act 2004, s 82, Sch 9, Pt 3.

to the other [spouse's or civil partner's home rights][291].

(2) If a spouse[, civil partner][292] or cohabitant is entitled to occupy a dwelling-house by virtue of a tenancy, the court's powers to make orders under this Schedule are additional to those conferred by sections 33, 35 and 36.

****

Schedule 9

Modifications, Saving and Transitional

Section 66(2)

1[293]   Transitional arrangements for those who have been living apart

(1)   The Lord Chancellor may by order provide for the application of Part II to marital proceedings which—

(a)   are begun during the transitional period, and
(b)   relate to parties to a marriage who immediately before the beginning of that period were living apart,

subject to such modifications (which may include omissions) as may be prescribed.

(2)   An order made under this paragraph may, in particular, make provision as to the evidence which a party who claims to have been living apart from the other party immediately before the beginning of the transitional period must produce to the court.

(3)   In this paragraph—

'marital proceedings' has the same meaning as in section 24;
'prescribed' means prescribed by the order; and
'transitional period' means the period of two years beginning with the day on which section 3 is brought into force.

Modifications of enactments etc

2[294]

(1)   The Lord Chancellor may by order make such consequential modifications of any enactment or subordinate legislation as appear to him necessary or expedient in consequence of Part II in respect of any reference (in whatever terms) to—

---

[291]   Amendment: Words inserted: Civil Partnership Act 2004, s 82, Sch 9, Pt 1, para 16(1), (19)(b), with effect from 5 December 2005; for transitional provisions see Civil Partnership Act 2004, s 82, Sch 9, Pt 3.

[292]   Amendment: Words inserted: Civil Partnership Act 2004, s 82, Sch 9, Pt 1, para 16(1), (20), with effect from 5 December 2005; for transitional provisions see Civil Partnership Act 2004, s 82, Sch 9, Pt 3.

[293]   Commencement: Not yet in force.

[294]   Commencement: Not yet in force.

(a)   a petition;
(b)   the presentation of a petition;
(c)   the petitioner or respondent in proceedings on a petition;
(d)   proceedings on a petition;
(e)   proceedings in connection with any proceedings on a petition;
(f)   any other matrimonial proceedings;
(g)   a decree; or
(h)   findings of adultery in any proceedings.

(2)   An order under sub-paragraph (1) may, in particular—

(a)   make provision applying generally in relation to enactments and subordinate legislation of a description specified in the order;
(b)   modify the effect of sub-paragraph (3) in relation to documents and agreements of a description so specified.

(3)   Otherwise a reference (in whatever terms) in any instrument or agreement to the presentation of a petition or to a decree has effect, in relation to any time after the coming into force of this paragraph—

(a)   in the case of a reference to the presentation of a petition, as if it included a reference to the making of a statement; and
(b)   in the case of a reference to a decree, as if it included a reference to a divorce order or (as the case may be) a separation order.

3[295]

If an Act or subordinate legislation—

(a)   refers to an enactment repealed or amended by or under this Act, and
(b)   was passed or made before the repeal or amendment came into force,

the Lord Chancellor may by order make such consequential modifications of any provision contained in the Act or subordinate legislation as appears to him necessary or expedient in respect of the reference.

4[296]   **Expressions used in paragraphs 2 and 3**

In paragraphs 2 and 3—

'decree' means a decree of divorce (whether a decree nisi or a decree which has been made absolute) or a decree of judicial separation;
'instrument' includes any deed, will or other instrument or document
'petition' means a petition for a decree of divorce or a petition for a decree of judicial separation; and
'subordinate legislation' has the same meaning as in the Interpretation Act 1978.

---

[295]   Commencement: 28 July 1997 (Family Law Act 1996 (Commencement No 2) Order 1997, SI 1997/1892).
[296]   Commencement: 28 July 1997 (Family Law Act 1996 (Commencement No 2) Order 1997, SI 1997/1892).

Proceedings under way

5[297]

(1)   Except for paragraph 6 of this Schedule, nothing in any provision of Part II, Part I of Schedule 8 or Schedule 10—

(a)   applies to, or affects—

   (i)   any decree granted before the coming into force of the provision;
   (ii)   any proceedings begun, by petition or otherwise, before that time; or
   (iii)   any decree granted in any such proceedings;

(b)   affects the operation of—

   (i)   the 1973 Act,
   (ii)   any other enactment, or
   (iii)   any subordinate legislation,

in relation to any such proceedings or decree or to any proceedings in connection with any such proceedings or decree; or

(c)   without prejudice to paragraph (b), affects any transitional provision having effect under Schedule 1 to the 1973 Act.

(2)   In this paragraph, 'subordinate legislation' has the same meaning as in the Interpretation Act 1978.

6[298]

(1)   Section 31 of the 1973 Act has effect as amended by this Act in relation to any order under Part II of the 1973 Act made after the coming into force of the amendments.

(2)   Subsections (7) to (7F) of that section also have effect as amended by this Act in relation to any order made before the coming into force of the amendments.

7[299]   **Interpretation**

In paragraphs 8 to 15 'the 1983 Act' means the Matrimonial Homes Act 1983.

8[300]   **Pending applications for orders relating to occupation and molestation**

(1)   In this paragraph and paragraph 10 'the existing enactments' means—

(a)   the Domestic Violence and Matrimonial Proceedings Act 1976;
(b)   sections 16 to 18 of the Domestic Proceedings and Magistrates' Courts Act 1978; and

---

[297]   Commencement: Not yet in force.
[298]   Commencement: Not yet in force.
[299]   Commencement: 1 October 1997 (SI 1997/1892).
[300]   Commencement: 1 October 1997 (SI 1997/1892).

(c)   sections 1 and 9 of the 1983 Act.

(2)   Nothing in Part IV, Part III of Schedule 8 or Schedule 10 affects any application for an order or injunction under any of the existing enactments which is pending immediately before the commencement of the repeal of that enactment.

9[301]   Pending applications under Schedule 1 to the Matrimonial Homes Act 1983

Nothing in Part IV, Part III of Schedule 8 or Schedule 10 affects any application for an order under Schedule 1 to the 1983 Act which is pending immediately before the commencement of the repeal of that Schedule.

10[302]   Existing orders relating to occupation and molestation

(1)   In this paragraph 'an existing order' means any order or injunction under any of the existing enactments which—

(a)   is in force immediately before the commencement of the repeal of that enactment; or
(b)   was made or granted after that commencement in proceedings brought before that commencement.

(2)   Subject to sub-paragraphs (3) and (4), nothing in Part IV, Part III of Schedule 8 or Schedule 10—

(a)   prevents an existing order from remaining in force; or
(b)   affects the enforcement of an existing order.

(3)   Nothing in Part IV, Part III of Schedule 8 or Schedule 10 affects any application to extend, vary or discharge an existing order, but the court may, if it thinks it just and reasonable to do so, treat the application as an application for an order under Part IV.

(4)   The making of an order under Part IV between parties with respect to whom an existing order is in force discharges the existing order.

Matrimonial home rights

11[303]

(1)   Any reference (however expressed) in any enactment, instrument or document (whether passed or made before or after the passing of this Act) to rights of occupation under, or within the meaning of, the 1983 Act shall be construed, so far as is required for continuing the effect of the instrument or document, as being or as the case requires including a reference to matrimonial home rights under, or within the meaning of, Part IV.

---

[301]   Commencement: 1 October 1997 (SI 1997/1892).
[302]   Commencement: 1 October 1997 (SI 1997/1892).
[303]   Commencement: 1 October 1997 (SI 1997/1892).

(2) Any reference (however expressed) in this Act or in any other enactment, instrument or document (including any enactment amended by Schedule 8) to matrimonial home rights under, or within the meaning of, Part IV shall be construed as including, in relation to times, circumstances and purposes before the commencement of sections 30 to 32, a reference to rights of occupation under, or within the meaning of, the 1983 Act.

12[304]

(1) Any reference (however expressed) in any enactment, instrument or document (whether passed or made before or after the passing of this Act) to registration under section 2(8) of the 1983 Act shall, in relation to any time after the commencement of sections 30 to 32, be construed as being or as the case requires including a reference to registration under section 31(10).

(2) Any reference (however expressed) in this Act or in any other enactment, instrument or document (including any enactment amended by Schedule 8) to registration under section 31(10) shall be construed as including a reference to—

(a) registration under section 2(7) of the Matrimonial Homes Act 1967 or section 2(8) of the 1983 Act, and

(b) registration by caution duly lodged under section 2(7) of the Matrimonial Homes Act 1967 before 14th February 1983 (the date of the commencement of section 4(2) of the Matrimonial Homes and Property Act 1981).

13[305]

In sections 30 and 31 and Schedule 4—

(a) any reference to an order made under section 33 shall be construed as including a reference to an order made under section 1 of the 1983 Act, and

(b) any reference to an order made under section 33(5) shall be construed as including a reference to an order made under section 1 of the 1983 Act by virtue of section 2(4) of that Act.

14[306]

Neither section 31(11) nor the repeal by the Matrimonial Homes and Property Act 1981 of the words 'or caution' in section 2(7) of the Matrimonial Homes Act 1967, affects any caution duly lodged as respects any estate or interest before 14th February 1983.

---

[304] Commencement: 1 October 1997 (SI 1997/1892).
[305] Commencement: 1 October 1997 (SI 1997/1892).
[306] Commencement: 1 October 1997 (SI 1997/1892).

15[307]

Nothing in this Schedule is to be taken to prejudice the operation of sections 16 and 17 of the Interpretation Act 1978 (which relate to the effect of repeals).

****

---

[307] Commencement: 1 October 1997 (SI 1997/1892).

Protection from Harassment Act 1997[308]

England and Wales

1[309]   Prohibition of harassment

(1)   A person must not pursue a course of conduct—

(a) which amounts to harassment of another, and

(b) which he knows or ought to know amounts to harassment of the other.

[(1A) A person must not pursue a course of conduct—

(a)   which involves harassment of two or more persons, and

(b)   which he knows or ought to know involves harassment of those persons, and

(c)   by which he intends to persuade any person (whether or not one of those mentioned above)—

(i)   not to do something that he is entitled or required to do, or

(ii)   to do something that he is not under any obligation to do.][310]

(2)   For the purposes of this section, the person whose course of conduct is in question ought to know that it amounts to [or involves][311] harassment of another if a reasonable person in possession of the same information would think the course of conduct amounted to [or involved][312] harassment of the other.

(3)   Subsection (1) [or (1A)][313] does not apply to a course of conduct if the person who pursued it shows—

(a)   that it was pursued for the purpose of preventing or detecting crime,

(b)   that it was pursued under any enactment or rule of law or to comply with any condition or requirement imposed by any person under any enactment, or

(c)   that in the particular circumstances the pursuit of the course of conduct was reasonable.

---

[308]   Act reference: 1997 c 40.
   Royal assent: 21 March 1997.
   Long title: An Act to make provision for protecting persons from harassment and similar conduct.
[309]   Commencement: 16 June 1997 (SI 1997/1418).
[310]   Amendment: Subsection inserted: Serious Organised Crime and Police Act 2005, s 125(1), (2)(a), with effect from 1 July 2005.
[311]   Amendment: Words inserted: Serious Organised Crime and Police Act 2005, s 125(1), (2)(b), with effect from 1 July 2005.
[312]   Amendment: Words inserted: Serious Organised Crime and Police Act 2005, s 125(1), (2)(b), with effect from 1 July 2005.
[313]   Amendment: Words inserted: Serious Organised Crime and Police Act 2005, s 125(1), (2)(c), with effect from 1 July 2005.

2[314] **Offence of harassment**

(1)   A person who pursues a course of conduct in breach of [section 1(1) or (1A)][315] is guilty of an offence.

(2)   A person guilty of an offence under this section is liable on summary conviction to imprisonment for a term not exceeding six months, or a fine not exceeding level 5 on the standard scale, or both.

(3)   ...[316]

3[317]   **Civil remedy**

(1)   An actual or apprehended breach of [section 1(1)][318] may be the subject of a claim in civil proceedings by the person who is or may be the victim of the course of conduct in question.

(2)   On such a claim, damages may be awarded for (among other things) any anxiety caused by the harassment and any financial loss resulting from the harassment.

(3)   Where—

(a)   in such proceedings the High Court or a county court grants an injunction for the purpose of restraining the defendant from pursuing any conduct which amounts to harassment, and

(b)   the plaintiff considers that the defendant has done anything which he is prohibited from doing by the injunction,

the plaintiff may apply for the issue of a warrant for the arrest of the defendant.

(4)   An application under subsection (3) may be made—

(a)   where the injunction was granted by the High Court, to a judge of that court, and

(b)   where the injunction was granted by a county court, to a judge or district judge of that or any other county court.

(5)   The judge or district judge to whom an application under subsection (3) is made may only issue a warrant if—

(a)   the application is substantiated on oath, and

---

[314]   Commencement: 16 June 1997 (SI 1997/1418).

[315]   Amendment: Words substituted: Serious Organised Crime and Police Act 2005, s 125(1), (3), with effect from 1 July 2005.

[316]   Amendment: Subsection repealed: Police Reform Act 2002, s 107(2), Sch 8, with effect from 1 October 2002 (Police Reform Act 2002 (Commencement No 1) Order 2002, SI 2002/2306).

[317]   Commencement: sub-ss (1), (2): 16 June 1997 (SI 1997/1498); sub-ss (3)–(9): 1 September 1998 (SI 1998/1902).

[318]   Amendment: Words substituted: Serious Organised Crime and Police Act 2005, s 125(1), (4), with effect from 1 July 2005.

(b)   the judge or district judge has reasonable grounds for believing that the defendant has done anything which he is prohibited from doing by the injunction.

(6)   Where—

(a)   the High Court or a county court grants an injunction for the purpose mentioned in subsection (3)(a), and
(b)   without reasonable excuse the defendant does anything which he is prohibited from doing by the injunction,

he is guilty of an offence.

(7)   Where a person is convicted of an offence under subsection (6) in respect of any conduct, that conduct is not punishable as a contempt of court.

(8)   A person cannot be convicted of an offence under subsection (6) in respect of any conduct which has been punished as a contempt of court.

(9)   A person guilty of an offence under subsection (6) is liable—

(a)   on conviction on indictment, to imprisonment for a term not exceeding five years, or a fine, or both, or
(b)   on summary conviction, to imprisonment for a term not exceeding six months, or a fine not exceeding the statutory maximum, or both.

[3A   Injunctions to protect persons from harassment within section 1(1A)][319]

[(1)   This section applies where there is an actual or apprehended breach of section 1(1A) by any person ('the relevant person').

(2)   In such a case—

(a)   any person who is or may be a victim of the course of conduct in question, or
(b)   any person who is or may be a person falling within section 1(1A)(c),

may apply to the High Court or a county court for an injunction restraining the relevant person from pursuing any conduct which amounts to harassment in relation to any person or persons mentioned or described in the injunction.

(3)   Section 3(3) to (9) apply in relation to an injunction granted under subsection (2) above as they apply in relation to an injunction granted as mentioned in section 3(3)(a).][320]

---

[319]   Amendment: Paragraph heading inserted: Serious Organised Crime and Police Act 2005, s 125(1), (5), with effect from 1 July 2005.
[320]   Amendment: Paragraph inserted: Serious Organised Crime and Police Act 2005, s 125(1), (5), with effect from 1 July 2005.

4[321] Putting people in fear of violence

(1)   A person whose course of conduct causes another to fear, on at least two occasions, that violence will be used against him is guilty of an offence if he knows or ought to know that his course of conduct will cause the other so to fear on each of those occasions.

(2)   For the purposes of this section, the person whose course of conduct is in question ought to know that it will cause another to fear that violence will be used against him on any occasion if a reasonable person in possession of the same information would think the course of conduct would cause the other so to fear on that occasion.

(3)   It is a defence for a person charged with an offence under this section to show that—

(a)   his course of conduct was pursued for the purpose of preventing or detecting crime,

(b)   his course of conduct was pursued under any enactment or rule of law or to comply with any condition or requirement imposed by any person under any enactment, or

(c)   the pursuit of his course of conduct was reasonable for the protection of himself or another or for the protection of his or another's property.

(4)   A person guilty of an offence under this section is liable—

(a)   on conviction on indictment, to imprisonment for a term not exceeding five years, or a fine, or both, or

(b)   on summary conviction, to imprisonment for a term not exceeding six months, or a fine not exceeding the statutory maximum, or both.

(5)   If on the trial on indictment of a person charged with an offence under this section the jury find him not guilty of the offence charged, they may find him guilty of an offence under section 2.

(6)   The Crown Court has the same powers and duties in relation to a person who is by virtue of subsection (5) convicted before it of an offence under section 2 as a magistrates' court would have on convicting him of the offence.

---

[321]   Commencement: 16 June 1997 (SI 1997/1418).

5[322]   **Restraining orders [*on conviction*]**[323]

(1)   A court sentencing or otherwise dealing with a person ('the defendant') convicted of an offence [*under section 2 or 4*][324] may (as well as sentencing him or dealing with him in any other way) make an order under this section.

(2)   The order may, for the purpose of protecting the victim [or victims][325] of the offence, or any other person mentioned in the order, from [*further*][326] conduct which—

(a)   amounts to harassment, or
(b)   will cause a fear of violence,

prohibit the defendant from doing anything described in the order.

(3)   The order may have effect for a specified period or until further order.

[*(3A) In proceedings under this section both the prosecution and the defence may lead, as further evidence, any evidence that would be admissible in proceedings for an injunction under section 3.*][327]

(4)   The prosecutor, the defendant or any other person mentioned in the order may apply to the court which made the order for it to be varied or discharged by a further order.

[*(4A) Any person mentioned in the order is entitled to be heard on the hearing of an application under subsection (4).*][328]

(5)   If without reasonable excuse the defendant does anything which he is prohibited from doing by an order under this section, he is guilty of an offence.

(6)   A person guilty of an offence under this section is liable—

---

[322]   Commencement: 16 June 1997 (SI 1997/1418).

[323]   Prospective amendment: Words prospectively inserted: Domestic Violence, Crime and Victims Act 2004, s 58(1), Sch 10, para 43(1), (2); for transitional and transitory provisions see s 59, Sch 12, para 5(3) thereto, with effect from a date to be appointed: see the Domestic Violence, Crime and Victims Act 2004, s 60.

[324]   Prospective amendment: Words prospectively inserted: Domestic Violence, Crime and Victims Act 2004, ss 12(1), 58(2), Sch 11; for transitional and transitory provisions see s 59, Sch 12, para 5(1) thereto, with effect from a date to be appointed: see the Domestic Violence, Crime and Victims Act 2004, s 60.

[325]   Amendment: Words inserted: Serious Organised Crime and Police Act 2005, s 125(1), (6), with effect from 1 July 2005.

[326]   Prospective amendment: Word prospectively repealed: Domestic Violence, Crime and Victims Act 2004, s 58(1), (2), Sch 10, para 43(1), (3), Sch 11; for transitional and transitory provisions see s 59, Sch 12, para 5(1) thereto, with effect from a date to be appointed: see the Domestic Violence, Crime and Victims Act 2004, s 60.

[327]   Prospective amendment: Sub-paragraph prospectively inserted: Domestic Violence, Crime and Victims Act 2004, s 12(2); for transitional and transitory provisions see s 59, Sch 12, para 5(2) thereto, with effect from a date to be appointed: see the Domestic Violence, Crime and Victims Act 2004, s 60.

[328]   Prospective amendment: Sub-paragraph prospectively inserted: Domestic Violence, Crime and Victims Act 2004, s 12(3), with effect from a date to be appointed: see the Domestic Violence, Crime and Victims Act 2004, s 60.

(a)   on conviction on indictment, to imprisonment for a term not exceeding five
       years, or a fine, or both, or

(b)   on summary conviction, to imprisonment for a term not exceeding six months,
       or a fine not exceeding the statutory maximum, or both.

*[(7) A court dealing with a person for an offence under this section may vary or discharge the order in
question by a further order.]*[329]

[5A Restraining orders on acquittal][330]

*[(1) A court before which a person ('the defendant') is acquitted of an offence may, if it considers it
necessary to do so to protect a person from harassment by the defendant, make an order prohibiting
the defendant from doing anything described in the order.*

*(2) Subsections (3) to (7) of section 5 apply to an order under this section as they apply to an order
under that one.*

*(3) Where the Court of Appeal allow an appeal against conviction they may remit the case to the
Crown Court to consider whether to proceed under this section.*

(4) Where—

(a)   the Crown Court allows an appeal against conviction, or

(b)   a case is remitted to the Crown Court under subsection (3),

*the reference in subsection (1) to a court before which a person is acquitted of an offence is to be read
as referring to that court.*

*(5) A person made subject to an order under this section has the same right of appeal against the
order as if—*

(a)   he had been convicted of the offence in question before the court which made the order, and

(b)   the order had been made under section 5.][331]

6[332]   Limitation

In section 11 of the Limitation Act 1980 (special time limit for actions in respect of
personal injuries), after subsection (1) there is inserted—

---

[329] Prospective amendment: Sub-paragraph prospectively inserted: Domestic Violence, Crime and Victims
       Act 2004, s 12(4); for transitional and transitory provisions see s 59, Sch 12, para 5(3) thereto, with
       effect from a date to be appointed: see the Domestic Violence, Crime and Victims Act 2004, s 60.
[330] Prospective amendment: Paragraph heading prospectively inserted: Domestic Violence, Crime and
       Victims Act 2004, s 12(4); for transitional and transitory provisions see s 59, Sch 12, para 5(5) thereto,
       with effect from a date to be appointed: see the Domestic Violence, Crime and Victims Act 2004, s 60.
[331] Prospective amendment: Paragraph prospectively inserted: Domestic Violence, Crime and Victims Act
       2004, s 12(4); for transitional and transitory provisions see s 59, Sch 12, para 5(5) thereto, with effect
       from a date to be appointed: see the Domestic Violence, Crime and Victims Act 2004, s 60.
[332] Commencement: 16 June 1997 (SI 1997/1498).

'(1A) This section does not apply to any action brought for damages under section 3 of the Protection from Harassment Act 1997.'

7[333]   Interpretation of this group of sections

(1)   This section applies for the interpretation of [sections 1 to 5] [*sections 1 to 5A*][334].

(2)   References to harassing a person include alarming the person or causing the person distress.

[(3) A 'course of conduct' must involve—

(a)   in the case of conduct in relation to a single person (see section 1(1)), conduct on at least two occasions in relation to that person, or
(b)   in the case of conduct in relation to two or more persons (see section 1(1A)), conduct on at least one occasion in relation to each of those persons.][335]

[(3A) A person's conduct on any occasion shall be taken, if aided, abetted, counselled or procured by another—

(a)   to be conduct on that occasion of the other (as well as conduct of the person whose conduct it is); and
(b)   to be conduct in relation to which the other's knowledge and purpose, and what he ought to have known, are the same as they were in relation to what was contemplated or reasonably foreseeable at the time of the aiding, abetting, counselling or procuring.][336]

(4)   'Conduct' includes speech.

[(5) References to a person, in the context of the harassment of a person, are references to a person who is an individual.][337]

Scotland

8–11

(*Applies to Scotland only*)

---

[333]   Commencement: 16 June 1997 (SI 1997/1418).

[334]   Prospective amendment: Words prospectively substituted: Domestic Violence, Crime and Victims Act 2004, s 58(1), Sch 10, para 44; for transitional and transitory provisions see s 59, Sch 12, para 5(3) thereto, with effect from a date to be appointed: see the Domestic Violence, Crime and Victims Act 2004, s 60.

[335]   Amendment: Sub-paragraph substituted: Serious Organised Crime and Police Act 2005, s 125(1), (7)(a), with effect from 1 July 2005.

[336]   Amendment: Sub-paragraph inserted: Criminal Justice and Police Act 2001, s 44, with effect from 1 August 2001, (Criminal Justice and Police Act 2001 (Commencement No 1) Order 2001, SI 2001/2223.

[337]   Amendment: Sub-paragraph inserted: Serious Organised Crime and Police Act 2005, s 125(1), (7)(b), with effect from 1 July 2005.

General

12[338]   National security etc

(1)   If the Secretary of State certifies that in his opinion anything done by a specified person on a specified occasion related to—

(a)   national security,
(b)   the economic well-being of the United Kingdom, or
(c)   the prevention or detection of serious crime,

and was done on behalf of the Crown, the certificate is conclusive evidence that this Act does not apply to any conduct of that person on that occasion.

(2)   In subsection (1), 'specified' means specified in the certificate in question.

(3)   A document purporting to be a certificate under subsection (1) is to be received in evidence and, unless the contrary is proved, be treated as being such a certificate.

13[339]   Corresponding provision for Northern Ireland

An Order in Council made under paragraph 1(1)(b) of Schedule 1 to the Northern Ireland Act 1974 which contains a statement that it is made only for purposes corresponding to those of sections 1 to 7 and 12 of this Act—

(a)   shall not be subject to sub-paragraphs (4) and (5) of paragraph 1 of that Schedule (affirmative resolution of both Houses of Parliament), but
(b)   shall be subject to annulment in pursuance of a resolution of either House of Parliament.

14[340]   Extent

(1)   Sections 1 to 7 extend to England and Wales only.

(2)   Sections 8 to 11 extend to Scotland only.

(3)   This Act (except section 13) does not extend to Northern Ireland.

15[341]   Commencement

(1)   Sections 1, 2, 4, 5 and 7 to 12 are to come into force on such day as the Secretary of State may by order made by statutory instrument appoint.

(2)   Sections 3 and 6 are to come into force on such day as the Lord Chancellor may by order made by statutory instrument appoint.

---

[338]   Commencement: 16 June 1997 (SI 1997/1418).
[339]   Commencement: 21 March 1997 (Royal Assent).
[340]   Commencement: 21 March 1997 (Royal Assent).
[341]   Commencement: 21 March 1997 (Royal Assent).

(3)   Different days may be appointed under this section for different purposes.

16[342]   Short title

This Act may be cited as the Protection from Harassment Act 1997.

---

[342]   Commencement: 21 March 1997 (Royal Assent).

APPENDIX 2

STATUTORY INSTRUMENTS

CIVIL PROCEDURE RULES 1998, SI 1998/3132

Sch 1 – RSC Order 94

Applications and Appeals to High Court under various Acts: Queen's Bench Division

1[1] Jurisdiction of High Court to quash certain orders, schemes, etc

(1)   Where by virtue of any enactment the High Court has jurisdiction, on the application of any person, to quash or prohibit any order, scheme, certificate or plan, any amendment or approval of a plan, any decision of a Minister or government department or any action on the part of a Minister or government department, the jurisdiction shall be exercisable by a single judge of the Queen's Bench Division.

(2)   The application must be made by claim form which must state the grounds of the application.

2[2] Filing and service of claim form

(1)   A claim form under rule 1 must be filed at the Crown Office, and served, within the time limited by the relevant enactment for making the application.

(2)   Subject to paragraph (4) the claim form must be served on the appropriate Minister or government department, and—

(a)   if the application relates to a compulsory purchase order made by an authority other than the appropriate Minister or government department, or to a clearance order under the Housing Act 1985, on the authority by whom the order was made;

(b)   if the application relates to a scheme or order to which Schedule 2 to the Highways Act 1980, applies made by an authority other than the Secretary of State, on that authority;

(c)   if the application relates to a structure plan, local plan or other development plan within the meaning of the Town and Country Planning Act 1990, on the local planning authority who prepared the plan;

(d)   if the application relates to any decision or order, or any action on the part of a Minister of the Crown to which section 21 of the Land Compensation Act 1961, or section 288 of the Town and Country Planning Act 1990, applies, on the authority directly concerned with such decision, order or action or, if that authority is the applicant, on every person who would, if he were aggrieved by the decision, order or action be entitled to apply to the High Court under the said section 21 or the said section 245, as the case may be;

---

[1]   Commencement: 26 April 1999 (SI 1998/3132).
[2]   Commencement: 26 April 1999 (SI 1998/3132).

(e)   if the application relates to a scheme to which Schedule 32 to the Local
        Government, Planning and Land Act 1980 applies, on the body which adopted
        the scheme.

(3)   In paragraph (2) 'the appropriate Minister or government department' means the
Minister of the Crown or government department by whom the order, scheme,
certificate, plan, amendment, approval or decision in question was or may be made,
authorised, confirmed, approved or given or on whose part the action in question was
or may be taken.

(4)   Where the application relates to an order made under the Road Traffic
Regulation Act 1984, the claim form must be served—

(a)   if the order was made by a Minister of the Crown, on that Minister;
(b)   if the order was made by a local authority with the consent, or in pursuance of a
        direction, of a Minister of the Crown, on that authority and also on that
        Minister;
(c)   in any other case, on the local authority by whom the order was made.

3[3]   Filing of witness statement or affidavits, etc

(1)   Evidence at the hearing of an application under rule 1 shall be by witness
statement or affidavit.

(2)   Any witness statement or affidavit in support of the application must be filed by
the applicant in the Crown Office within 14 days after service of the claim form and
the applicant must, at the time of filing, serve a copy of the witness statement or
affidavit and of any exhibit thereto on the respondent.

(3)   Any witness statement or affidavit in opposition to the application must be filed
by the respondent in the Crown Office within 21 days after the service on him under
paragraph (2) of the applicant's witness statement or affidavit and the respondent
must, at the time of filing, serve a copy of his witness statement or affidavit and of any
exhibit thereto on the applicant.

(4)   When filing a witness statement or affidavit under this rule a party must leave a
copy thereof and of any exhibit thereto at the Crown Office for the use of the Court.

(5)   Unless the Court otherwise orders, an application under rule 1 shall not be heard
earlier than 14 days after the time for filing a witness statement or affidavit by the
respondent has expired.

4[4]   Rectification of register of deeds of arrangement

(1)   Every application to the Court under section 7 of the Deeds of Arrangement
Act, 1914, for an order—

---

[3]   Commencement: 26 April 1999 (SI 1998/3132).
[4]   Commencement: 26 April 1999 (SI 1998/3132).

(a) that any omission to register a deed of arrangement within the time prescribed by that Act be rectified by extending the time for such registration, or

(b) that any omission or mis-statement of the name, residence or description of any person be rectified by the insertion in the register of his true name, residence or description,

must be made by witness statement or affidavit without notice being served on any other party to a master of the Queen's Bench Division.

(2) The witness statement or affidavit must set out particulars of the deed of arrangement and of the omission or mis-statement in question and must state the grounds on which the application is made.

5[5] Exercise of jurisdiction under Representation of the People Acts

(1) Proceedings in the High Court under the Representation of the People Acts shall be assigned to the Queen's Bench Division.

(2) Subject to paragraphs (3) and (4) the jurisdiction of the High Court under the said Acts in matters relating to parliamentary and local government elections shall be exercised by a Divisional Court.

(3) Paragraph (2) shall not be construed as taking away from a single judge or a master any jurisdiction under the said Acts which, but for that paragraph, would be exercisable by a single judge or, as the case may be, by a Master.

(4) Where the jurisdiction of the High Court under the said Acts is by a provision of any of those Acts made exercisable in matters relating to parliamentary elections by a single judge, that jurisdiction in matters relating to local government elections shall also be exercisable by a single judge.

(5) ...[6]

6, 7 ...[7]

[8 Tribunals and Inquiries Act 1992: appeal from tribunal

(1) A person who was a party to proceedings before any such tribunal as is mentioned in section 11(1) of the Tribunals and Inquiries Act 1992 and is dissatisfied in point of law with the decision of the tribunal may appeal to the High Court.

(2) The appellant's notice must be served—

(a) on the chairman of the tribunal;

---

[5] Commencement: 26 April 1999 (SI 1998/3132).

[6] Paragraph revoked: Civil Procedure (Amendment) Rules 1999, SI 1999/1008, with effect from 26 April 1999.

[7] Rules revoked: Civil Procedure (Amendment) Rules 2000, SI 2000/221, with effect from 2 May 2000 except where a person seeks to appeal a judgment or order made before that date.

(b) in the case of a tribunal which has no chairman or member who acts as a chairman, on the member or members of that tribunal; or

(c) in the case of any such tribunal as is specified in paragraph 16 of Schedule 1 to the said Act of 1992, on the secretary of the tribunal.

(3) Where an appeal is against the decision of a tribunal constituted under section 46 of the National Health Service Act 1977 the appellant's notice must be filed at the High Court within 14 days after the date of that decision.

(4) Where an appeal is against the decision of a tribunal established under section 1 of the Employment Tribunals Act 1996 the appellant's notice must be filed at the High Court within 42 days after the date of that decision.][8]

9[9] Tribunals and Inquiries Act 1992: case stated by tribunal

(1) Any such tribunal as is mentioned in section 11(1) of the Tribunals and Inquiries Act 1992 may, of its own initiative or at the request of any party to proceedings before it, state in the course of proceedings before it in the form of a special case for the decision of the High Court any question of law arising in the proceedings.

(2) Any party to proceedings before any such tribunal who is aggrieved by the tribunal's refusal to state such a case may apply to the High Court for an order directing the tribunal to do so.

(3) A case stated by any such tribunal which has no chairman or member who acts as a chairman must be signed by the member or members of the tribunal.

10, 10A, 11 …[10]

12[11] Applications for permission under section 289(6) of the Town and Country Planning Act 1990 and section 65(5) of the Planning (Listed Buildings and Conservation Areas) Act 1990

(1) An application for permission to appeal to the High Court under section 289 of the Town and Country Planning Act 1990 or section 65 of the Planning (Listed Buildings and Conservation Areas) Act 1990 shall be made within 28 days after the date on which notice of the decision was given to the applicant.

(2) An application shall—

(a) include, where necessary, any application to extend the time for applying,

(b) be in writing setting out the reasons why permission should be granted, and if the time for applying has expired, the reasons why the application was not made within that time,

---

[8] Rule substituted: Civil Procedure (Amendment) Rules 2000, SI 2000/221, with effect from 2 May 2000.

[9] Commencement: 26 April 1999 (SI 1998/3132).

[10] Rules revoked: Civil Procedure (Amendment) Rules 2000, SI 2000/221, with effect from 2 May 2000 except where a person seeks to appeal a judgment or order made before that date.

[11] Commencement: 26 April 1999 (SI 1998/3132).

(c)   be made by filing it in the Crown Office together with the decision, a draft [appellant's notice][12], and a witness statement or affidavit verifying any facts relied on,

(d)   before being filed under sub-paragraph (c), be served together with the draft [appellant's notice][13] and a copy of the witness statement or affidavit to be filed with the application, upon the persons who are referred to in rule 13(5), and

(e)   be accompanied by a witness statement or affidavit giving the names and addresses of, and the places and dates of service on, all persons who have been served with the application and, if any person who ought to be served has not been served, the witness statement or affidavit must state that fact and the reason for it.

(3) An application shall be heard—

(a)   by a single judge …[14];

(b)   unless the Court otherwise orders, not less than 21 days after it was filed at the Crown Office.

Any person served with the application shall be entitled to appear and be heard.

(4) If on the hearing of an application the Court is of opinion that any person who ought to have been served has not been served, the Court may adjourn the hearing on such terms (if any) as it may direct in order that the application may be served on that person.

(5) If the Court grants permission—

(a)   it may impose such terms as to costs and as to giving security as it thinks fit;

(b)   it may give directions; and

(c)   the [appellant's notice][15] by which the appeal is to be brought shall be served and filed within 7 days of the grant.

(6) Any respondent who intends to use a witness statement or affidavit at the hearing shall file it in the Crown Office and serve a copy thereof on the applicant as soon as is practicable and in any event, unless the Court otherwise allows, at least 2 days before the hearing. The Court may allow the applicant to use a further witness statement or affidavit.

---

[12]   Words substituted: Civil Procedure (Amendment) Rules 2000, SI 2000/221, with effect from 2 May 2000.

[13]   Words substituted: Civil Procedure (Amendment) Rules 2000, SI 2000/221, with effect from 2 May 2000.

[14]   Words revoked: Civil Procedure (Amendment) Rules 1999, SI 1999/1008, with effect from 26 April 1999.

[15]   Words substituted: Civil Procedure (Amendment) Rules 2000, SI 2000/221, with effect from 2 May 2000.

13[16]   Proceedings under sections 289 and 290 of the Town and Country Planning Act 1990 and under section 65 of the Planning (Listed Buildings and Conservation Areas) Act 1990

(1)   In this rule a reference to 'section 65' is a reference to section 65 of the Planning (Listed Buildings and Conservation Areas) Act 1990, but, save as aforesaid, a reference to a section by number is a reference to the section so numbered in the Town and Country Planning Act 1990.

(2)   An appeal shall lie to the High Court on a point of law against a decision of the Secretary of State under subsection (1) or (2) of section 289 or under subsection (1) of section 65 at the instance of any person or authority entitled to appeal under any of those subsections respectively.

(3)   In the case of a decision to which section 290 applies, the person who made the application to which the decision relates, or the local planning authority, if dissatisfied with the decision in point of law, may appeal against the decision to the High Court.

(4)   Any appeal under section 289(1) or (2), section 65(1) or section 290, and any case stated under section 289(3) or section 65(2), shall be heard and determined by a single judge unless the Court directs that the matter shall be heard and determined by a Divisional Court.

(5)   The persons to be served with the [appellant's notice][17] by which an appeal to the High Court is brought by virtue of section 289(1) or (2), section 65(1) or section 290 are—

(a)   the Secretary of State;
(b)   the local planning authority who served the notice or gave the decision, as the case may be, or, where the appeal is brought by that authority, the appellant or applicant in the proceedings in which the decision appealed against was given;
(c)   in the case of an appeal brought by virtue of section 289(1) or section 65(1), any other person having an interest in the hand to which the notice relates, and;
(d)   in the case of an appeal brought by virtue of section 289(2), any other person on whom the notice to which those proceedings related was served.

(6)   The Court hearing any such appeal may remit the matter to the Secretary of State to the extent necessary to enable him to provide the Court with such further information in connection with the matter as the Court may direct.

(7)   Where the Court is of opinion that the decision appealed against was erroneous in point of law, it shall not set aside or vary that decision but shall remit the matter to the Secretary of State with the opinion of the Court for re-hearing and determination by him.

---

[16]   Commencement: 26 April 1999 (SI 1998/3132).
[17]   Words substituted: Civil Procedure (Amendment) Rules 2000, SI 2000/221, with effect from 2 May 2000.

(8) ...[18]

(9) The Court may give directions as to the exercise, until an appeal brought by virtue of section 289(1) is finally concluded and any re-hearing and determination by the Secretary of State has taken place, of the power to serve, and institute proceedings (including criminal proceedings) concerning—

(a) a stop notice under section 183, and
(b) a breach of condition notice under section 187A.

14[19] Applications under section 13 Coroners Act 1988

(1) Any application under section 13 of the Coroners Act 1988 shall be heard and determined by a Divisional Court.

(2) The application must be made by claim form and the claim form must state the grounds of the application and, unless the application is made by the Attorney General, shall be accompanied by his fiat.

(3) The claim form must be filed in the Crown Office and served upon all persons directly affected by the application within six weeks after the grant of the fiat.

15[20] Applications under section 42, Supreme Court Act 1981

(1) Every application to the High Court by the Attorney General under section 42 of the Supreme Court Act 1981 shall be heard and determined by a Divisional Court.

(2) The application must be made by claim form which, together with a witness statement or affidavit in support, shall be filed in the Crown Office and served on the person against whom the order is sought.

16 [...][21]

---

[18] Paragraph revoked: Civil Procedure (Amendment) Rules 2000, SI 2000/221, with effect from 2 May 2000.
[19] Commencement: 26 April 1999 (SI 1998/3132).
[20] Commencement: 26 April 1999 (SI 1998/3132).
[21] Provision revoked: Civil Procedure (Amendment) Rules 2004, SI 2004/1306, with effect from 30 June 2004.

Family Proceedings Rules 1991, SI 1991/1247[22]

****

Part III

Other Matrimonial etc Proceedings

****

[3.8 Applications under Part IV of the Family Law Act 1996 (Family Homes and Domestic Violence)

(1) An application for an occupation order or a non-molestation order under Part IV of the Family Law Act 1996 shall be made in Form FL401.

(2) An application for an occupation order or a non-molestation order made by a child under the age of sixteen shall be made in Form FLA401 but shall be treated, in the first instance, as an application to the High Court for leave.

(3) An application for an occupation order or a non-molestation order which is made in other proceedings which are pending shall be made in Form FL401.

(4) An application in Form FL401 shall be supported by a statement which is signed by the applicant and is sworn to be true.

(5) Where an application is made without giving notice, the sworn statement shall state the reasons why notice was not given.

(6) An application made on notice (together with the sworn statement and a notice in Form FL402) shall be served by the applicant on the respondent personally not less than 2 days before the date on which the application will be heard.

(7) The court may abridge the period specified in paragraph (6).

(8) Where the applicant is acting in person, service of the application shall be effected by the court if the applicant so requests.

This does not affect the court's power to order substituted service.

---

[22] SI reference: SI 1991/1247.
  Made under: Matrimonial and Family Proceedings Act 1984, s 40(1).

(9)   Where an application for an occupation order or a non-molestation order is pending, the court shall consider (on the application of either party or of its own motion) whether to exercise its powers to transfer the hearing of that application to another court and shall make an order for transfer in Form FL417 if it seems necessary or expedient to do so.

(10)   Rule 9.2A shall not apply to an application for an occupation order or a non-molestation order under Part IV of the Family Law Act 1996.

(11)   A copy of an application for an occupation order under section 33, 35 or 36 of the Family Law Act 1996 shall be served by the applicant by first-class post on the mortgagee or, as the case may be, the landlord of the dwelling-house in question, with a notice in Form FL416 informing him of his right to make representations in writing or at any hearing.

(12)   Where the application is for the transfer of a tenancy, notice of the application shall be served by the applicant on the other cohabitant[, spouse or civil partner]²³ and on the landlord (as those terms are defined by paragraph 1 of Schedule 7 to the Family Law Act 1996) and any person so served shall be entitled to be heard on the application.

(13)   [Paragraph 7 of Appendix 4 shall apply]²⁴ to—

(a)   an application for an occupation order under section 33, 35 or 36 of the Family Law Act 1996, and

(b)   an application for the transfer of a tenancy ...²⁵

(14)   Rule 3.6(7) to (9) (...²⁶) shall apply, with the necessary modifications, to an application for the transfer of a tenancy, as they apply to an application under rule 3.6.

(15)   The applicant shall file a statement in Form FL415 after he has served the application.]²⁷

[3.9   Hearing of applications under Part IV of the Family Law Act 1996

(1)   An application for an occupation order or a non-molestation order under Part IV of the Family Law Act 1996 shall be dealt with in chambers unless the court otherwise directs.

---

²³   Words substituted: Family Proceedings (Amendment) (No 5) Rules 2005, SI 2005/2922, with effect from 5 December 2005.

²⁴   Words substituted: Family Proceedings (Amendment) (No 5) Rules 2005, SI 2005/2922, with effect from 5 December 2005.

²⁵   Words revoked: Family Proceedings (Amendment) (No 5) Rules 2005, SI 2005/2922, with effect from 5 December 2005.

²⁶   Words revoked: Family Proceedings (Amendment) (No 5) Rules 2005, SI 2005/2922, with effect from 5 December 2005.

²⁷   Rule substituted: Family Proceedings (Amendment No 3) Rules 1997, SI 1997/1893, with effect from 1 October 1997.
     [NB references to rr 2.62 and 2.63 in this rule shall be read as if the amendments to those rules by Family Proceedings (Amendment No 2) Rules 1999, SI 1999/3491 had not been made: Family Proceedings (Amendment No 2) Rules 1999, SI 1999/3491].

(2)   Where an order is made on an application made ex parte, a copy of the order together with a copy of the application and of the sworn statement in support shall be served by the applicant on the respondent personally.

(3)   Where the application is for an occupation order under section 33, 35 or 36 of the Family Law Act 1996, a copy of any order made on the application shall be served by the applicant by first-class post on the mortgagee or, as the case may be, the landlord of the dwelling-house in question.

(4)   A copy of an order made on an application heard inter partes shall be served by the applicant on the respondent personally.

(5)   Where the applicant is acting in person, service of a copy of any order made on the hearing of the application shall be effected by the court if the applicant so requests.

(6)   The following forms shall be used in connection with hearings of applications under Part IV of the Family Law Act 1996—

(a)   a record of the hearing shall be made on Form FL405, [and][...][28]

(b)   any [*occupation*][29] order made on the hearing shall be issued in Form FL404[.][, *and*][30]

[(c)   *any non-molestation order made on the hearing shall be issued in Form FL404a*][31]

(7)   The court may direct that a further hearing be held in order to consider any representations made by a mortgagee or a landlord.

(8)   An application to vary, extend or discharge an order made under Part IV of the Family Law Act 1996 shall be made in Form FL403 and this rule shall apply to the hearing of such an application.

3.9A   Enforcement of orders made on applications under Part IV of the Family Law Act 1996

[(1)   Where a power of arrest is attached to one or more of the provisions ('the relevant provisions') of an order made under Part IV of the Family Law Act 1996—

(a)   the relevant provisions shall be set out in Form FL406 and the form shall not include any provisions of the order to which the power of arrest was not attached; and

---

28   Prospective amendment: Word prospectively revoked: Family Proceedings (Amendment No [-]) Rules 2005, r 2(a), with effect from a date to be appointed.

29   Prospective amendment: Word prospectively inserted: Family Proceedings (Amendment No [-]) Rules 2005, r 2(b)(i), with effect from a date to be appointed.

30   Prospective amendment: Word prospectively substituted: Family Proceedings (Amendment No [-]) Rules 2005, r 2(b)(ii), with effect from a date to be appointed.

31   Prospective amendment: Sub-paragraph prospectively inserted: Family Proceedings (Amendment No [-]) Rules 2005, r 2(c), with effect from a date to be appointed.

(b)   a copy of the form shall be delivered to the officer for the time being in charge
       of any police station for the applicant's address or of such other police station as
       the court may specify.

The copy of the form delivered under sub-paragraph (b) shall be accompanied by a
statement showing that the respondent has been served with the order or informed of
its terms (whether by being present when the order was made or by telephone or
otherwise).]

*[(1) Where the court makes an occupation order under the Family Law Act 1996 and a power of
arrest is attached to one or more of the provisions ('the relevant provisions') of the order, the relevant
provisions shall be set out in Form FL406 and the form shall not include any provisions of the order
to which the power of arrest was not attached.]*[32]

*[(1A) Where the court makes a non-molestation order under that Act, all the provisions of that
order shall be set out in Form [FL406a].*

*(1B) Where paragraph (1) or (1A) applies, the following documents shall be delivered to the officer
for the time being in charge of any police station for the applicant's address or of such other police
station as the court may specify—*

(a)   a copy of Form FL406 or [FL406a], as the case may be; and
*(b)   a statement showing that the respondent has been served with the order or informed of its terms
       (whether by being present when the order was made or by telephone or otherwise).]*[33]

(2)   Where an order is made varying or discharging the relevant provisions *[of the
occupation order or, as the case may be, any provisions of the non-molestation order]*[34], the proper
officer shall—

(a)   immediately inform the officer who received a copy of the form under
       paragraph [(1)][*1B*][35] and, if the applicant's address has changed, the officer for
       the time being in charge of the police station for the new address; and
(b)   deliver a copy of the order to any officer so informed.

(3)   An application for the issue of a warrant for the arrest of the respondent [*under
section 47(8) of the Family Law Act 1996*][36] shall be made in Form FL407 and the
warrant shall be issued in Form FL408.

(4)   The court before whom a person is brought following his arrest may—

---

[32]   Prospective amendment: Sub-paragraph prospectively substituted: Family Proceedings (Amendment
       No [-]) Rules 2005, r 3(a), with effect from a date to be appointed.
[33]   Prospective amendment: Sub-paragraphs prospectively inserted: Family Proceedings (Amendment No
       [-]) Rules 2005, r 3(b), with effect from a date to be appointed.
[34]   Prospective amendment: Words prospectively inserted: Family Proceedings (Amendment No [-]) Rules
       2005, r 3(c)(i), with effect from a date to be appointed.
[35]   Prospective amendment: Word prospectively substituted: Family Proceedings (Amendment No [-])
       Rules 2005, r 3(c)(ii), with effect from a date to be appointed.
[36]   Prospective amendment: Words prospectively inserted: Family Proceedings (Amendment No [-]) Rules
       2005, r 3(d), with effect from a date to be appointed.

(a)   determine whether the facts, and the circumstances which led to the arrest, amounted to disobedience of the order, or

(b)   adjourn the proceedings and, where such an order is made, the arrested person may be released and—

    (i)   be dealt with within 14 days of the day on which he was arrested; and

    (ii) be given not less than 2 days' notice of the adjourned hearing.

Nothing in this paragraph shall prevent the issue of a notice under CCR Order 29, rule 1(4) if the arrested person is not dealt with within the period mentioned in sub-paragraph (b)(i) above.

(5)   The following provisions shall apply, with the necessary modifications, to the enforcement of orders made ...[37] under Part IV of the Family Law Act 1996—

(a)   RSC Order 52, rule 7 (powers to suspend execution of committal order);

(b)   (in a case where an application for an order of committal is made to the High Court) RSC Order 52, rule 2 (application for leave);

(c)   CCR Order 29, rule 1 (committal for breach of order);

(d)   CCR Order 29, rule 1A (undertakings);

(e)   CCR Order 29, rule 3 (discharge of person in custody); and CCR Order 29, rule 1 shall have effect, as if for paragraph (3), there were substituted the following—

'(3)   At the time when the order is drawn up, the proper officer shall—

(a) where the order made is (or includes) a non-molestation order and

(b) where the order made is an occupation order and the court so directs,

issue a copy of the order, indorsed with or incorporating a notice as to the consequences of disobedience, for service in accordance with paragraph (2).'.

(6)   The court may adjourn consideration of the penalty to be imposed for contempts found provided and such consideration may be restored if the respondent does not comply with any conditions specified by the court.

(7)   Where the court makes a hospital order in Form FL413 or a guardianship order in Form FL414 under the Mental Health Act 1983, the proper officer shall—

(a)   send to the hospital any information which will be of assistance in dealing with the patient;

(b)   inform the applicant when the respondent is being transferred to hospital.

(8)   Where a transfer direction given by the Secretary of State under section 48 of the Mental Health Act 1983 is in force in respect of a person remanded in custody by the court under Schedule 5 to the Family Law Act 1996, the proper officer shall notify—

(a)   the governor of the prison to which that person was remanded; and

(b)   the hospital where he is detained,

---

[37]   Words revoked: Family Proceedings (Amendment No 3) Rules 2005, SI 2005/559, with effect from 4 April 2005.

of any committal hearing which that person is required to attend and the proper officer shall give notice in writing to the hospital where that person is detained of any further remand under paragraph 3 of Schedule 5 to the Family Law Act 1996.

(9)   An order for the remand of the respondent shall be in Form FL409.

(10)   In paragraph (4) 'arrest' means arrest under a power of arrest attached to [an order][*an occupation order under section 47(2) or (3) of the Family Law Act 1996*][38] or under a warrant of arrest [*issued on an application under section 47(8) of that Act*][39].][40]

[3.10   Applications under Part IV of the Family Law Act 1996: bail

(1)   An application for bail made by a person arrested under a power of arrest [*attached to an occupation order under section 47(2) or (3) of the Family Law Act 1996*][41] or a warrant of arrest [*issued on an application under section 47(8) of that Act*][42] may be made either orally or in writing.

(2)   Where an application is made in writing, it shall contain the following particulars—

(a)   the full name of the person making the application;

(b)   the address of the place where the person making the application is detained at the time when the application is made;

(c)   the address where the person making the application would reside if he were to be granted bail;

(d)   the amount of the recognizance in which he would agree to be bound; and

(e)   the grounds on which the application is made and, where a previous application has been refused, full particulars of any change in circumstances which has occurred since that refusal.

(3)   An application made in writing shall be signed by the person making the application or by a person duly authorised by him in that behalf or, where the person making the application is a minor or is for any reason incapable of acting, by a guardian ad litem acting on his behalf and a copy shall be served by the person making the application on the applicant for the Part IV order.

(4)   The persons prescribed for the purposes of paragraph 4 of Schedule 5 to the Family Law Act 1996 (postponement of taking of recognizance) are—

(a)   a district judge,

---

[38]   Prospective amendment: Words prospectively substituted: Family Proceedings (Amendment No [-]) Rules 2005, r 3(e)(i), with effect from a date to be appointed.

[39]   Prospective amendment: Words prospectively inserted: Family Proceedings (Amendment No [-]) Rules 2005, r 3(e)(ii), with effect from a date to be appointed.

[40]   Rules 3.9, 3.9A substituted for r 3.9 as originally enacted: Family Proceedings (Amendment No 3) Rules 1997, SI 1997/1893, with effect from 1 October 1997.

[41]   Prospective amendment: Words prospectively inserted: Family Proceedings (Amendment No [-]) Rules 2005, r 4(a), with effect from a date to be appointed.

[42]   Prospective amendment: Words prospectively inserted: Family Proceedings (Amendment No [-]) Rules 2005, r 4(b), with effect from a date to be appointed.

(b)   a justice of the peace,

(c)   a justices' clerk,

(d)   a police officer of the rank of inspector or above or in charge of a police station, and

(e)   (where the person making the application is in his custody) the governor or keeper of a prison.

(5)   The person having custody of the person making the application shall—

(a)   on receipt of a certificate signed by or on behalf of the district judge stating that the recognizance of any sureties required have been taken, or on being otherwise satisfied that all such recognizances have been taken; and

(b)   on being satisfied that the person making the application has entered into his recognizance,

release the person making the application.

(6)   The following forms shall be used—

(a)   the recognizance of the person making the application shall be in Form FL410 and that of a surety in Form FL411;

(b)   a bail notice in Form FL412 shall be given to the respondent where he is remanded on bail.][43]

****

Part IV

Proceedings under the Children Act 1989

****

[4.24A Exclusion requirements: interim care orders and emergency protection orders

(1)   This rule applies where the court includes an exclusion requirement in an interim care order or an emergency protection order.

(2)   The applicant for an interim care order or emergency protection order shall—

(a)   prepare a separate statement of the evidence in support of the application for an exclusion requirement;

(b)   serve the statement personally on the relevant person with a copy of the order containing the exclusion requirement (and of any power of arrest which is attached to it);

(c)   inform the relevant person of his right to apply to vary or discharge the exclusion requirement.

---

[43]   Rule substituted: Family Proceedings (Amendment No 3) Rules 1997, SI 1997/1893, with effect from 1 October 1997.

(3) Where a power of arrest is attached to an exclusion requirement in an interim care order or an emergency protection order, a copy of the order shall be delivered to the officer for the time being in charge of the police station for the area in which the dwelling-house in which the child lives is situated (or of such other station as the court may specify) together with a statement showing that the relevant person has been served with the order or informed of its terms (whether by being present when the order was made or by telephone or otherwise).

(4)　Rules 3.9(5), 3.9A (except paragraphs (1) and (3)) and 3.10 shall apply, with the necessary modifications, for the service, variation, discharge and enforcement of any exclusion requirement to which a power of arrest is attached as they apply to an order made on an application under Part IV of the Family Law Act 1996.

(5)　The relevant person shall serve the parties to the proceedings with any application which he makes for the variation or discharge of the exclusion requirement.

(6)　Where an exclusion requirement ceases to have effect whether—

(a)　as a result of the removal of a child under section 38A(10) or 44A(10),
(b)　because of the discharge of the interim care order or emergency protection order, or
(c)　otherwise,

the applicant shall inform—

    (i)　the relevant person,
    (ii)　the parties to the proceedings,
    (iii)　any officer to whom a copy of the order was delivered under paragraph (3), and
    (iv)　(where necessary) the court.

(7)　Where the court includes an exclusion requirement in an interim care order or an emergency protection order of its own motion, paragraph (2) shall apply with the omission of any reference to the statement of the evidence.][44]

****

Part VIII

Appeals

****

---

[44]　Rule inserted: Family Proceedings (Amendment No 3) Rules 1997, SI 1997/1893, with effect from 1 October 1997.

[8.1A Appeals from orders made under Part IV of the Family Law Act 1996

(1)   This rule applies to all appeals from orders made under Part IV of the Family Law Act 1996 and on such an appeal—

(a)   paragraphs (2), (3), (4), (5), (7) and (8) of rule 4.22,
(b)   paragraphs (5) and (6) of rule 8.1, and
(c)   paragraphs (4)(e) and (6) of rule 8.2,

shall apply subject to the following provisions of this rule and with the necessary modifications.

(2)   The [[designated officer]⁴⁵ for]⁴⁶ the magistrates' court from which an appeal is brought shall be served with the documents mentioned in rule 4.22(2).

(3)   Where an appeal lies to the High Court, the documents required to be filed by rule 4.22(2) shall be filed in the registry of the High Court which is nearest to the magistrates' court from which the appeal is brought.

(4)   Where the appeal is brought against the making of a hospital order or a guardianship order under the Mental Health Act 1983, a copy of any written evidence considered by the magistrates' court under section 37(1)(a) of the 1983 Act shall be sent by the [[designated officer]⁴⁷]⁴⁸ to the registry of the High Court in which the documents relating to the appeal are filed in accordance with paragraph (3).

(5)   A district judge may dismiss an appeal to which this rule applies for want of prosecution and may deal with any question of costs arising out of the dismissal or withdrawal of an appeal.

(6)   Any order or decision granting or varying an order (or refusing to do so) in proceedings in which an application is made in accordance with rule 3.8 for—

(a)   an occupation order as described in section 33(4) of the Family Law Act 1996,
(b)   an occupation order containing any of the provisions specified in section 33(3) where the applicant or the respondent has matrimonial home rights, or
(c)   a transfer of tenancy,

---

45   Words substituted: Courts Act 2003 (Consequential Provisions) (No 2) Order 2005, SI 2005/617 with effect from 1 April 2005.
46   Words substituted: Family Proceedings (Amendment) Rules 2001, SI 2001/821, with effect from 1 April 2001.
47   Words substituted: Courts Act 2003 (Consequential Provisions) (No 2) Order 2005, SI 2005/617 with effect from 1 April 2005.
48   Words substituted: Family Proceedings (Amendment) Rules 2001, SI 2001/821, with effect from 1 April 2001.

shall be treated as a final order for the purposes of CCR Order 37, rule 6 and, on an appeal from such an order, the judge may exercise his own discretion in substitution for that of the district judge and the provisions of CCR Order 37, rule 6 shall apply.][49]

---

[49] Rule inserted: Family Proceedings (Amendment No 3) Rules 1997, SI 1997/1893, with effect from 1 October 1997.

Family Proceedings (Amendment No [ ]) Rules 2005 (draft)

Made	*[ ] 2005*
Laid before Parliament	*[ ] 2005*
Coming into force	*[ ] 2005*

We, the authority having power under section 40(1) of the Matrimonial and Family Proceedings Act 1984 to make rules of court for the purposes of family proceedings in the High Court and county courts, in the exercise of the powers conferred by that section, make the following Rules:

Citation, Commencement and Interpretation

1.—(1)   These Rules may be cited as the Family Proceedings (Amendment No [ ]) Rules 2005 and shall come into force on [ ] 2005.

(2)   In these Rules a reference to a rule or Appendix by number alone is a reference to the rule or Appendix so numbered in the Family Proceedings Rules 1991.

Amendments to the Family Proceedings Rules 1991

2.   In rule 3.9(6)—

(a)   in paragraph (a), omit 'and';
(b)   in paragraph (b)—
    (i)   after 'any', insert 'occupation'; and
    (ii)   after 'FL404', omit the full-stop and insert ', and'; and
(c)   after paragraph (b), insert—

'(c) any non-molestation order made on the hearing shall be issued in Form FL404a.'.

3.   In rule 3.9A—

(a)   for paragraph (1), substitute—

'(1)   Where the court makes an occupation order under the Family Law Act 1996 and a power of arrest is attached to one or more of the provisions ("the relevant provisions") of the order, the relevant provisions shall be set out in Form FL406 and the form shall not include any provisions of the order to which the power of arrest was not attached.'

(b)   after paragraph (1), insert—

'(1A)   Where the court makes a non-molestation order under that Act, all the provisions of that order shall be set out in Form [FL406a].

(1B)   Where paragraph (1) or (IA) applies, the following documents shall be delivered to the officer for the time being in charge of any police station for the applicant's address or of such other police station as the court may specify—

(a)   a copy of Form FL406 or [FL406a], as the case may be; and
(b)   a statement showing that the respondent has been served with the order or informed of its terms (whether by being present when the order was made or by telephone or otherwise).'

(c)   in paragraph (2)—
   (i)   after 'relevant provisions', insert 'of the occupation order or, as the case may be, any provisions of the non-molestation order'; and
   (ii)   in sub-paragraph (a), for '(1)', substitute '(1B)'.
(d)   in paragraph (3), after 'the respondent', insert 'under section 47(8) of the Family Law Act 1996'; and
(e)   in paragraph (10)—
   (i)   for 'an order', substitute 'an occupation order under section 47(2) or (3) of the Family Law Act 1996'; and
   (ii)   after 'warrant of arrest', insert 'issued on an application under section 47(8) of that Act'.

4.   In rule 3.10(1)—

(a)   after 'power of arrest', insert 'attached to an occupation order under section 47(2) or (3) of the Family Law Act 1996'; and
(b)   after 'warrant of arrest', insert 'issued on an application under section 47(8) of that Act'.

5.   In Appendix 1—

(a)   for Form FL401, substitute the form set out in Schedule 1 to these Rules;
(b)   for Form FL404, substitute the form set out in Schedule 2 to these Rules;
(c)   after Form FL404, insert Form FL404a as set out in Schedule 3 to these Rules;
(d)   for Form FL406, substitute the form set out in Schedule 4 to these Rules; and
(e)   after Form FL406, insert Form FL406a as set out in Schedule 5 to these Rules.

Signatory text

Address

Date

Name

Parliamentary Under Secretary of State

Department

Family Proceedings Courts (Matrimonial Proceedings etc) Rules 1991, SI 1991/1991

Part II

Matrimonial Proceedings under the Domestic Proceedings and Magistrates' Courts Act 1978[, Proceedings under Section 55A of the [Family Law Act 1986,][50][51] [[-][52] Proceedings under Part IV of the Family Law Act 1996][53] [and Proceedings under the Civil Partnership Act 2004][54]

[3A   Applications under Part IV of the Family Law Act 1996

(1)   An application for an occupation order or a non-molestation order under Part IV of the Family Law Act 1996 (Family Homes and Domestic Violence) shall be made in Form FL401.

(2)   An application for an occupation order or a non-molestation order which is made in other proceedings which are pending shall be made in Form FL401.

(3)   An application in Form FL401 shall be supported—

(a)   by a statement which is signed and is declared to be true; or
(b)   with the leave of the court, by oral evidence.

(4)   An application in Form FL401 may, with the leave of the justices' clerk or of the court, be made ex parte, in which case—

(a)   the applicant shall file with the [[designated officer for the court][55][56] or the court the application at the time when the application is made or as directed by the justices' clerk; and
(b)   the evidence in support of the application shall state the reasons why the application is made ex parte.

---

50   Words substituted: Magistrates' Courts (Miscellaneous Amendments) Rules 2005, SI 2005/2930, with effect from 5 December 2005.
51   Words inserted: Family Proceedings Courts (Family Law Act 1986) Rules 2001, SI 2001/778, with effect from 1 April 2001.
52   Word revoked: Magistrates' Courts (Miscellaneous Amendments) Rules 2005, SI 2005/2930, with effect from 5 December 2005.
53   Words inserted: Family Proceedings Courts (Matrimonial Proceedings etc) (Amendment) Rules 1997, SI 1997/1894, with effect from 1 October 1997.
54   Words inserted: Magistrates' Courts (Miscellaneous Amendments) Rules 2005, SI 2005/2930, with effect from 5 December 2005.
55   Words substituted: Courts Act 2003 (Consequential Provisions) (No 2) Order 2005 SI 2005/617, with effect from 1 April 2005.
56   Words substituted: Magistrates' Courts (Transfer of Justices' Clerks' Functions) (Miscellaneous Amendments) Rules 2001, SI 2001/615, with effect from 1 April 2001.

(5)   An application made on notice (together with any statement supporting it and a notice in Form FL402) shall be served by the applicant on respondent personally not less than 2 business days prior to the date on which the application will be heard.

(6)   The court or the justices' clerk may abridge the period specified in paragraph (5).

(7)   Where the applicant is acting in person, service of the application may, with the leave of the justices' clerk, be effected in accordance with rule 4.

(8)   Where an application for an occupation order or a non-molestation order is pending, the court shall consider (on the application of either party or of its own motion) whether to exercise its powers to transfer the hearing of that application to another court and the justices' clerk or the court shall make an order for transfer in Form FL417 if it seems necessary or expedient to do so.

(9)   Where an order for transfer is made, the [[designated officer for the court][57]][58] shall send a copy of the order—

(a)   to the parties, and
(b)   to the family proceedings court or to the county court to which the proceedings are to be transferred.

(10)   A copy of an application for an occupation order under section 33, 35 or 36 of the Family Law Act 1996 shall be served by the applicant by first-class post on the mortgagee or, as the case may be, the landlord of the dwelling-house in question, with a notice in Form FL416 informing him of his right to make representations in writing or at any hearing.

(11)   The applicant shall file a statement in Form FL415 after he has served the application.

(12)   Rule 33A of the Family Proceedings Courts (Children Act 1989) Rules 1991 (disclosure of addresses) shall apply for the purpose of preventing the disclosure of addresses where an application is made in Form FL401 as it applies for that purpose in proceedings under the Children Act 1989.][59]

[12A   Hearing of applications under Part IV of the Family Law Act 1996

(1)   This rule applies to the hearing of applications under the Part IV of the Family Law Act 1996 and the following forms shall be used in connection with such hearings—

---

[57]   Words substituted: Courts Act 2003 (Consequential Provisions) (No 2) Order 2005 SI 2005/617,.with effect from 1 April 2005.

[58]   Words substituted: Magistrates' Courts (Transfer of Justices' Clerks' Functions) (Miscellaneous Amendments) Rules 2001, SI 2001/615, with effect from 1 April 2001.

[59]   Rule inserted: Family Proceedings Courts (Matrimonial Proceedings etc) (Amendment) Rules 1997, SI 1997/1894, with effect from 1 October 1997.

(a)   a record of the hearing shall be made on Form FL405, [and][60]

(b)   any [*occupation*][61] order made on the hearing shall be issued in Form FL404[.][, *and*][62]

[*(c)   any non-molestation order made on the hearing shall be issued in Form FL404a.*][63]

(2)   Where an order is made on an application made ex parte, a copy of the order together with a copy of the application and of any statement supporting it shall be served by the applicant on the respondent personally.

(3)   Where the applicant is acting in person, service of a copy of an order made on an application made ex parte shall be effected by the [[designated officer for the court][64]][65] if the applicant so requests.

(4)   Where the application is for an occupation order under section 33, 35 or 36 of the Family Law Act 1996, a copy of any order made on the application shall be served by the applicant by first-class post on the mortgagee or, as the case may be, the landlord of the dwelling-house in question.

(5)   A copy of an order made on an application heard inter partes shall be served by the applicant on the respondent personally.

(6)   Where the applicant is acting in person, service of a copy of the order made on an application heard inter partes may, with the leave of the justices' clerk, be effected in accordance with rule 4.

(7)   The court may direct that a further hearing be held in order to consider any representations made by a mortgagee or a landlord.

12B   Applications to vary etc orders made under Part IV of the Family Law Act 1996

An application to vary, extend or discharge an order made under Part IV of the Family Law Act 1996 shall be made in Form FL403 and rules 12 and 12A shall apply to the hearing of such an application.][66]

---

60   Prospective amendment: Word prospectively revoked: Family Proceedings Courts Matrimonial Proceedings etc.) (Amendment) Rules 2005, r 2(a), with effect from a date to be appointed.

61   Prospective amendment: Word prospectively inserted: Family Proceedings Courts Matrimonial Proceedings etc.) (Amendment) Rules 2005, r 2(b)(i), with effect from a date to be appointed.

62   Prospective amendment: Word prospectively inserted: Family Proceedings Courts Matrimonial Proceedings etc.) (Amendment) Rules 2005, r 2(b)(ii), with effect from a date to be appointed.

63   Prospective amendment: Sub-paragraph prospectively inserted: Family Proceedings Courts Matrimonial Proceedings etc.) (Amendment) Rules 2005, r 2(c), with effect from a date to be appointed.

64   Words substituted: Courts Act 2003 (Consequential Provisions) (No 2) Order 2005 SI 2005/617, with effect from 1 April 2005.

65   Words substituted: Magistrates' Courts (Transfer of Justices' Clerks' Functions) (Miscellaneous Amendments) Rules 2001, SI 2001/615, with effect from 1 April 2001.

66   Rules inserted: Family Proceedings Courts (Matrimonial Proceedings etc) (Amendment) Rules 1997, SI 1997/1894, with effect from 1 October 1997.

[20 Enforcement of orders made on applications under Part IV of the Family Law Act 1996

[(1) Where a power of arrest is attached to one or more of the provisions ('the relevant provisions') of an order made under Part IV of the Family Law Act 1996—

(a) the relevant provisions shall be set out in Form FL406 and the form shall not include any provisions of the order to which the power of arrest was not attached; and

(b) a copy of the appropriate form shall be delivered to the officer for the time being in charge of any police station for the applicant's address or of such other police station as the court may specify.

The copy of the appropriate form delivered under paragraph (b) shall be accompanied by a statement showing that the respondent has been served with the order or informed of its terms (whether by being present when the order was made or by telephone or otherwise).]

[(1) Where a power of arrest is attached to one or more of the provisions ('the relevant provisions') of an occupation order under the Family Law Act 1996, the relevant provisions shall be set out in Form FL406 and the form shall not include any provisions of the order to which the power of arrest was not attached.][67]

[(1A) Where a non-molestation order is made under that Act, all the provisions of the order shall be set out in Form [FL406a].

(1B) Where paragraph (1) or (1A) applies, the following documents shall be delivered to the officer for the time being in charge of any police station for the applicant's address or of such other police station as the court may specify—

(a) a copy of Form FL406 or [FL406a], as the case may be; and

(b) a statement showing that the respondent has been served with the order or informed of its terms (whether by being present when the order was made or by telephone or otherwise).][68]

(2) Where an order is made varying or discharging the relevant provisions *[of the occupation order or, as the case may be, any provisions of the non-molestation order]*[69], the [[designated officer of the court][70]][71] shall—

---

[67] Prospective amendment: Sub-paragraph prospectively substituted: Family Proceedings Courts Matrimonial Proceedings etc.) (Amendment) Rules 2005, r 3(a), with effect from a date to be appointed.

[68] Prospective amendment: Sub-paragraphs prospectively inserted: Family Proceedings Courts Matrimonial Proceedings etc.) (Amendment) Rules 2005, r 3(b), with effect from a date to be appointed.

[69] Prospective amendment: Words prospectively inserted: Family Proceedings Courts Matrimonial Proceedings etc.) (Amendment) Rules 2005, r 3(c)(i), with effect from a date to be appointed.

[70] Words substituted: Courts Act 2003 (Consequential Provisions) (No 2) Order 2005, SI 2005/617, with effect from 1 April 2005.

[71] Words substituted: Magistrates' Courts (Transfer of Justices' Clerks' Functions) (Miscellaneous Amendments) Rules 2001, SI 2001/615, with effect from 1 April 2001.

(a)   immediately inform the officer who received a copy of the form under paragraph [(1)][*1B*][72] and, if the applicant's address has changed, the officer for the time being in charge of the police station for the new address; and

(b)   deliver a copy of the order to any officer so informed.

(3) An application for the issue of a warrant for the arrest of the respondent [*under section 47(8) of the Family Law Act 1996*][73] shall be made in Form FL407 and the warrant shall be issued in Form FL408 and delivered by the [[designated officer of the court][74]][75] to the officer for the time being in charge of any police station for the respondent's address or of such other police station as the court may specify.

(4) The court before whom a person is brought following his arrest may—

(a)   determine whether the facts, and the circumstances which led to the arrest, amounted to disobedience of the order, or

(b)   adjourn the proceedings and, where such an order is made, the arrested person may be released and—

    (i)   be dealt with within 14 days of the day on which he was arrested; and

    (ii)   be given not less than 2 business days' notice of the adjourned hearing.

Nothing in this paragraph shall prevent the issue of a notice under paragraph (8) if the arrested person is not dealt with within the period mentioned in sub-paragraph (b)(i) above.

(5)   Paragraphs (6) to (13) shall apply for the enforcement of orders made on applications under Part IV of the Family Law Act 1996 by committal order.

(6)   Subject to paragraphs (11) and (12), an order shall not be enforced by committal order unless—

(a)   a copy of the order in Form FL404 [*or FL404a*][76] has been served personally on the respondent; and

(b)   where the order requires the respondent to do an act, the copy has been so served before the expiration of the time within which he was required to do the act and was accompanied by a copy of any order, made between the date of the order and the date of service, fixing that time.

---

[72]   Prospective amendment: Word prospectively substituted: Family Proceedings Courts Matrimonial Proceedings etc.) (Amendment) Rules 2005, r 3(c)(ii), with effect from a date to be appointed.

[73]   Prospective amendment: Words prospectively inserted: Family Proceedings Courts Matrimonial Proceedings etc.) (Amendment) Rules 2005, r 3(d), with effect from a date to be appointed.

[74]   Words substituted: Courts Act 2003 (Consequential Provisions) (No 2) Order 2005, SI 2005/617, with effect from 1 April 2005.

[75]   Words substituted: Magistrates' Courts (Transfer of Justices' Clerks' Functions) (Miscellaneous Amendments) Rules 2001, SI 2001/615, with effect from 1 April 2001.

[76]   Prospective amendment: Words prospectively inserted: Family Proceedings Courts Matrimonial Proceedings etc.) (Amendment) Rules 2005, r 3(e), with effect from a date to be appointed.

(7)   At the time when the order is drawn up, the [[designated officer of the court]⁷⁷]⁷⁸ shall—

(a)   where the order made is (or includes) a non-molestation order, and
(b)   where the order made is an occupation order and the court so directs,

issue a copy of the order, indorsed with or incorporating a notice as to the consequences of disobedience, for service in accordance with paragraph (6).

(8)   If the respondent fails to obey the order, the [[designated officer of the court]⁷⁹]⁸⁰ shall, at the request of the applicant, issue a notice in Form FL418 warning the respondent that an application will be made for him to be committed and, subject to paragraph (12), the notice shall be served on him personally.

(9)   The request for issue of the notice under paragraph (8) shall be treated as a complaint and shall—

(a)   identify the provisions of the order or undertaking which it is alleged have been disobeyed or broken;
(b)   list the ways in which it is alleged that the order or undertaking has been disobeyed or broken;
(c)   be supported by a statement which is signed and is declared to be true and which states the grounds on which the application is made,

and, unless service is dispensed with under paragraph (12), a copy of the statement shall be served with the notice.

(10)   If an order in Form FL419 (a committal order) is made, it shall include provision for the issue of a warrant of committal in Form FL420 and, unless the court otherwise orders—

(a)   a copy of the order shall be served personally on the person to be committed either before or at the time of the execution of the warrant; or
(b)   the order for the issue of the warrant may be served on the person to be committed at any time within 36 hours after the execution of the warrant.

(11)   An order requiring a person to abstain from doing an act may be enforced by committal order notwithstanding that a copy of the order has not been served personally if the court is satisfied that, pending such service, the respondent had notice thereof either—

(a)   by being present when the order was made;
(b)   by being notified of the terms of the order whether by telephone or otherwise.

---

⁷⁷   Words substituted: Courts Act 2003 (Consequential Provisions) (No 2) Order 2005, SI 2005/617, with effect from 1 April 2005.
⁷⁸   Words substituted: Magistrates' Courts (Transfer of Justices' Clerks' Functions) (Miscellaneous Amendments) Rules 2001, SI 2001/615, with effect from 1 April 2001.
⁷⁹   Words substituted: Courts Act 2003 (Consequential Provisions) (No 2) Order 2005, SI 2005/617, with effect from 1 April 2005.
⁸⁰   Words substituted: Magistrates' Courts (Transfer of Justices' Clerks' Functions) (Miscellaneous Amendments) Rules 2001, SI 2001/615, with effect from 1 April 2001.

(12)   The court may dispense with service of a copy of the order under paragraph (6) or a notice under paragraph (8) if the court thinks it just to do so.

(13)   Where service of a notice to show cause is dispensed with under paragraph (12) and a committal order is made, the court may of its own motion fix a date and time when the person to be committed is to be brought before the court.

(14)   Paragraphs (6) to (10), (12) and (13) shall apply to the enforcement of undertakings with the necessary modifications and as if—

(a)   for paragraph (6) there were substituted the following—

'(6)   A copy of Form FL422 recording the undertaking shall be delivered by the [[designated officer of the court][81]][82] to the party giving the undertaking—

(a) by handing a copy of the document to him before he leaves the court building; or

(b) where his place of residence is known, by posting a copy to him at his place of residence; or

(c) through his solicitor,

and, where delivery cannot be effected in this way, the [[designated officer of the court][83]][84] shall deliver a copy of the document to the party for whose benefit the undertaking is given and that party shall cause it to be served personally as soon as is practicable.';

(b)   in paragraph (12), the words from 'a copy' to 'paragraph (6) or' were omitted.

(15)   Where a person in custody under a warrant or order, desires to apply to the court for his discharge, he shall make his application in writing attested by the governor of the prison showing that he has purged or is desirous of purging his contempt and the [[designated officer of the court][85]][86] shall, not less than one day before the application is heard, serve notice of it on the party (if any) at whose instance the warrant or order was issued.

(16)   The court by whom an order of committal is made may by order direct that the execution of the order of committal shall be suspended for such period or on such terms or conditions as it may specify.

---

81   Words substituted: Courts Act 2003 (Consequential Provisions) (No 2) Order 2005, SI 2005/617, with effect from 1 April 2005.

82   Words substituted: Magistrates' Courts (Transfer of Justices' Clerks' Functions) (Miscellaneous Amendments) Rules 2001, SI 2001/615, with effect from 1 April 2001.

83   Words substituted: Courts Act 2003 (Consequential Provisions) (No 2) Order 2005, SI 2005/617, with effect from 1 April 2005.

84   Words substituted: Magistrates' Courts (Transfer of Justices' Clerks' Functions) (Miscellaneous Amendments) Rules 2001, SI 2001/615, with effect from 1 April 2001.

85   Words substituted: Courts Act 2003 (Consequential Provisions) (No 2) Order 2005, SI 2005/617, with effect from 1 April 2005.Words substituted: Courts Act 2003 (Consequential Provisions) (No 2) Order 2005, SI 2005/617, with effect from 1 April 2005.

86   Words substituted: Magistrates' Courts (Transfer of Justices' Clerks' Functions) (Miscellaneous Amendments) Rules 2001, SI 2001/615.

(17)   Where execution of an order of committal is suspended by an order under paragraph (16), the applicant for the order of committal must, unless the court otherwise directs, serve on the person against whom it was made a notice informing him of the making and terms of the order under that paragraph.

(18)   The court may adjourn consideration of the penalty to be imposed for contempts found proved and such consideration may be restored if the respondent does not comply with any conditions specified by the court.

(19)   Where the court makes a hospital order in Form FL413 or a guardianship order in Form FL414 under the Mental Health Act 1983, the [[designated officer of the court][87]][88] shall—

(a)   send to the hospital any information which will be of assistance in dealing with the patient;

(b)   inform the applicant when the respondent is being transferred to hospital.

(20)   Where a transfer direction given by the Secretary of State under section 48 of the Mental Health Act 1983 is in force in respect of a person remanded in custody by the court, the [[designated officer of the court][89]] shall notify—

(a)   the governor of the prison to which that person was remanded; and

(b)   the hospital where he is detained,

of any committal hearing which that person is required to attend and the [designated officer of the court][90]shall give notice in writing to the hospital where that person is detained of any further remand.

(21)   An order for the remand of the respondent shall be in Form FL409 and an order discharging the respondent from custody shall be in Form FL421.

(22)   In paragraph (4) 'arrest' means arrest under a power of arrest [*attached to an occupation order under section 47(2) or (3) of the Family Law Act 1996*][91] attached to an order or under a warrant of arrest [*issued on an application under section 47(8) of that Act*][92].

---

[87]   Words substituted: Courts Act 2003 (Consequential Provisions) (No 2) Order 2005, SI 2005/617, with effect from 1 April 2005.

[88]   Words substituted: Magistrates' Courts (Transfer of Justices' Clerks' Functions) (Miscellaneous Amendments) Rules 2001, SI 2001/615, with effect from 1 April 2001.

[89]   Words substituted: Courts Act 2003 (Consequential Provisions) (No 2) Order 2005, SI 2005/617, with effect from 1 April 2005.

[90]   Words substituted: Courts Act 2003 (Consequential Provisions) (No 2) Order 2005, SI 2005/617, with effect from 1 April 2005.

[91]   Prospective amendment: Words prospectively inserted: Family Proceedings Courts Matrimonial Proceedings etc.) (Amendment) Rules 2005, r 3(f)(i), with effect from a date to be appointed.

[92]   Prospective amendment: Words prospectively inserted: Family Proceedings Courts Matrimonial Proceedings etc.) (Amendment) Rules 2005, r 3(f)(ii), with effect from a date to be appointed.

21   Applications under Part IV of the Family Law Act 1996: bail

(1)   An application for bail made by a person arrested under a power of arrest [*attached to an occupation order under section 47(2) or (3) of the Family Law Act 1996*][93] or a warrant of arrest [*issued on an application under section 47(8) of that Act*][94] may be made either orally or in writing.

(2)   Where an application is made in writing, it shall contain the following particulars—

(a)   the full name of the person making the application;

(b)   the address of the place where the person making the application is detained at the time when the application is made;

(c)   the address where the person making the application would reside if he were to be granted bail;

(d)   the amount of the recognizance in which he would agree to be bound; and

(e)   the grounds on which the application is made and, where a previous application has been refused, full particulars of any change in circumstances which has occurred since that refusal.

(3)   An application made in writing shall be signed by the person making the application or by a person duly authorised by him in that behalf or, where the person making the application is a minor or is for any reason incapable of acting, by a guardian ad litem acting on his behalf and a copy shall be served by the person making the application on the applicant for the Part IV order.

(4)   The following form shall be used—

(a)   the recognizance of the person making the application shall be in Form FL410 and that of a surety in Form FL411;

(b)   a bail notice in Form FL412 shall be given to the respondent where he is remanded on bail.][95]

---

[93]   Prospective amendment: Words prospectively inserted: Family Proceedings Courts Matrimonial Proceedings etc.) (Amendment) Rules 2005, r 4(a), with effect from a date to be appointed.

[94]   Prospective amendment: Words prospectively inserted: Family Proceedings Courts Matrimonial Proceedings etc.) (Amendment) Rules 2005, r 4(B), with effect from a date to be appointed.

[95]   Rules substituted: Family Proceedings Courts (Matrimonial Proceedings etc) (Amendment) Rules 1997, SI 1997/1894, with effect from 1 October 1997.

Family Proceedings Courts (Matrimonial Proceedings etc) (Amendment) Rules 2005 (draft)

Made	*[ ] 2005*
Laid before Parliament	*[ ] 2005*
Coming into force	*[ ] 2005*

The Lord Chancellor, in exercise of the powers conferred upon him by section 144 of the Magistrates' Courts Act 1981, and after consultation with the rule committee appointed under that sections, makes the following Rules:

Citation, commencement and interpretation

1.—(1) These Rules may be cited as the Family Proceedings Courts (Matrimonial Proceedings etc.) (Amendment) Rules 2005 and shall come into force on [ ] 2005.

(2) In these Rules, unless the context otherwise requires, a reference to a rule or Schedule by number alone is a reference to the rule or Schedule so numbered in the Family Proceedings Courts (Matrimonial Proceedings etc.) Rules 1991.

Amendments to the Family Proceedings Courts (Matrimonial Proceedings etc.) Rules 1991

2.   In rule 12A(1)—

(a)   in paragraph (a), omit 'and'; (b) in paragraph (b)—
  (i)   after 'any', insert 'occupation'; and
  (ii)   after 'FL404', omit the full-stop and insert ', and'; and (c) after paragraph (b), insert—

'(c) any non-molestation order made on the hearing shall be issued in Form FL404a.'.

3.   In rule 20—

(a)   for paragraph (1), substitute—

'(1) Where a power of arrest is attached to one or more of the provisions ("the relevant provisions") of an occupation order under the Family Law Act 1996, the relevant provisions shall be set out in Form FL406 and the form shall not include any provisions of the order to which the power of arrest was not attached.';

(b)   after paragraph (1), insert—

'(I A) Where a non-molestation order is made under that Act, all the provisions of the order shall be set out in Form [FL406a].

(1B) Where paragraph (1) or (IA) applies, the following documents shall be delivered to the officer for the time being in charge of any police station for the applicant's address or of such other police station as the court may specify—

(a)   a copy of Form FL406 or [FL406a], as the case may be; and

(b)   a statement showing that the respondent has been served with the order or informed of its terms (whether by being present when the order was made or by telephone or otherwise).'

(c)   in paragraph (2)—

    (i)   after 'relevant provisions', insert 'of the occupation order or, as the case may be, any provisions of the non-molestation order'; and

    (ii)   in sub-paragraph (a), for '(1)', substitute '(1B)'.

(d)   in paragraph (3), after 'the respondent', insert 'under section 47(8) of the Family Law Act 1996';

(e)   in paragraph (6)(a), after 'FL404', insert 'or FL404a, as the case may be,';

(f)   in paragraph (22)—

    (i)   after 'power of arrest', insert 'attached to an occupation order under section 47(2) or (3) of the Family Law Act 1996'; and

    (ii)   after 'warrant of arrest', insert 'issued on an application under section 47(8) of that Act'.

4.   In rule 21(1)—

(a)   after 'power of arrest', insert 'attached to an occupation order under section 47(2) or (3) of the Family Law Act 1996'; and

(b)   after 'warrant of arrest', insert 'issued on an application under section 47(8) of that Act'.

5.   In Schedule I—

(a) for Form FL401, substitute the form set out in Schedule 1 to these Rules;

(b) for Form FL404, substitute the form set out in Schedule 2 to these Rules;

(c) after Form FL404, insert Form FL404a as set out in Schedule 3 to these Rules;

(d) for Form FL406, substitute the form set out in Schedule 4 to these Rules; and

(e) after Form FL 406, insert Form 406a as set out in Schedule 5 to these Rules.

Signatory text

Address

Date

Name

Parliamentary Under Secretary of State

Department

Family Law Act 1996 (Part IV) (Allocation of Proceedings) Order 1997, SI 1997/1896[96]

1[97]

(1)   This Order may be cited as the Family Law Act 1996 (Part IV) (Allocation of Proceedings) Order 1997 and shall come into force on 1st October 1997.

(2)   In this Order, unless the context otherwise requires—

'county court' means a county court of one of the classes specified in article 2;
'family proceedings' has the meaning assigned by section 63 and includes proceedings which are family business within the meaning of section 32 of the Matrimonial and Family Proceedings Act 1984;
'family proceedings court' has the meaning assigned by article 3;
'the Act' means the Family Law Act 1996 and a section, Part or Schedule referred to by number alone means the section, Part or Schedule so numbered in that Act.

2[98] Classes of county court

The classes of county court specified for the purposes of this Order are—

(a)   designated county courts, being those courts designated for the time being—

   (i)   as divorce county courts by an order under section 33 of the Matrimonial and Family Proceedings Act 1984; or

   (ii)   as civil partnership proceedings county courts by an order under section 36A of the Matrimonial and Family Proceedings Act 1984; or

   (iii)   as both divorce county courts and civil partnership proceedings county courts by such orders][99];

(b)   family hearing centres, being those courts set out in Schedule 1 to the Children (Allocation of Proceedings) Order 1991; and

(c)   care centres, being those courts set out in column (ii) of Schedule 2 to that Order.

---

96   SI reference: SI 1997/1896.
    Made under: Family Law Act 1996, s 57.
97   Commencement: 1 October 1997 (art 1(1)).
98   Commencement: 1 October 1997 (art 1(1)).
99   Subsection inserted: Family Law Act 1996 (Part IV).(Allocation of Proceedings) (Amendment) Order 2005, SI 2005/2924, with effect from 5 December 2005.

3[100] Classes of magistrates' court

The classes of magistrates' court specified for the purposes of this Order are family proceedings courts, being those courts constituted in accordance with section 67 of the Magistrates' Courts Act 1980.

Commencement of Proceedings

4[101] Commencement of proceedings

(1) Subject to section 59, paragraph 1 of Schedule 7 and the provisions of this article, proceedings under Part IV may be commenced in a county court or in a family proceedings court.

(2) An application—

(a)   under Part IV brought by an applicant who is under the age of eighteen; and
(b)   for the grant of leave under section 43 (Leave of court required for applications by children under sixteen),

shall be commenced in the High Court.

(3) Where family proceedings are pending in a county court or a family proceedings court, an application under Part IV may be made in those proceedings.

5[102] Application to extend, vary or discharge order

(1) Proceedings under Part IV—

(a)   to extend, vary or discharge an order, or
(b)   the determination of which may have the effect of varying or discharging an order,

shall be made to the court which made the order.

(2) A court may transfer proceedings made in accordance with paragraph (1) to any other court in accordance with the provisions of articles 6 to 14.

Transfer of Proceedings

6[103] Disapplication of enactments about transfer

Sections 38 and 39 of the Matrimonial and Family Proceedings Act 1984 shall not apply to proceedings under Part IV.

---

[100]   Commencement: 1 October 1997 (art 1(1)).
[101]   Commencement: 1 October 1997 (art 1(1)).
[102]   Commencement: 1 October 1997 (art 1(1)).
[103]   Commencement: 1 October 1997 (art 1(1)).

7[104] Transfer from one family proceedings court to another

A family proceedings court ('the transferring court') shall (on application or of its own motion) transfer proceedings under Part IV to another family proceedings court ('the receiving court') where—

(a)   the transferring court considers that it would be appropriate for those proceedings to be heard together with other family proceedings which are pending in the receiving court; and

(b)   the receiving court, by its justices' clerk (as defined by rule 1(2) of the Family Proceedings Courts (Children Act 1989) Rules 1991), consents to the transfer.

8[105]   Transfer from family proceedings court to county court

(1)   A family proceedings court may, on application or of its own motion, transfer proceedings under Part IV to a county court where it considers that—

(a)   it would be appropriate for those proceedings to be heard together with other family proceedings which are pending in that court; or

(b)   the proceedings involve—

   (i)   a conflict with the law of another jurisdiction;
   (ii)   some novel and difficult point of law;
   (iii)   some question of general public interest; or

(c)   the proceedings are exceptionally complex.

(2)   A family proceedings court must transfer proceedings under Part IV to a county court where—

(a)   a child under the age of eighteen is the respondent to the application or wishes to become a party to the proceedings; or

(b)   a party to the proceedings is a person who, by reason of mental disorder within the meaning of the Mental Health Act 1983, is incapable of managing and administering his property and affairs.

(3)   Except where transfer is ordered under paragraph (1)(a), the proceedings shall be transferred to the nearest county court.

9[106]   Transfer from family proceedings court to High Court

A family proceedings court may, on application or of its own motion, transfer proceedings under Part IV to the High Court where it considers that it would be appropriate for those proceedings to be heard together with other family proceedings which are pending in that Court.

---

[104]   Commencement: 1 October 1997 (art 1(1)).
[105]   Commencement: 1 October 1997 (art 1(1)).
[106]   Commencement: 1 October 1997 (art 1(1)).

10[107]   Transfer from one county court to another

A county court may, on application or of its own motion, transfer proceedings under Part IV to another county court where—

(a)   it considers that it would be appropriate for those proceedings to be heard together with other family proceedings which are pending in that court;

(b)   the proceedings involve the determination of a question of a kind mentioned in section 59(1) and the property in question is situated in the district of another county court; or

(c)   it seems necessary or expedient so to do.

11[108]   Transfer from county court to family proceedings court

A county court may, on application or of its own motion, transfer proceedings under Part IV to a family proceedings court where—

(a)   it considers that it would be appropriate for those proceedings to be heard together with other family proceedings which are pending in that court; or

(b)   it considers that the criterion

(i)   in article 8(1)(a) no longer applies because the proceedings with which the transferred proceedings were to be heard have been determined;

(ii)   in article 8(1)(b) or (c) does not apply.

12[109]   Transfer from county court to High Court

A county court may, on application or of its own motion, transfer proceedings under Part IV to the High Court where it considers that the proceedings are appropriate for determination in the High Court.

13[110]   Transfer from High Court to family proceedings court

The High Court may, on application or of its own motion, transfer proceedings under Part IV to a family proceedings court where it considers that it would be appropriate for those proceedings to be heard together with other family proceedings which are pending in that court.

14[111]   Transfer from High Court to county court

The High Court may, on application or of its own motion, transfer proceedings under Part IV to a county court where it considers that—

(a)   it would be appropriate for those proceedings to be heard together with other family proceedings which are pending in that court;

---

[107]   Commencement: 1 October 1997 (art 1(1)).
[108]   Commencement: 1 October 1997 (art 1(1)).
[109]   Commencement: 1 October 1997 (art 1(1)).
[110]   Commencement: 1 October 1997 (art 1(1)).
[111]   Commencement: 1 October 1997 (art 1(1)).

(b)   the proceedings are appropriate for determination in a county court; or

(c)   it is appropriate for an application made by a child under the age of eighteen to be heard in a county court.

15[112]   Disposal following arrest

Where a person is brought before—

(a)   a relevant judicial authority in accordance with section 47(7)(a), or

(b)   a court by virtue of a warrant issued under section 47(9),

and the matter is not disposed of forthwith, the matter may be transferred to be disposed of by the relevant judicial authority or court which issued the warrant or, as the case may be, which attached the power of arrest under section 47(2) or (3), if different.

Miscellaneous

16[113]   Principal Registry of the Family Division

(1)   The principal registry of the Family Division of the High Court shall be treated, for the purposes of this Order, as if it were a [designated county court,][114] a family hearing centre and a care centre.

(2)   Without prejudice to article 10, the principal registry may transfer an order made in proceedings which are pending in the principal registry to the High Court for enforcement.

17[115]   Lambeth, Shoreditch and Woolwich County Courts

Proceedings under Part IV may be commenced in, transferred to and tried in Lambeth, Shoreditch or Woolwich County Court.

18[116]   Contravention of provisions of this Order

Where proceedings are commenced or transferred in contravention of a provision of this Order, the contravention shall not have the effect of making the proceedings invalid.

---

[112]   Commencement: 1 October 1997 (art 1(1)).

[113]   Commencement: 1 October 1997 (art 1(1)).

[114]   Words substituted: Family Law Act 1996 (Part IV) (Allocation of Proceedings) (Amendment) Order 2005, SI 2005/2924, with effect from 5 December 2005.

[115]   Commencement: 1 October 1997 (art 1(1)).

[116]   Commencement: 1 October 1997 (art 1(1)).

APPENDIX 3

FORMS

FORM FL401 – APPLICATION FOR A NON-MOLESTATION ORDER / AN OCCUPATION ORDER

Application for:	**To be completed by the court**
a non-molestation order	Date issued
an occupation order	
Family Law Act 1996 (Part IV)	Case number
The court	

Please read the accompanying notes as you complete this form.

1 About you (the applicant)

State your title (Mr, Mrs etc), full name, address,
telephone number and date of birth (if under 18):

State your solicitor's name, address, reference,
telephone, FAX and DX numbers:

2 About the respondent

State the respondent's name, address and date of
birth (if known):

3 The Order(s) for which you are applying

This application is for:

☐ a non-molestation order

☐ an occupation order

☐ Tick this box if you wish the court to hear
your application without notice being given
to the respondent. The reasons relied on for an
application being heard without notice must be
stated in the statement in support.

1

---

4 Your relationship to the respondent (the person to be served with this application)

Your relationship to the respondent is:
Please tick only one of the following

1 ☐ Married

2 ☐ Were married

3 ☐ Cohabiting

4 ☐ Were cohabiting

5 ☐ Both of you live or have lived in the same
      household

6 ☐ Relative
      State how related:

7 ☐ Agreed to marry.
      Give the date the agreement was made. If the
      agreement has ended, state when.

8 ☐ Both of you are parents of or have
      parental responsibility for a child

9 ☐ One of you is a parent of a child and the
      other has parental responsibility
      for that child

---

10 ☐ One of you is the natural parent or
grandparent of a child adopted or
freed for adoption, and the other is:
    (i)   the adoptive parent
 or (ii) a person who has applied for
           an adoption order for the child
 or (iii) a person with whom the child
           has been placed for adoption
 or (iv) the child who has been adopted
           or freed for adoption.
State whether (i), (ii), (iii) or (iv):

11 ☐ Both of you are parties to the same family
proceedings (see also Section 11 below).

5 Application for a non-molestation order

If you wish to apply for a non-molestation order,
state briefly in this section the order you want.

Give full details in support of your application in
your supporting evidence

6 Application for an occupation order

*If you do not wish to apply for an occupation
order, please go to section 9 of this form.*

(A) State the address of the dwelling house to which
your application relates:

(B) State whether it is occupied by you or the
respondent now or in the past, or whether it was
intended to be occupied by you or the respondent:

3

(C) State whether you are entitled to occupy
the dwelling-house: ☐ Yes   ☐ No

If yes, explain why:

(D) State whether the respondent is entitled to
occupy the dwelling-house: ☐ Yes   ☐ No

If yes, explain why:

**On the basis of your answer to (C) and (D)
above, tick one of the boxes 1 to 5 below to
show the category into which you fit**

1 ☐ a spouse who has matrimonial home rights in
the dwelling-house, or a person who is
entitled to occupy it by virtue of a beneficial
estate or interest or contract or by virtue of
any enactment giving him or her the right to
remain in occupation.

If you tick box 1, state whether there is a
dispute or pending proceedings between you
and the respondent about your right to occupy
the dwelling-house.

2 ☐ a former spouse with no existing right to
occupy, where the respondent spouse is
entitled.

3 ☐ a cohabitant or former cohabitant with no
existing right to occupy, where the respondent
cohabitant or former cohabitant is so entitled.

4 ☐ a spouse or former spouse who is not entitled
to occupy, where the respondent spouse or
former spouse is also not entitled.

5 ☐ a cohabitant or former cohabitant who is not
entitled to occupy, where the respondent
cohabitant or former cohabitant is also not
entitled.

Matrimonial Home Rights

If you do have matrimonial home rights please:

State whether the title to the land is registered or unregistered (if known):

If registered, state the Land Registry title number (if known):

If you wish to apply for an occupation order, state briefly here the order you want. Give full details in support of your application in your supporting evidence.

7 Application for additional order(s) about the dwelling house

If you want to apply for any of the orders listed in the notes to this section, state what order you would like the court to make:

8 Mortgage and rent

Is the dwelling house subject to a mortgage?

☐ Yes   ☐ No

If yes, please provide the name and address of the mortgagee:

Is the dwelling house rented?

☐ Yes   ☐ No

If yes, please provide the name and address of the landlord:

9 At the court

Will you need an interpreter at court?

☐ Yes   ☐ No

If 'Yes', specify the language:

If you need an interpreter because you do not
speak English, you are responsible for providing
your own.

If you need an interpreter or other facilities
because of a disability, please contact the court
to ask what help is available.

10 Other information

State the name and date of birth of any child
living with or staying with, or likely to live with
or stay with, you or the respondent:

State the name of any other person living in the
same household as you and the respondent, and
say why they live there:

11 Other Proceedings and Orders

If there are any other current family proceedings
or orders in force involving you and the
respondent, state the type of proceedings or
orders, the court and the case number. This
includes any application for an occupation order
or non-molestation order against you by the
respondent.

This application is to be served upon the respondent

Signed   Date

Application for a non-molestation order or occupation order
Notes for Guidance

Section 1

If you do not wish your address to be made known to the respondent, leave the space on the form blank and complete Confidential Address Form C8. The court can give you this form.

If you are under 18, someone over 18 must help you make this application. That person, who might be one of your parents, is called a 'next friend'.

If you are under 16 you need permission to make this application. You must apply to the High Court for permission, using this form. If the High Court gives you permission to make this application, it will then either hear the application itself or transfer it to a county court.

Section 3

An urgent order made by the court before notice of the application is served on the respondent is called an ex-parte order. In deciding whether to make an ex-parte order the court will consider all the circumstances of the case, including:

◻ *any risk of significant harm to the applicant or a relevant child, attributable to conduct of the respondent, if the order is not made immediately*

◻ *whether it is likely that the applicant will be deterred or prevented from pursuing the application if an order is not made immediately*

◻ *whether there is reason to believe that the respondent is aware of the proceedings but is deliberately evading service and that the applicant or a relevant child will be seriously prejudiced by the delay involved.*

If the court makes an ex-parte order, it must give the respondent an opportunity to make representations about the order as soon as just and convenient at a full hearing.

'Harm' in relation to a person who has reached the age of 18 means ill-treatment or the impairment of health, and in relation to a child means ill-treatment or the impairment of health and development. 'Ill-treatment' includes forms of ill-treatment which are not physical and, in relation to a child, includes sexual abuse. The court will require evidence of any harm which you allege in support of your application. This evidence should be included in the statement accompanying this application.

Section 4

For you to be able to apply for an order you must be related to the respondent in one of the ways listed in this section of the form. If you are not related in one of these ways you should seek legal advice.

Cohabitants are a man and a woman who, although not married to each other, are living or have lived together as husband and wife. People who have cohabited, but have then married will not fall within this category, but will fall within the category of married people.

Those who live or have lived in the same household do not include people who share the same household because one of them is the other's employee, tenant, lodger or boarder.

You will only be able to apply as a relative of the respondent if you are:

(A) the father, mother, stepfather, stepmother, son, daughter, stepson, stepdaughter, grandmother, grandfather, grandson or granddaughter of the respondent or of the respondent's spouse or former spouse.

(B) the brother, sister, uncle, aunt, niece or nephew (whether of the full blood or of the half blood or by marriage) of the respondent or of the respondent's spouse or former spouse.

This includes, in relation to a person who is living or has lived with another person as husband and wife, any person who would fall within (A) or (B) if the parties were married to each other (for example, your cohabitee's father or brother).

Agreements to marry: You will fall within this category only if you make this application within three years of the termination of the agreement. The court will require the following evidence of the agreement:

> *evidence in writing*

or the gift of an engagement ring in contemplation of marriage

or evidence that a ceremony has been entered into in the presence of one or more other persons assembled for the purpose of witnessing it.

Parents and parental responsibility: You will fall within this category if

> *both you and the respondent are either the parents of a child or have parental responsibility for that child*

or if one of you is the parent and the other has parental responsibility.

Under the Children Act 1989, parental responsibility is held automatically by a child's mother, and by the child's father if he and the mother were married to each other at the time of the child's birth or have married subsequently. Where this is not the case, parental responsibility can be acquired by the father in accordance with the provisions of the Children Act 1989.

Section 5

A non-molestation order can forbid the respondent to molest you or a relevant child. Molestation can include, for example, violence, threats, pestering and other forms of harassment. The court can forbid particular acts of the respondent, molestation in general, or both.

Section 6

If you wish to apply for an occupation order but you are uncertain about your answer to any of the questions in this part of the application form, you should seek legal advice.

(A) A dwelling-house includes any building or part of a building which is occupied as a dwelling; any caravan, houseboat or structure which is occupied as a dwelling; and any yard, garden, garage or outhouse belonging to it and occupied with it.

Section 6 (continued)

(C) & (D) *The following questions give examples to help you to decide if you or the respondent, or both of you, are entitled to occupy the dwelling-house:*

(a)   *Are you the sole legal owner of the dwelling-house?*

(b)   *Are you and the respondent joint legal owners of the dwelling-house?*

(c)   *Is the respondent the sole legal owner of the dwelling-house?*

(d)   *Do you rent the dwelling-house as sole tenant?*

(e)   *Do you and the respondent rent the dwelling-house as joint tenants?*

(f)   *Does the respondent rent the dwelling house as sole tenant?*

If you answer ☐ **Yes** *to (a), (b), (d) or (e) you are likely to be entitled to occupy the dwelling-house*

☐ **Yes** *to (c) or (f) you may not be entitled (unless, for example, you are a spouse and have matrimonial home rights - see the notes under 'Matrimonial Home Rights' below)*

☐ **Yes** *to (b), (c), (e) or (f), the respondent is likely to be entitled to occupy the dwelling-house.*

☐ **Yes** *to (a) or (d) the respondent may not be entitled (unless, for example, he is a spouse and has matrimonial home rights).*

Box 1 *For example, if you are sole owner, joint owner, or if you rent the property. If you are not a spouse, former spouse, cohabitant or former cohabitant of the respondent, you will only be able to apply for an occupation order if you fall within this category.*

If you answer Yes to this question, it will not be possible for a magistrates' court to deal with the application, unless the court decides that it is unnecessary for it to decide this question in order to deal with the application or make an order. If the court decides that it cannot deal with the application, it will transfer the application to a county court.

Box 2 *For example, if the respondent was married to you and is sole owner or rents the property.*

Box 3 *For example, if the respondent is or was cohabiting with you and is sole owner or rents the property.*

Matrimonial Home Rights

Where one spouse is entitled to occupy the dwelling-house by virtue of a beneficial estate or interest or contract or by virtue of any enactment giving him or her the right to remain in occupation, and the other spouse is not so entitled, the spouse who is not entitled has matrimonial home rights. These are a right, if the spouse is in occupation, not to be evicted or excluded from the dwelling house except with the leave of the court and, if the spouse is not in occupation, the right with the leave of the court to enter into and occupy the dwelling-house.

Matrimonial home rights do not exist if the dwelling-house has never been, and was never intended to be, the matrimonial home of the two spouses. If the marriage has come to an end, matrimonial home rights will also have ceased, unless a court order has been made during the marriage for the rights to continue after the end of the marriage.

Occupation Orders *The possible orders are:*

If you have ticked box 1 above, an order under section 33 of the Act may:

☐   *enforce the applicant's entitlement to remain in occupation as against the respondent*

☐   *require the respondent to permit the applicant to enter and remain in the dwelling-house or part of it*

☐   *regulate the occupation of the dwelling-house by either or both parties*

☐   *if the respondent is also entitled to occupy, the order may prohibit, suspend or restrict the exercise by him, of that right*

☐   *restrict or terminate any matrimonial home rights of the respondent*

☐   *require the respondent to leave the dwelling-house or part of it*

☐   *exclude the respondent from a defined area around the dwelling-house*

☐   *declare that the applicant is entitled to occupy the dwelling-house or has matrimonial home rights in it*

☐   *provide that matrimonial home rights of the applicant are not brought to an end by the death of the other spouse or termination of the marriage.*

If you have ticked box 2 or box 3 above, an order under section 35 or 36 of the Act may:

☐   *give the applicant the right not to be evicted or excluded from the dwelling-house or any part of it by the respondent for a specified period*

☐   *prohibit the respondent from evicting or excluding the applicant during that period*

☐   *give the applicant the right to enter and occupy the dwelling house for a specified period*

☐   *require the respondent to permit the exercise of that right*

☐   *regulate the occupation of the dwelling-house by either or both of the parties*

☐   *prohibit, suspend or restrict the exercise by the respondent of his right to occupy*

☐   *require the respondent to leave the dwelling-house or part of it*

☐   *exclude the respondent from a defined area around the dwelling-house.*

If you have ticked box 4 or box 5 above, an order under section 37 or 38 of the Act may:

☐   *require the respondent to permit the applicant to enter and remain in the dwelling-house or part of it*

☐   *regulate the occupation of the dwelling-house by either or both of the parties*

☐   *require the respondent to leave the dwelling-house or part of it*

☐   *exclude the respondent from a defined area around the dwelling-house.*

Section 6 (continued)

You should provide any evidence which you have on the following matters in your evidence in support of this application. If necessary, further statements may be submitted after the application has been issued.

If you have ticked box 1, 4 or 5 above, the court will need any available evidence of the following:

- the housing needs and resources of you, the respondent and any relevant child
- the financial resources of you and the respondent
- the likely effect of any order, or of any decision not to make an order, on the health, safety and well-being of you, the respondent and any relevant child
- the conduct of you and the respondent in relation to each other and otherwise.

If you have ticked box 2 above, the court will need any available evidence of:

- the housing needs and resources of you, the respondent and relevant child
- the financial resources of you and the respondent
- the likely effect of any order, or of any decision not to make an order on the health, safety and well-being of you, the respondent and any relevant child
- the conduct of you and the respondent in relation to each other and otherwise.
- the length of time that has elapsed since you and the respondent ceased to live together
- the length of time that has elapsed since the marriage was dissolved or annulled
- the existence of any pending proceedings between you and the respondent:
  - under section 23A of the Matrimonial Causes Act 1973 (property adjustment orders in connection with divorce proceedings etc.
  - or under Schedule 1 para 1(2)(d) or (e) of the Children Act 1989 (orders for financial relief against parents)
  - or relating to the legal or beneficial ownership of the dwelling-house.

If you have ticked box 3 above, the court will need any available evidence of:

- the housing needs and resources of you, the respondent and any relevant child
- the financial resources of you and the respondent
- the likely effect of any order, or of any decision not to make an order, on the health, safety and well-being of you, the respondent and any relevant child
- the conduct of you and the respondent in relation to each other and otherwise
- the nature of you and the respondent's relationship

- the length of time during which you have lived together as husband and wife
- whether you and the respondent have had any children, or have both had parental responsibility for any children
- the length of time which has elapsed since you and the respondent ceased to live together
- the existence of any pending proceedings between you and the respondent under Schedule 1 para 1(2)(d) or (e) of the Children Act 1989 or relating to the legal or beneficial ownership of the dwelling-house.

Section 7

Under section 40 of the Act the court may make the following additional orders when making an occupation order:

- impose on either party obligations as to the repair and maintenance of the dwelling-house
- impose on either party obligations as to the payment of rent, mortgage or other outgoings affecting it
- order a party occupying the dwelling-house to make periodical payments to the other party in respect of the accommodation, if the other party would (but for the order) be entitled to occupy it
- grant either party possession or use of furniture or other contents
- order either party to take reasonable care of any furniture or other contents
- order either party to take reasonable steps to keep the dwelling-house and any furniture or other contents secure.

Section 8

If the dwelling-house is rented or subject to a mortgage, the landlord or mortgagee must be served with notice of the proceedings in Form FL416. He or she will then be able to make representations to the court regarding the rent or mortgage.

Section 10

A person living in the same household may, for example, be a member of the family or a tenant or employee of you or the respondent.

FORM FL401 – APPLICATION FOR A NON-MOLESTATION ORDER / AN OCCUPATION ORDER (DRAFT)

Application for: a non-molestation order an occupation order *Family Law Act 1996 (Part IV)* **The court**	**To be completed by the court** **ANNEX F** Date issued Case number

Please read the accompanying notes as you complete this form.

1   About you (the applicant)

State your title (Mr, Mrs etc), full name, address, telephone number and date of birth (if under 18):

State your solicitor's name, address, reference, telephone, FAX and DX numbers:

2   About the respondent

State the respondent's name, address and date of birth (if known):

3   The Order(s) for which you are applying

This application is for:

☐ a non-molestation order

☐ an occupation order

☐ Tick this box if you wish the court to hear your application without notice being given to the respondent. The reasons relied on for an application being heard without notice must be stated in the statement in support.

4   Your relationship to the respondent (the person to be served with this applicatio

Your relationship to the respondent is:
Please tick only one of the following

1 ☐ Married

2 ☐ Were married

3 ☐ Cohabiting

4 ☐ Were cohabiting

5 ☐ Have or have had an intimate personal
      relationship with each other that is or was
      of significant duration

6 ☐ Both of you live or have lived in the same
      household

7 ☐ Relative
      State how related:

8 ☐ Agreed to marry.
      Give the date the agreement was made. If the
      agreement has ended, state when.

9 ☐ Both of you are parents of or have
      parental responsibility for a child

10 ☐ One of you is a parent of a child and the
       other has parental responsibility
       for that child

11 ☐ One of you is the natural parent or
grandparent of a child adopted or
freed for adoption, and the other is:

    (i)   the adoptive parent

  or (ii)   a person who has applied for
an adoption order for the child

  or (iii) a person with whom the child
has been placed for adoption

  or (iv) the child who has been adopted
or freed for adoption.

State whether (i), (ii), (iii) or (iv):

12 ☐ Both of you are parties to the same family
proceedings (see also Section 11 below).

5 Application for a non-molestation order

If you wish to apply for a non-molestation order,
state briefly in this section the order you want.

Give full details in support of your application in
your supporting evidence

6 Application for an occupation order

*If you do not wish to apply for an occupation
order, please go to section 9 of this form.*

(A) State the address of the dwelling house to which
your application relates:

(B) State whether it is occupied by you or the
respondent now or in the past, or whether it was
intended to be occupied by you or the respondent:

3

(C) State whether you are entitled to occupy
the dwelling-house: ☐ Yes   ☐No

If yes, explain why:

(D) State whether the respondent is entitled to
occupy the dwelling-house: ☐ Yes   ☐No

If yes, explain why:

**On the basis of your answer to (C) and (D)
above, tick one of the boxes 1 to 5 below to
show the category into which you fit**

1 ☐ a spouse who has matrimonial home rights in
the dwelling-house, or a person who is
entitled to occupy it by virtue of a beneficial
estate or interest or contract or by virtue of
any enactment giving him or her the right to
remain in occupation.

If you tick box 1, state whether there is a
dispute or pending proceedings between you
and the respondent about your right to occupy
the dwelling-house.

2 ☐ a former spouse with no existing right to
occupy, where the respondent spouse is
entitled.

3 ☐ a cohabitant or former cohabitant with no
existing right to occupy, where the respondent
cohabitant or former cohabitant is so entitled.

4 ☐ a spouse or former spouse who is not entitled
to occupy, where the respondent spouse or
former spouse is also not entitled.

5 ☐ a cohabitant or former cohabitant who is not
entitled to occupy, where the respondent
cohabitant or former cohabitant is also not
entitled.

Matrimonial Home Rights

If you do have matrimonial home rights please:

State whether the title to the land is registered or unregistered (if known):

If registered, state the Land Registry title number (if known):

If you wish to apply for an occupation order, state briefly here the order you want. Give full details in support of your application in your supporting evidence.

7 Application for additional order(s) about the dwelling house

If you want to apply for any of the orders listed in the notes to this section, state what order you would like the court to make:

8 Mortgage and rent

Is the dwelling house subject to a mortgage?

☐ Yes ☐ No

If yes, please provide the name and address of the mortgagee:

Is the dwelling house rented?

☐ Yes ☐ No

If yes, please provide the name and address of the landlord:

9 At the court

Will you need an interpreter at court?

☐ Yes   ☐ No

If 'Yes', specify the language:

If you require an interpreter you must notify the
court immediately so that one can be arranged.

If you have a disability for which you require
special assistance or special facilities, please state
what your needs are. The court staff will get in
touch with you about your requirements.

10 Other information

State the name and date of birth of any child
living with or staying with, or likely to live with
or stay with, you or the respondent:

State the name of any other person living in the
same household as you and the respondent, and
say why they live there:

11 Other Proceedings and Orders

If there are any other current family proceedings
or orders in force involving you and the
respondent, state the type of proceedings or
orders, the court and the case number. This
includes any application for an occupation order
or non-molestation order against you by the
respondent.

This application is to be served upon the respondent

Signed   Date

Application for a non-molestation order or occupation order
Notes for Guidance

Section 1

If you do not wish your address to be made known to the respondent, leave the space on the form blank and complete Confidential Address Form C8. The court can give you this form.

If you are under 18, someone over 18 must help you make this application. That person, who might be one of your parents, is called a 'next friend'.

If you are under 16 you need permission to make this application. You must apply to the High Court for permission, using this form. If the High Court gives you permission to make this application, it will then either hear the application itself or transfer it to a county court.

Section 3

An urgent order made by the court before notice of the application is served on the respondent is called an ex-parte order. In deciding whether to make an ex-parte order the court will consider all the circumstances of the case, including:

- *any risk of significant harm to the applicant or a relevant child, attributable to conduct of the respondent, if the order is not made immediately*

- *whether it is likely that the applicant will be deterred or prevented from pursuing the application if an order is not made immediately*

- *whether there is reason to believe that the respondent is aware of the proceedings but is deliberately evading service and that the applicant or a relevant child will be seriously prejudiced by the delay involved.*

If the court makes an ex-parte order, it must give the respondent an opportunity to make representations about the order as soon as just and convenient at a full hearing.

'Harm' in relation to a person who has reached the age of 18 means ill-treatment or the impairment of health, and in relation to a child means ill-treatment or the impairment of health and development. 'Ill-treatment' includes forms of ill-treatment which are not physical and, in relation to a child, includes sexual abuse. The court will require evidence of any harm which you allege in support of your application. This evidence should be included in the statement accompanying this application.

Section 4

For you to be able to apply for an order you must be related to the respondent in one of the ways listed in this section of the form. If you are not related in one of these ways you should seek legal advice.

Cohabitants are two persons who, although not married to each other, are living together as husband and wife or (if of the same sex) in an equivalent relationship. People who have cohabited, but have then married will not fall within this category, but will fall within the category of married people.

Those who live or have lived in the same household do not include people who share the same household because one of them is the other's employee, tenant, lodger or boarder.

You will only be able to apply as a relative of the respondent if you are:

(A) the father, mother, stepfather, stepmother, son, daughter, stepson, stepdaughter, grandmother, grandfather, grandson or granddaughter of the respondent or of the respondent's spouse or former spouse.

(B) the brother, sister, uncle, aunt, niece, nephew or first cousin (whether of the full blood or of the half blood or by marriage) of the respondent or of the respondent's spouse or former spouse.

This includes, in relation to a person who is living or has lived with another person as husband and wife, any person who would fall within (A) or (B) if the parties were married to each other (for example, your cohabitee's father or brother).

Agreements to marry: You will fall within this category only if you make this application within three years of the termination of the agreement. The court will require the following evidence of the agreement:

> *evidence in writing*

or the gift of an engagement ring in contemplation of marriage

or evidence that a ceremony has been entered into in the presence of one or more other persons assembled for the purpose of witnessing it.

Parents and parental responsibility: You will fall within this category if

> *both you and the respondent are either the parents of a child or have parental responsibility for that child*

or if one of you is the parent and the other has parental responsibility.

Under the Children Act 1989, parental responsibility is held automatically by a child's mother, and by the child's father if he and the mother were married to each other at the time of the child's birth or have married subsequently. Where this is not the case, parental responsibility can be acquired by the father in accordance with the provisions of the Children Act 1989.

Section 5

A non-molestation order can forbid the respondent to molest you or a relevant child. Molestation can include, for example, violence, threats, pestering and other forms of harassment. The court can forbid particular acts of the respondent, molestation in general, or both.

Section 6

If you wish to apply for an occupation order but you are uncertain about your answer to any of the questions in this part of the application form, you should seek legal advice.

(A) A dwelling-house includes any building or part of a building which is occupied as a dwelling; any caravan, houseboat or structure which is occupied as a dwelling; and any yard, garden, garage or outhouse belonging to it and occupied with it.

Section 6 (continued)

(C) & (D) *The following questions give examples to help you to decide if you or the respondent, or both of you, are entitled to occupy the dwelling-house:*

(a)   Are you the sole legal owner of the dwelling-house?

(b)   Are you and the respondent joint legal owners of the dwelling-house?

(c)   Is the respondent the sole legal owner of the dwelling-house?

(d)   Do you rent the dwelling-house as sole tenant?

(e)   Do you and the respondent rent the dwelling-house as joint tenants?

(f)   Does the respondent rent the dwelling house as sole tenant?

If you answer   ■ **Yes** *to (a), (b), (d) or (e) you are likely to be entitled to occupy the dwelling-house*

       ■ **Yes** *to (c) or (f) you may not be entitled (unless, for example, you are a spouse and have matrimonial home rights - see the notes under 'Matrimonial Home Rights' below)*

       ■ **Yes** *to (b), (c), (e) or (f), the respondent is likely to be entitled to occupy the dwelling-house.*

       ■ **Yes** *to (a) or (d) the respondent may not be entitled (unless, for example, he is a spouse and has matrimonial home rights).*

Box 1 *For example, if you are sole owner, joint owner, or if you rent the property. If you are not a spouse, former spouse, cohabitant or former cohabitant of the respondent, you will only be able to apply for an occupation order if you fall within this category.*

If you answer **Yes** *to this question, it will not be possible for a magistrates' court to deal with the application, unless the court decides that it is unnecessary for it to decide this question in order to deal with the application or make an order. If the court decides that it cannot deal with the application, it will transfer the application to a county court.*

Box 2 *For example, if the respondent was married to you and is sole owner or rents the property.*

Box 3 *For example, if the respondent is or was cohabiting with you and is sole owner or rents the property.*

Matrimonial Home Rights

Where one spouse is entitled to occupy the dwelling-house by virtue of a beneficial estate or interest or contract or by virtue of any enactment giving him or her the right to remain in occupation, and the other spouse is not so entitled, the spouse who is not entitled has matrimonial home rights. These are a right, if the spouse is in occupation, not to be evicted or excluded from the dwelling house except with the leave of the court and, if the spouse is not in occupation, the right with the leave of the court to enter into and occupy the dwelling-house.

Matrimonial home rights do not exist if the dwelling-house has never been, and was never intended to be, the matrimonial home of the two spouses. If the marriage has come to an end, matrimonial home rights will also have ceased, unless a court order has been made during the marriage for the rights to continue after the end of the marriage.

Occupation Orders *The possible orders are:*

If you have ticked box 1 above, an order under section 33 of the Act may:

- *enforce the applicant's entitlement to remain in occupation as against the respondent*

- *require the respondent to permit the applicant to enter and remain in the dwelling-house or part of it*

- *regulate the occupation of the dwelling-house by either or both parties*

- *if the respondent is also entitled to occupy, the order may prohibit, suspend or restrict the exercise by him, of that right*

- *restrict or terminate any matrimonial home rights of the respondent*

- *require the respondent to leave the dwelling-house or part of it*

- *exclude the respondent from a defined area around the dwelling-house*

- *declare that the applicant is entitled to occupy the dwelling-house or has matrimonial home rights in it*

- *provide that matrimonial home rights of the applicant are not brought to an end by the death of the other spouse or termination of the marriage.*

If you have ticked box 2 or box 3 above, an order under section 35 or 36 of the Act may:

- *give the applicant the right not to be evicted or excluded from the dwelling-house or any part of it by the respondent for a specified period*

- *prohibit the respondent from evicting or excluding the applicant during that period*

- *give the applicant the right to enter and occupy the dwelling house for a specified period*

- *require the respondent to permit the exercise of that right*

- *regulate the occupation of the dwelling-house by either or both of the parties*

- *prohibit, suspend or restrict the exercise by the respondent of his right to occupy*

- *require the respondent to leave the dwelling-house or part of it*

- *exclude the respondent from a defined area around the dwelling-house.*

If you have ticked box 4 or box 5 above, an order under section 37 or 38 of the Act may:

- *require the respondent to permit the applicant to enter and remain in the dwelling-house or part of it*

- *regulate the occupation of the dwelling-house by either or both of the parties*

- *require the respondent to leave the dwelling-house or part of it*

- *exclude the respondent from a defined area around the dwelling-house.*

Section 6 (continued)

You should provide any evidence which you have on the following matters in your evidence in support of this application. If necessary, further statements may be submitted after the application has been issued.

If you have ticked box 1, 4 or 5 above, the court will need any available evidence of the following:

- *the housing needs and resources of you, the respondent and any relevant child*
- *the financial resources of you and the respondent*
- *the likely effect of any order, or of any decision not to make an order, on the health, safety and well-being of you, the respondent and any relevant child*
- *the conduct of you and the respondent in relation to each other and otherwise.*

If you have ticked box 2 above, the court will need any available evidence of:

- *the housing needs and resources of you, the respondent and relevant child*
- *the financial resources of you and the respondent*
- *the likely effect of any order, or of any decision not to make an order on the health, safety and well-being of you, the respondent and any relevant child*
- *the conduct of you and the respondent in relation to each other and otherwise.*
- *the length of time that has elapsed since you and the respondent ceased to live together*
- *the length of time that has elapsed since the marriage was dissolved or annulled*
- *the existence of any pending proceedings between you and the respondent:*
    under section 23A of the Matrimonial Causes Act 1973 (property adjustment orders in connection with divorce proceedings etc.
    or under Schedule 1 para 1(2)(d) or (e) of the Children Act 1989 (orders for financial relief against parents)
    or relating to the legal or beneficial ownership of the dwelling-house.

If you have ticked box 3 above, the court will need any available evidence of:

- *the housing needs and resources of you, the respondent and any relevant child*
- *the financial resources of you and the respondent*
- *the likely effect of any order, or of any decision not to make an order, on the health, safety and well-being of you, the respondent and any relevant child*
- *the conduct of you and the respondent in relation to each other and otherwise*
- *the nature of you and the respondent's relationship*

- *the length of time during which you have lived together as husband and wife*
- *whether you and the respondent have had any children, or have both had parental responsibility for any children*
- *the length of time which has elapsed since you and the respondent ceased to live together*
- *the existence of any pending proceedings between you and the respondent under Schedule 1 para 1(2)(d) or (e) of the Children Act 1989 or relating to the legal or beneficial ownership of the dwelling-house.*

Section 7

Under section 40 of the Act the court may make the following additional orders when making an occupation order:

- *impose on either party obligations as to the repair and maintenance of the dwelling-house*
- *impose on either party obligations as to the payment of rent, mortgage or other outgoings affecting it*
- *order a party occupying the dwelling-house to make periodical payments to the other party in respect of the accommodation, if the other party would (but for the order) be entitled to occupy it*
- *grant either party possession or use of furniture or other contents*
- *order either party to take reasonable care of any furniture or other contents*
- *order either party to take reasonable steps to keep the dwelling-house and any furniture or other contents secure.*

Section 8

If the dwelling-house is rented or subject to a mortgage, the landlord or mortgagee must be served with notice of the proceedings in Form FL416. He or she will then be able to make representations to the court regarding the rent or mortgage.

Section 10

A person living in the same household may, for example, be a member of the family or a tenant or employee of you or the respondent.

FORM FL404 – ORDER OR DIRECTION

 In the

Case Number

[Order]   [Direction]   Sheet   of

Family Law Act 1996

In the

Case Number

[Order] [Direction] Sheet of

Family Law Act 1996

Ordered by [Mr] [Mrs] Justice

[His] [Her] Honour Judge

[Deputy] District Judge [of the Family Division]

Justice[s] of the Peace

[Assistant] Recorder

Clerk of the Court

on

FL404 Order or Direction

Orders under Family Law Act 1996 Part IV

*(General heading followed by Notice A **or** Notice B and numbered options as appropriate)*

Notice A – order includes non-molestation order – penal notice mandatory

Important Notice to the Respondent [name]

This order gives you instructions which you must follow. You should read it all carefully. If you do not understand anything in this order you should go to a solicitor, Legal Advice Centre or Citizens Advice Bureau. You have a right to ask the court to change or cancel the order but you must obey it unless the court does change or cancel it.

You must obey the instructions contained in this order. If you do not, you will be guilty of contempt of court, and you may be sent to prison.

Notice B – order does not include non-molestation order – *penal notice discretionary

Important Notice to the Respondent [name]

This order gives you instructions which you must follow. You should read it all carefully. If you do not understand anything in this order you should go to a solicitor, Legal Advice Centre or Citizens Advice Bureau. You have a right to ask the court to change or cancel the order but you must obey it unless the court does change or cancel it.

You must obey the instructions contained in this order. *[If you do not, you will be guilty of contempt of court, and you may be sent to prison.]

Occupation orders under s33 of the Family Law Act 1996

1.   The court declares that the applicant [name] is entitled to occupy [*address of home or intended home*] as [*his/her*] home. **OR**

2.   The court declares that the applicant [name] has matrimonial home rights in [*address of home or intended home*]. **AND/OR**

3.   The court declares that the applicant [name]'s matrimonial home rights shall not end when the respondent [name] dies or their marriage is dissolved and shall continue until … or further order.

It is ordered that:

4.   The respondent [name] shall allow the applicant [name] to occupy [*address of home or intended home*] **OR**

5.   The respondent [name] shall allow the applicant [name] to occupy part of [*address of home or intended home*] namely: [*specify part*]

6.   The respondent [name] shall not obstruct, harass or interfere with the applicant [name]'s peaceful occupation of [*address of home or intended home*]

7.   The respondent [name] shall not occupy [*address of home or intended home*] **OR**

8.   The respondent [name] shall not occupy [*address of home or intended home*] from [*specify date*] until [*specify date*] **OR**

9.   The respondent [name] shall not occupy [*specify part of address of home or intended home*] **AND/OR**

10.   The respondent [name] shall not occupy [*address or part of address*] between [*specify dates or times*]

11.   The respondent [name] shall leave [*address or part of address*] [forthwith] [within ___ [*hours/days*] of service on [*him/her*] of this order.] **AND/OR**

12.   Having left [*address or part of address*], the respondent [name] shall not return to, enter or attempt to enter [or go within [*specify distance*] of] it.

Occupation orders under ss35 & 36 of the Family Law Act 1996

It is ordered that:

13.   The applicant [name] has the right to occupy [*address of home or intended home*] and the respondent [name] shall allow the applicant [name] to do so. **OR**

14.   The respondent [name] shall not evict or exclude the applicant [name] from [*address of home or intended home*] or any part of it namely [*specify part*]. **AND/OR**

15.   The respondent [name] shall not occupy [*address of home or intended home*]. **OR**

16.   The respondent [name] shall not occupy [*address of home or intended home*] from [*specify date*] until [*specify date*] **OR**

17.   The respondent [name] shall not occupy [*specify part of address of home or intended home*] **OR**

18.   The respondent [name] shall leave [*address or part of address*] [forthwith] [within ___ [*hours/days*] of service on [*him/her*] of this order.] **AND/OR**

19.   Having left [*address or part of address*], the respondent [name] shall not return to, enter or attempt to enter [or go within [*specify distance*] of] it.

Occupation orders under ss37 & 38 of the Family Law Act 1996

It is ordered that:

20.   The respondent [name] shall allow the applicant [name] to occupy [*address of home or intended home*] or part of it namely: [*specify*]. **AND/OR**

21.   [One or both of the provisions in paragraphs 6 & 10 above may be inserted] **AND/OR**

22.   The respondent [name] shall leave [*address or part of address*] [forthwith] [within ___ [*hours/days*] of service on [*him/her*] of this order.] **AND/OR**

23.   Having left [*address or part of address*], the respondent [name] may not return to, enter or attempt to enter [or go within [*specify distance*] of] it.

Additional provisions which may be included in occupation orders made under ss33, 35 or 36 of Family Law Act 1996

It is ordered that:

24.   The *[applicant [name]]* *[respondent [name]]* shall maintain and repair *[address of home or intended home]* **AND/OR**

25.   The *[applicant [name]]* *[respondent [name]]* shall pay the rent for *[address of home or intended home]* **OR**

26.   The *[applicant [name]]* *[respondent [name]]* shall pay the mortgage payments on *[address of home or intended home]*. **OR**

27.   The *[applicant [name]]* *[respondent [name]]* shall pay the following for *[address of home or intended home]*: [specify outgoings as bullet points].

28.   The *[party in occupation]* shall pay to the *[other party]* £   each *[week, month, etc]* for *[address of home etc]*.

29.   The *[party in occupation]* shall keep and use the *[furniture]* [contents] *[specify if necessary]* of *[address of home or intended home]* and the *[applicant [name]]* *[respondent [name]]* shall return to the *[party in occupation]* the *[furniture]* [contents] *[specify if necessary]* *[no later than [date/time]]*.

30.   The *[party in occupation]* shall take reasonable care of the *[furniture]* [contents] *[specify if necessary]* of *[address of home or intended home]*.

31.   The *[party in occupation]* shall take all reasonable steps to keep secure *[address of home or intended home]* and the furniture or other contents *[specify if necessary]*.

Duration

Occupation orders under s33 of the Family Law Act 1996

32.   This order shall last until [*specify event or date*]. **OR**

33.   This order shall last until a further order is made.

Occupation orders under ss35 & 37 of the Family Law Act 1996

34.   This order shall last until [*state date which must not be more than 6 months from the date of this order*].

35.   The occupation order made on [*state date*] is extended until [*state date which must not be more than 6 months from the date of this extension*].

Occupation orders under ss36 & 38 Family Law Act 1996

36.   This order shall last until [*state date which must not be more than 6 months from the date of this order*].

35.   The occupation order made on [*state date*] is extended until [*state date which must not be more than 6 months from the date of this extension*] and must end on that date.

Non-molestation orders

It is ordered that:

38.   The respondent [name] is forbidden to use or threaten violence against the applicant [name] [and must not instruct, encourage or in any way suggest that any other person should do so]. **AND/OR**

39.   The respondent [name] is forbidden to intimidate, harass or pester [*or [specify]*] the applicant [name] [and must not instruct, encourage or in any way suggest that any other person should do so]. **AND/OR**

40.   The respondent [name] is forbidden to use or threaten violence against the relevant child(ren) [name(s) and date(s) of birth] [and must not instruct, encourage or in any way suggest that any other person should do so]. **AND/OR**

41.   The respondent [name] is forbidden to intimidate, harass or pester [*or [specify]*] [the relevant child(ren) [name(s) and date(s) of birth] [and must not instruct, encourage or in any way suggest that any other person should do so].

FORM FL404 – ORDER OR DIRECTION (DRAFT)

Occupation Order
(Under Part 4 of the
Family Law Act 1996)

In the	
	Court
Case No.	
Applicant	
Ref	
Respondent	
Ref	

To

of

Important Notice to the Respondent [name]

This order gives you instructions which you must follow. You should read it carefully. If you do not understand anything in this order you should go to a solicitor, Legal Advice Centre or Citizens Advice Bureau. You have a right to ask the court to change or cancel the order by way of formal application to the court.

You **must** obey the instructions contained in this order. If you do not, you will be guilty of contempt of court, and you may be sent to prison.

On   20   , District Judge

Sitting at

considered an application for an injunction and **ordered that** [name]
is forbidden (and must not instruct, encourage or in any way suggest that any other person should do so) **from:-**

until [   ] [further order]

[Notice of further hearing [(see also note overleaf)]
The court will re-consider the application and whether the order should continue at a further hearing at

on   the   day of   20 at   o'clock

If you do not attend at the time shown the court may make an order in your absence.]

DRAFT FL404

FORM FL404a – NON-MOLESTATION ORDER (DRAFT)

Non - Molestation Order
(Under Part 4 of the
Family Law Act 1996)

In the	
	Court
Case No.	
Applicant	
Ref	
Respondent	
Ref	

To

of

Important Notice to the Respondent [name]

This order gives you instructions which you must follow. You should read it carefully. If you do not understand anything in this order you should go to a solicitor, Legal Advice Centre or Citizens Advice Bureau. You have a right to ask the court to change or cancel the order by way of a formal application to the court.

You **must** obey this order. If, without reasonable excuse, you do anything which you are forbidden from doing by this order, you will be committing a criminal offence and liable on conviction to a term of imprisonment not exceeding five years or to a fine or to both or alternatively be guilty of contempt of court and may be sent to prison for a period not exceeding two years.

On   20   , District Judge

Sitting at

considered an application for an injunction and **ordered that** [name]
is forbidden from (and must not instruct, encourage or in any way suggest that any other person should do so):-

until [   ] [further order]

[Notice of further hearing [(see also note overleaf)]
The court will re-consider the application and whether the order should continue at a further hearing at

on   the   day of   20 at   o'clock

If you do not attend at the time shown the court may make an order in your absence.]

DRAFT FL404a

FORM FL406a – RECORD OF NON-MOLESTATION ORDER (DRAFT)

Record of
Non – Molestation Order

In the	
	Court
Case No.	
Applicant	
Ref	
Respondent	
Ref	

On   20   , District Judge

Sitting at

considered an application for an injunction and **ordered that** [name]
is forbidden from (and must not instruct, encourage or in any way suggest that any other person should do so):-

(here set out the provisions of the non-molestation order)

This order expires on:

Note to the Arresting Officer

Under the Domestic Violence, Crime and Victims Act 2004, which amends Part 4 of the Family Law Act 1996 (section 42), breach of a non-molestation order is a criminal offence and punishable for up to five years imprisonment.

> "A person who without reasonable excuse does anything that he is prohibited from doing by a non-molestation order is guilty of an offence."

> *Part 4 Family Law Act 1996, Section 42A (1)*

INDEX

References are to paragraph numbers.